I0888863

# Broadening the Horizon: Critical Introductions to Amma Darko

Edited by

Vincent O. Odamtten

ayebia

An Adinkra symbol meaning

*Ntesie matemasie*

A symbol of knowledge and wisdom

ARTS COUNCIL ENGLAND

This edition published by Ayebia Clarke Limited
7 Syringa Walk
Banbury
OX16 1FR
Oxfordshire
UK

First published in the UK by Ayebia Clarke Publishing Limited, 2007
Ayebia Clarke Literary Agency & Publishing Limited

And distributed outside Africa, Europe and the United Kingdom exclusively by
Lynne Rienner Publishers, Inc.
1800 30th St., Ste. 314
Boulder, CO 80301
USA
www.rienner.com



British Library Cataloguing-in-Publication Data
A catalogue record of this book is available from the British Library.

Cover design by Amanda Carroll at Millipedia
Eye design, by permission from GTP Ghana, Real Wax Design No. 5025 "Eyes"

Typeset by FiSH Books, Enfield, Middlesex.
Printed and bound in Great Britain by Mackays of Chatham, Chatham, Kent.

The publisher wishes to acknowledge the help of Arts Council Funding

**ISBN 978-0-9547023-8-0**

Available from www.ayebia.co.uk or email info@ayebia.co.uk
Distributed in Africa, Europe & the UK by TURNAROUND at www.turnaround-uk.com

# Broadening the Horizon: Critical Introductions to Amma Darko

In memory of
Vincentia Charity Odamtten,
both my mother and
mother-midwife to countless others, and
who gave and cared about our lives
beyond our naming.

# CONTENTS

# BIOGRAPHIES OF CONTRIBUTORS

**Louise Allen Zak** was awarded a BA in English at the University of Toronto, her MA and Ph.D., also in English from the University of Massachusetts at Amherst. She was Associate Dean for Academic Affairs at Marlboro College Vermont, and also served as Associate Dean for Internships and Study Abroad. She has published and spoken on topics connected with her research and professional experience including West African women writers, college accreditation, and studying and living abroad. She is currently Associate Director of the Higher Education Commission of the New England Association of Schools and Colleges (NEASC).

**Rev. Fr. Gervais Angsotinge** is a lecturer at the Department of English, University of Ghana, Legon. He has published in journals including the University of Ghana *Institute of African Studies Research Review.* He was awarded a BA from the University of Ghana at Legon, an M.Litt. from Sterling University and MA and Ph.D. from UCLA.

**Kari Dako** is Associate professor at the Department of English, University of Ghana. She has written and published widely on sociolinguistics, Ghanaian English, and African literature in publications such as *English Worldwide, Modern Fiction Studies, Arms Akimbo,* and the University of Ghana's *Institute of African Studies Research Review*. Her books include *The Baobabs of Tete and Other Stories* (Michigan State University Press), an English translation of Thorkild Hansen's classic trilogy on the Atlantic Slave Trade (*Coast of Slaves, Ships of Slaves,* and *Islands of Slaves*) from Danish (Sub-Saharan Publishers, Accra), and a dictionary of "Ghanaianisms".

**Aloysius Denkabe** obtained his BA at the University of Ghana, Legon and his MA from Cambridge University. Although a specialist in the English Renaissance period and Shakespeare, he also publishes on Ghanaian literature and has contributed to a number of anthologies including *English In Ghana*. He is a Senior Lecturer in the Department of English and also the current Director of Sports at the University of Ghana.

**Helen Yitah** has a Ph.D. in post-colonial literature at the University of South Carolina, Columbia, where she is now a Visiting Assistant Professor. She has published in *The Encyclopedia for Post-colonial Literatures in English, The Bilingual Review, Oral Tradition, The Research Review,* and the University of Ghana's *Language Centre Journal.*

**Sean P. O'Connell** is a recent graduate of Hamilton College, New York, concentrating in Africana Studies and Government. O'Connell is currently completing an MA in African-American Studies at Columbia University's Institute for Research in African-American Studies (IRAAS). The focus of his research is on the rise of Black towns and settlements in America's Western Frontier during the second wave of the great migration.

**Monica Bungaro** lectures at the University of Birmingham, England, and is a researcher in African and Caribbean literatures, as well as Black British women writers and post-colonial studies. She has contributed to a number of anthologies including *The Historical Companion to Post-colonial Literatures in English*, ed. David Johnson, Edinburgh UP and Columbia UP (2005) and *Gender, Body and Sexuality in African Cultures and Literatures*, ed. Flora Veit-Wild, New York/Amsterdam: Rodopi (2005). She is presently completing a book on *Images of Women in Recent African Fiction in English* and editing a book on *Post-colonial Pedagogy*.

**Carmela Garritano** is an Assistant Professor of English at the University of St. Thomas in St. Paul, Minnesota. She has published 'Women Melodrama, and Political Critique: A Feminist Reading of *Hostages, Dust to Dust,* and *True Confessions*' for *Nigerian Video Films,* edited by Jonathan Haynes, University of Ohio Press (2000), and *'A Feminist Reading of Ellen Kuzwayo's "Call Me Woman"* for *The Post-colonial Condition of African Literature*', Trenton, NJ (2000). She is currently completing a book on the Ghanaian film and video industries. Her research interests include African literature and film, global media, cultural studies, and the intersection of discourses of gender and modernity.

**Mary Ellen (Ellie) Higgins** is Assistant Professor of English at the McKeesport Campus of the Pennsylvania State University. She published an interview with Amma Darko in the *Journal of Commonwealth Literature* and an article on *Beyond the Horizon* in *Tulsa Studies in Women's Literature*. She has written about African cinema in *Research in African Literatures*, and has contributed chapters to the forthcoming books *Writing Gender, Race, and Diaspora* and *Perspectives on African Literatures at the Millennium*.

**Naana Banyiwa Horne** received her BA from the University of Cape Coast, Ghana and her Ph.D. from the University of Wisconsin in Madison. She taught in the Humanities Department at Indiana University, Kokomo. Horne is a poet, her collection of poems, *Sunkwa: Clingings onto Life* will shortly be reissued in a second edition. She is a scholar of African women writers and currently teaches at Santa Fe Community College in Gainesville, Florida.

# INTRODUCTION

## Beyond the Comfort Zone: Relations Between African Writers and Audience

In late July of 2005 I had a series of conversations with the well-known Ghanaian writer and activist, Ama Ata Aidoo. We discussed issues of human, and especially women's, rights in the context of the *right to freedom of expression*. These conversations came up as we talked about *Mbaasem*, the NGO that Aidoo had set up in Ghana to help aspiring women writers develop their craft as well as to address *women's matters*. The idea of pushing such an agenda was not new, and I do not presume to be the first man to see common ground between the discussions of women's rights, in particular their freedom of expression and the fundamental rights of all human beings – children, women and men. Such dialogues with Aidoo and others began to inform a project I had been working on, an anthology of criticism on the work of Amma Darko, another Ghanaian woman writer whose voice is firm enough to articulate, without compromise, the expectations and hurdles facing a new generation of Africa's children in a new century.

As the editor of this first collected volume of literary criticism focused on the novels of Amma Darko, one of Ghana's and Africa's most exciting and challenging "new" writers, I feel privileged to be the facilitator of a series of conversations on the subject of Darko's works and conversations that took me deeper both into her work and into the works of her Ghanaian literary foremothers. What became clear to me as the months passed on this project, was that *freedom of expression*, especially that of women, was as necessary to the health of a society and this world as are the other *rights* we so often proclaim. Yet, those rights, so long sought and at so great a cost, are void of meaning without an audience, a community or communities that are willing to enter into a dialogue, to actively participate in conversations that move us beyond the comfort zone.

I use the phrase *beyond the comfort zone* as the desiderata of our critical projects, because there are many histories, often voiced-over in the discourses of academe and elsewhere, that valorise *semantic acrobatics* over engagement with both the literature and the sordid realities of our neocolonial, post-colonial, globalised lives. One can take her or his pick of terms to describe the political, socio-economic, and gendered relationships that characterise our lived actualities. Yet the fact remains that the writer, whether on the Continent or in the Diaspora, struggles to give artistic form to our collective needs and to describe the often half-perceived possibilities and dangers, even as she outlines a safe harbour far from the storms of a homogenising globalisation. Indeed, over the last half-century our writers have cut a literary path out of the forests of colonialism, celebrated our independence, mourned our loss of revolutionary innocence and now ask us to reflect with maturity and the 'knowledge gained since', upon this new dispensation, this so-called new order with its hegemonic neo-conservative, or maybe neo-liberal, global agenda. In the context of this era of heightened paranoia, insecurities and growing inequalities of wealth and well-being within and between nation-states, our storytellers give us hope against the erosion of the few institutions that once inspired faith in an unbounded future.

Because it strengthens our sense of the continuity of the line of strong women storytellers in the Ghanaian tradition, let us consider the significance of two of the earlier writers in that tradition before moving into a discussion of Amma Darko and her work and of the critical perspectives on that work contained in this volume. First, as we move towards the subject of our concern, we should pause to honour and to acknowledge Efua T. Sutherland, whose words and actions made a difference in our perception of the past – with her development of the Anansegoro, amongst other theatrical innovations; of the present – in the haunting drama of greed, duplicity and sacrifice: *Edufa*; and of the future – in *New Life at Kyerefaso*, even as that early short story revealed the persistence of hope, despite a poverty of spirit. And so, in the tenth anniversary year of Auntie Efua's passing, I note:

For Efua Sutherland, there are not words enough . . .
(1924–1996)

Auntie Efua,
I thank you for teaching me
to be an honest man/woman
who knows the pleasure
of plays and . . .
who knows the worth
of the work and . . .
who knows the love
of these words, these deeds and . . .
who learnt that
new life comes with pain
who learnt that
new earth is turned with care
who learnt that
the new will seed into our harvest
your promise of visions
flowering into
thank you's for being . . .

> Auntie Efua, you are always with us
> *m'daase pii!*

Her influence on the development of contemporary Ghanaian drama and literature is both profound and far-reaching. As I noted in my volume on the work of Ama Ata Aidoo, *The Art of Ama Ata Aidoo* (1994), '[Efua Sutherland's] influence . . . may be more correctly acknowledged in terms of the *psychological space* [she fashioned] by [her] advocacy of the creative use of the rich Ghanaian orature in the contemporary context' (199).

This habit of speaking to the 'here and now', even as the writer listens to the ancestral and traditional voices of yesterday with her eyes scanning the path ahead, makes room for a dynamic writer like Ama Ata Aidoo, who is the second guiding figure I would like to discuss in the context of Amma Darko's work. I have suggested elsewhere that Aidoo's concerns as an artist and a woman engaged in her world have given rise to literary works that demand that we recognise the complexity of the historical matrix in which those works are embedded. In addition, we must understand that each of Aidoo's works, in addressing specific ideological and sociopolitical issues, exists as both a development from and a development to another ground. That ground, I suggest, is conditioned by the neocolonial reality in which the texts are rooted and have their circulation, and which in turn overdetermines both artist and audience.

I further suggested that Aidoo's work actively sought to engage her audience in a process of self-criticism and education. The desired objective of the engagement between audience and Aidoo's multiple texts was and is the radical transformation of the audience's consciousness of personal and public histories. My focus then highlighted what I saw as a deft deployment of structural and thematic elements arising from Ghana's rich orature, as Aidoo appropriated and transformed Western literary genres. Yet the catalyst for my critical intervention grew out of the *dis*ease I experienced in reading some of the critical audience's responses to her work. These *partial* readings revealed as much about their authors' subject-positions as was revealed by my desire to address this problem of a fragmentary discourse, even as I recognized that it was symptomatic of our neocolonial times.

My contribution was then in the context of Aidoo's work, as it is now in the context of Darko's, the intention of beginning a conversation, or rather multiple conversations around the significance of this writer. Amma Darko has a grassroots following of readers from all walks of life and, as the essays included in this volume testify, both a strong national and international audience. Critical to the healthy development of a relationship between writer and reader, between the storyteller and her audience is a free flow and exchange of ideas.

Darko, whose first novel *Beyond the Horizon* was already a subject of international attention even before its publication,[1] is not readily classifiable under any of the rubrics hasty critics might like to use, and in the articles which follow we will see how and why that is so. In order to put the critical discussions collected here in the broadest possible context, however, I would like to suggest that we best understand the life and reputation of a book or a body of an author's work as being inextricably enmeshed within a series of open conversations. Lest we forget the obvious, the initiating conversation, from which all subsequent conversations arise, is between the writer and the material itself. For that reason, and in order to connect that first discussion with all subsequent conversations – that is those between the writer and publisher; reader and book, therefore, between the reader and the writer in the book; and between literary critics and the work – I have asked Amma Darko to participate in the construction of this introduction as respondent and commentator. It seems particularly appropriate that her voice be present at a time when the critical response to her writing has not yet calcified into the fossilised rankings of canon construction.[2] Upon our understanding of that first conversation, then, the Introduction seeks to build a platform for the critical discussions that follow.

## THE FIRST CONVERSATION

Perhaps the most mysterious of the relationships from which all of these conversations have arisen is that between the writer and the material with which she works. Certainly Amma Darko appears to be someone who emerged at the right moment in her nation's cultural history and someone with the kind of abilities and training that enabled her to recognise the need for new and different stories to be told. The ones still in circulation were only partial in their ability to reveal the new topographies of illicit flows of people, goods and capital that made dependency theories and oppositional models of centre and periphery seem obsolete. Darko's launching onto the literary scene in Ghana, as well as in Europe and the rest of the world, came as the much-needed panacea for a nervous critical community. As the poet and critic, Kofi Anyidoho, noted in his introduction to Darko's third published novel, *Faceless*:[3]

> Students and scholars of African Literature who, like me, have often wondered about the apparent absence of any major female Ghanaian writers following the remarkable pioneering work of Efua T. Sutherland and Ama Ata Aidoo, can now rest assured that a worthy successor has emerged in the person of Amma Darko.

But Darko was not Athena, born fully grown and armed out of the top of Zeus's head, ready to take the literary world by storm. Born in 1956, a year before Ghana's independence from colonial rule in Tamale, northern Ghana, she grew up in Accra under the care of her adoptive parents. After completing her secondary education, she attended the University of Science and Technology in Kumasi where in 1980 she obtained a degree from the College of Arts with a minor in English. After working for a year in Kumasi with the Technology Consultancy Centre, she left for Germany like many young Ghanaians who were part of the exodus to the West in search of further education, better prospects and the pot of gold. What she and many others found was a life of menial jobs in order to survive and maintain some modicum of dignity in a market place that was ruthlessly indifferent to those without power or wealth.

Unlike many who found themselves in such a wilderness, Darko was able to carve out the space and time from which she could write the kind of narrative about the sort of people she knew and met. Unlike her literary predecessors, who often wrote about individuals torn by the contradictions of negotiating the highways and byways of tradition and modernity – lonely angst-ridden souls embarrassed and haunted by their superior awareness of the fragility of the fictions upon which they had built their lives – Darko rejected such self-absorbed characters. Instead, she wrote about the experiences of ordinary people, not the ones who won scholarships to go abroad, not the ones whose journey to Europe could be described as a *Season of Migration to the North*,[4] but the ones who were too poor or unfortunate to know anything other than what society made apparent, never mind that it was all an elaborate illusion that some would call the dominant ideology or discourse.

Ultimately, of course, there is a distinctive alchemy or, alternatively, a strange attraction between the author and the material that is responsible for the stories that form in her head, her desire to tell them, and the manner in which the telling is done. This ongoing conversation between the author and the materials that speak to her and through her is what we are invited to overhear and share. Darko assures us: 'I harbour an unflinching conviction that I am filling a void with the stories I tell. I have faith and confidence in myself about my art. My love for my stories entrenches that.' Because she is secure in the significance of the stories she tells, Darko is also acutely conscious of the relationship between the focus of her work and the nature of her approach to it. 'I want to delve deeper into the intimacies and emotions of womanhood under the various conditions that many African women find themselves in. Please note that I didn't say "the intricacies and emotions of the African woman". I said "of womanhood under the various conditions that African women find themselves in". Women are women everywhere. It is the conditions they find themselves in, in their various cultures, that determine their reactions and attitudes.' Darko's nuanced distinction suggests to me, and this seems to be borne out in the varied array of critical apparatus employed in the following critical approaches, that we must resist the homogenising of women, as we must resist the totalizing of critical discourse under the tutelage of a Western feminist schoolmistress. Indeed, Darko would want us to jettison our assumptions about the predictability of human behaviour absent of the knowledge of the particularities of the individual's experiences.

Despite a style that has been characterized as direct and straightforward, her narratives have an irony of tone and are set against a complex sociological background. Indeed, she is remarkable for her ability to build a multiplicity of narratives and psychological perspectives into a given story, which is perhaps predictable, since she tells us: 'The mystery of the workings of the mind also fascinates me an awful lot.' Nor is Darko unconscious of the way in which her relationship to her material and to the stories she constructs from it is the first step in an unfolding process:

> To create a story in one's head and tell it in the form of writing is not always only for the pleasure of it. Writing is an outpouring. So sometimes it is also therapeutic. To have someone else enjoy it, identify with it, laugh or cry along with it is a bonding between writer and reader. My audience [the readers] rejuvenates me. By virtue of who they are, they tell me that something I created for myself is also good for them and worthy of their time and money. What more can I wish for?... Others liking my stories enough to want to spend their money to acquire and read them and [still] others [the critics] deeming my stories worthy of their valuable time or knowledge to assess them with a critical mind become a valuable bonus. The absolute icing on the cake!

It is impossible to ignore what she says here, the dialogical emphasis she puts upon the communal nature of the literary experience. It confirms that what we do, what we are capable of doing at our best, is of social importance. After all, a writer is also seeking an audience with *us*, even as we become her audience in the acts of critical reading and response.

## THE READER AND THE BOOK

From the conversations within an individual work and between the work and its creator, the community of the book moves out toward the reader. But Darko would suggest that for this process to work effectively and with integrity, the first 'reader' must be herself.

> I acknowledge the essential and crucial need of a readership in the art that I practise. Because of that, basically I write for myself. I can hope for but cannot dictate the size or mode or whatever of my readership. For which reason I must necessarily like a story I create in order to dare hope that another would also like it enough to want to spend precious time to read it.

Darko suggests here the importance that the integrity and directness of that first exchange between author and material has in regard to all subsequent conversations with and about the work, but it may well be that it is on the level of the exchange between the reader and the work that the sincerity and power of the author's tone and voice become most crucial.

The accessibility of Darko's language does not preclude the use of humour and irony in her work, and these qualities serve to temper her unflinching presentation of stark circumstances and human suffering and folly. Indeed, she sees the use of humour as being inherent in the Ghanaian narrative tradition and crucial to her relationship with the reader:

> Humour is strength. The ability to laugh at one's self and crack jokes at one's own expense is a healthy balm for the soul. Our Ananse stories are full of humour even when the subject matter is suffering and death. (Take this version of why Kweku Ananse, the spider is bald: He attends the funeral of his in-law; pretends to be in deep mourning and refuses food. But he is very hungry. So, in the middle of the night he steals some hot boiled beans. At the point of being caught red-handed, he pours the beans into his hat and wears it.) Humour is inherent in the fabric of the Ghanaian storyteller. And that is how I view myself. I am a storyteller who employs the mode of writing to reach a wider audience. Maybe the regular practice of my art has further sharpened my wits. Laughter is good for the soul . . . Reading (a story) should relax the reader. A story must be enjoyed. Even when it's a sad one and bogging down the reader's emotions, the reader should be helped to balance that heaviness with good doses of humour.

As she suggests here, perhaps her use of humour to leaven the weightiness of her subject matter explains the distinctiveness of the Darko voice and the marked success of her relationship to her readers as attested to by their growing numbers and enthusiasm.

## THE CRITIC, THE AUTHOR AND THE WORK

In contrast to the desired relationship between reader and writer, however, that between the author and the critic is notoriously vexed. Since the present volume represents the first collection of Darko criticism to date, it seemed to offer an opportunity for a balancing of evaluations. The insights of the critics who discuss her work in the ensuing pages can also be contextualised from the writer's perspective. For this reason Darko was invited to respond to a query about the effects of literary criticism upon her work; here is Darko's lively response on the nature of the interaction between the two:

> A Critic's attention to a work of mine is the employment of that Critic's time

> and the utilization of his acquired knowledge to assess something I have created. It is absolutely relevant and worthy of deep appreciation. But I pay heed only to what I deem to be constructive criticism. It is I who am the storyteller, not the Critic. I never lose sight of that. And as the creative writer, I must necessarily create a work, a piece before the Critic can play the role of criticising my creation. Yet the Critic is the proverbial observer of the one clearing the path, i.e. the Writer. So it is the Critic who may alert the path clearer, should the path that the clearer is clearing go crooked. Even then, who knows? Maybe the Writer does even want a crooked path. Otherwise, of course the Writer seeks then to straighten the path. In the end however, it is all up to the Writer. Yet, if the Critic praises and applauds (constructively) a piece of work, he does good justice to the morale and spirits of the creator. If I put my head and heart and mind and all into creating a piece of work, my faith in the work empowers me to endure unfavourable criticisms. But praise and applause would also not sway me in a direction I am not convinced about tackling at any particular time. Neither would it tempt me to stick in a particular 'comfort zone' as a result of the praise and applause.

If we accept the reasonable nature of Darko's response and hope that the critics responses will never interfere with the stories she chooses to tell by trying to straighten the paths that are crooked by design, or, perhaps to urge her to stick to the broad and safe well-travelled avenues when she seeks to lead us across more difficult terrain or down more dangerous byways and meaner streets, then we may be inclined to ask what purposes literary criticism can serve in the elucidation of Darko's work and career as a writer to this date.

And here I come into my own as the editor of this volume and writer of this introduction. The essays collected here are the result of readers, many of whom felt alone in their attraction to Darko's work, but were compelled, as I was, to mention her and her work at every opportunity that presented itself. Over the last ten years I have read papers and participated in conferences at which Darko's name slowly became almost as familiar to American critical readers as she was to European and Ghanaian audiences. At the African Literature Association meeting in Madison-Wisconsin in 2004, I attempted to organise an insurgent double session on Amma Darko; although I failed in pulling that off, the one session we did have gave rise to this volume.

It is clear by now that Amma Darko is recognised as a significant writer whose storytelling talent documents, for generations of African and other readers, the continent's globalisation pains *par excellence*. What is revealed through the critical responses in this collection is a complex and complicated writer who knows how to tell a good story and yet is confident enough in her art to deliver stinging and unflinching criticism of what Ghana has become as it and its people are ever more enmeshed in the web of global capitalism. Essays like Louise Zak's 'Amma Darko: Writing Her Way' meticulously document the Ghanaian novelist's genesis as a writer and introduce the unfamiliar reader to an artist who, in many ways, is already fulfilling the promise of her first novel, *Beyond the Horizon*, and whose own authorial development mirrors, in some regard, the harsh landscapes through which the characters of her many novels have travelled.

African critics such as Gervase Angsotinge, Kari Dako, Aloysius Denkabe and Helen Yitah critically situate the work of Amma Darko within the contexts of post-independence Ghanaian and continental writers like Ayi Kwei Armah, Ama Ata Aidoo, Miriama Bâ and Flora Nwapa. As fitting a new and challenging voice in the arena of literary production, Amma Darko's novels have elicited sophisticated readings that represent a variety of ideological perspectives and, to some extent, divergent positions in feminist, deconstructive and post-colonial criticisms. Bungaro, Garritano and Higgins, although focusing upon different issues and works, all examine *The Housemaid*, arguably a pivotal novella in Darko's *oeuvre*, from often radically opposed locations, underscoring the complexity of Darko's own feminism and dialogic imagination. Moreover, in considering the essays in this anthology, it is apparent that critics like Horne, O'Connell and myself are struck by Darko's keen sense of observation, as the writer exposes human foibles and the conflicting nature of characters caught in a nation and world where personal, political, economic and historical forces threaten to destroy the fabric of communities fascinated and often blinded by the dazzle of globalisation and materialism.

## CONVERSATIONS YET TO COME

It is always a challenge to attempt to evaluate the work of a writer who is at the height of her career. I hope that the critical essays collected here will shed some light on where the author has been and what she has accomplished. That is not to say that we can attempt to predict what other paths she may choose to follow in the future. Darko's is not a closed canon; in fact this volume will be published at about the same time that yet another novel will be appearing. In a strange echo of the past, it seems at this time that once again the work, with a projected title in English of *Not Without Flowers*, will be appearing in a German translation before it appears in the original English. This information emerged as part of Darko's response to an innocent inquiry as to whether she was the sort of writer who did research before writing any of her books?

> I did some research work at the Accra Psychiatric Hospital for my new unpublished story *Not Without Flowers*. I was shocked to find out how many women were there due to the emotional abuse they suffered at the hands of their spouses who were having affairs with young women their daughters'

ages. Such young women have no idea about some of the horrendous rippling effects of this 'sugar-daddy cum chicken-soup' mania on entire families. Little pleasures and petty financial gains that tear families apart; there is so much out there to write about: unbelievable stories.

I also think that knowingly or not, the whole AIDS yelling is not paying attention at all to the new trend of male prostitution. Not homosexuality. Male prostitution. Clients? Older females mostly, but not necessarily. Some are wealthy and single or divorced. Others are married and sexually unfulfilled for various reasons, e.g. polygamy. Thorny sensitive taboo issues. It's all in *Not Without Flowers*... dubious prayer camps; false prophets. Hot. I love it. And I think it is going to travel the same route as my first book: *Beyond the Horizon* did. It may get published first in German. My German publishers are thrilled with it. They are not waiting for it to be out first in the original. They are translating it straight from the manuscript for publishing in Autumn. But I think my publisher here is a little jittery. Already she doesn't think it would be out in time for the ALA conference in May. And I think she would be more comfortable if I tone down some places and turn it into something that will go down well with the Ministry of Education for it to be recommended for use in the classrooms. That won't happen.

And so it would appear that I might have omitted a significant actor in all of these conversations, namely the Publisher, the midwife of a writer's creation, the conduit or gatekeeper between the author and her public. Yet, however the discussion alluded to by Darko above may be resolved, it is my hope that the present volume may be productive of ever expanding circles of conversations that open up the world of Darko's fiction to an increasing, and increasingly aware, audience of readers. In focusing on dialogues, we assert that without the guarantees of freedom of expression, of conscience, our storytellers will be silenced and we shall be poorer for it. In this age, when a reluctance to speak out against what one perceives as the kernel of an injustice may grow into state sanctioned rape, violence and even genocide, we must trust that others, like us, will join in the conversation and pass on the word, and that a community of conscience may grow up around the figure of the unsilenced and un-silencible storyteller.

And beyond that soon to be published latest work, I asked Darko if there were other paths and other potential projects of a different nature. She replied:

I will love to dabble in film scripts one day. I think that when the right time comes I will simply find myself doing it. The urge will be too strong to ignore. Maybe what I should do now is to find time to study the basic technicalities of it.

We must wait for that treat; but in the meantime, let us turn our attention to the here and now. This anthology of criticism is a thoroughgoing and interdisciplinary look at the accomplishments of one of Ghana's, indeed Africa's, most outspoken writers of the present generation. A writer like Amma Darko, who is willing and able to move beyond the comfort zone, deserves a reader who is engaged and is also willing to move beyond the comfort zone. *Broadening the Horizon: Critical Introductions to Amma Darko* celebrates and introduces Amma Darko, whose work looks further because it stands on the shoulders of the best of Africa's anti-colonial and post-independence writers.

# Louise Allen Zak

## Amma Darko: Writing Her Way, Creating a Writing Life

How does an African woman writer actually live in her day-to-day world, find space and time to write and develop a relationship with publishers? How does her work appear on bookshelves and develop an audience? As critics read her work, how do they take note of that sometimes neglected person, who Ama Ata Aidoo once called 'the living me', the writer behind her text?[1] These questions are particularly relevant as one considers the unique context in which emerging African women writers function today.

Ghanaian novelist Amma Darko tackles themes that have long occupied writers from the African continent: the psychological and economic impact of colonialism on women, the injustices of patriarchal society, the conflict between the traditional values of the village and the pressures of urban life, and recently, critiques of pressing social problems. In addition to her fiction, her artistic life exemplifies perennial issues for African writers: inadequate time for solitude, inadequate supply and distribution of published works, the struggle to gain a readership in her own country, lack of awareness of the women writers who preceded her, lack of connection with others who are writing now, lack of critical attention at home and in the West. But chance and persistence have brought her some recent attention, and her reputation is gradually beginning to grow. She seems to be representative of a new generation of West African women writers who follow in the footsteps of their predecessors but are faced with new challenges and opportunities.

Ophelia Amma Darko was born in 1956, a year before Ghanaian independence, in Ghana's Northern region. A member of the Fanti ethnic group, she was one of seven children and was raised from babyhood by her aunt and uncle.[2] When she was ten, her uncle, a hospital pharmacist, was transferred and the family moved to Accra. Although she was a bright and successful student in school, she did no creative writing at that time. She headed for the University of Science and Technology in Kumasi intent on a career in industrial design. Quite by chance, she became involved with a student drama group and experimented briefly with writing scenes for them. Unlike many of the 'matriarchs' of African literature – Ama Ata Aidoo, Buchi Emecheta, Aminata Sow Fall, for example – Darko had no writing ambitions in her youth. She put away her dramatic dialogues and forgot about them. The writing bug had not yet bitten her.

After graduation from university in 1980, Darko decided to visit a pen pal in Germany, hoping to find interesting work. She had already worked for a year in Ghana but was dissatisfied. 'Home was suffocating me,' she said.[3] The economic situation in Ghana at the time was so dismal that many of her compatriots did the same. Several seasons of drought and bush fires had created severe food shortages. The re-absorption of one million Ghanaians expelled from Nigeria had put a strain on an already tight labour market. The government had instituted strict measures to comply with the International Monetary Fund's requirements for economic restructuring. All these circumstances left the country in the 1980s with few employment options even for university graduates. Many young Ghanaians saw the opportunity to better themselves by going to *aburokyire*, the Akan word for 'beyond the horizon', or overseas.

Darko was shocked when she arrived in Germany and found that the only jobs available to African women were in menial service and prostitution. She took a job as a domestic and made very little money. Unable to send money home, as was expected by many in her family, she felt a humiliating sense of failure, frustration, and anger. Still, there was one benefit. Her time abroad, alone and unmoored from the familiar, provided her with the opportunity to begin writing, which she did whenever she was not working. This experience of leaving home in order to come into writing is common to many writers, in Africa and elsewhere, and in fact seems almost an archetypal theme in the development of voice. Time abroad provides not only time and psychic distance but also the emotional impetus to begin to write. Chastened by what she saw of the lives of African women in Germany, Darko found she had a message:

> If you go abroad and return, you are worshipped irrespective of who you are... I did menial work and didn't make very much money. I saw girls making so much more on prostitution. Their families were happy because they sent so much money back home. Some of mine thought I was a failure. This was something that needed to be told (28 May 1998).

Armed with this message and writing in every spare moment, Darko created a manuscript in which she depicted the life of a young village girl married off to settle a debt of her father's, following her ambitious husband to the city and from there to Germany, where she is forced into prostitution to support him. The scenes in Germany take up the greater part of the work and reflect a reality Darko found easy to portray while she was there. She acknowledges freely: 'If I hadn't left Ghana and come to Germany, I would never have written' (28 May 1998).

Darko stayed in Germany until 1987. While she was unable to get her manuscript published in that time, it did begin circulating. Leaving it behind,

Darko returned home to Ghana and began her career as a tax inspector. She married and had two sons over the next decade, while also raising her husband's daughter from a previous marriage. By her account, her re-integration into her home culture was successful and without the sense of fractured identity that characterised the experience of earlier writers. Darko continued to write, drawing her inspiration from scenes around her in Accra.

The trajectory of Amma Darko's life is not so different from that of many women in Ghana who have gone on to higher education, travelled abroad once or twice, returned, married and then settled down at home. What is distinctive is that she began writing her experience into novels as an adult, eventually found an audience abroad in another language, persisted in writing despite a lack of recognition in her own culture and language, and has at last achieved some success.

The process of coming to writing varies, naturally, but there are some striking similarities among the West African women writers I have studied. First and foremost, they had supportive families, good education, and exposure to books. They often cited an encouraging teacher who helped them to develop the confidence to write. Secondly, for most of the writers, the motivation to begin writing was deeply personal. An issue, story, problem, question existed within their own lives that the writers felt had to be expressed. Darko herself acknowledges: 'I have to deal with issues I feel passionately about. I write first for me. If any other person finds it likeable, that's a bonus' (5 December 2000). Strong feeling, plus the confidence to render that feeling in words, is essential. For Amma Darko, the writing urge eventually is beyond one's control, almost like a voice from the subconscious, and it is deeply connected to her emotional state.

> Sometimes when I'm very depressed, that's when the urge comes . . . It's when I'm under pressure or when I'm going through bad times that I write a lot. Because then I have to write to survive. And when things are so smooth, I don't know, maybe it kills the urge or dampens it a little (3 December 1999).

A third commonality emerges: writing as an outlet of the emotions is both political and personal. Generations of African women writers have expressed a sense of social obligation and a hope that their writing, even in the early stages, might bring a positive benefit to someone besides themselves. Part of this social commitment results from the African worldview that recognises the artist's obligation to his or her community. Recording and re-living her experience and translating it into a lesson her society needs to learn, Darko willingly takes on sensitive subjects, saying: 'When I feel strongly about an issue, I write. It's educating others and therapy for me' (28 May 1998). This sense of connection with readers runs deep, and seems to come from women's complex role as caretakers for their societies, both preservers and critics of tradition. Those two roles inevitably come into conflict and require much of women writers, particularly in the post-colonial context. As Darko says,

> Because colonialism degraded our traditions, we now find ourselves too protective of them. We stubbornly refuse to look objectively at our culture. We have so little left, we can't afford to. But you get blackmailed if you say we should look twice at parts of our culture. People say you are not African. But with globalisation, we can no longer pretend that we live in our own village (2 June 1999).

Support, strong feeling and social commitment alone are not enough to make a writer. One must develop a sustainable writing practice that allows pages to accumulate. One needs time and focus, and there is a sense among many women working in West Africa that the demands of daily life are simply too great to allow the mental or physical energy to write. Even for the educated elite with household help, duties to the extended family, unpredictable transportation and communication systems, ever-rising inflation that makes imported goods ever more expensive if they can be found at all, frequent power outages, even regular bouts of malaria all take their toll. The focus required to dedicate oneself to an artistic process is harder to maintain in such a society. Making a living from writing is not even on the landscape. Women, who play multiple roles in keeping the social fabric of their societies together, find it particularly difficult to find time to write on a regular basis. Each day is filled with family and work responsibilities. Psychic energy and focus are depleted by the end of the day, so that even if one can find an hour before bed, there is little strength to use the hour well. Furthermore, extended African family networks must be maintained by routines of visits and involvements that place additional responsibilities on women. As a Fanti, Darko's children belong to her husband's lineage. Once a month, the entire family goes to her husband's hometown of Larteh, a small village in the Akwapim region, to connect with the extended family. Darko calls it 're-tanking', refreshing oneself after the stresses of a busy city life, and it provides connection to traditional ways that are still highly valued. Such connection is important but may also work against finding the necessary solitude to write. This social burden on women, in particular, along with the economic and logistical challenges of life in Ghana, makes finding time and space to write a lifelong struggle for women writers.

Darko has dealt with the problem in a unique way, by stealing hours from sleep in order to maintain a consistent writing practice. She developed an extremely disciplined schedule of three times a week getting up in the middle of the night at 2 a.m., working for an hour, and then going back to bed. Once she had been doing this for a while, it no longer seemed as disruptive as it was in the beginning. She also managed to carve out some time from her job at the

Internal Revenue Service, taking breaks between reviewing files. Darko uses any gap in her schedule to write, even for a few minutes. Working little by little, gathering bits of time from the fringes of other parts of her life, she manages to accumulate at least an hour a day to devote to her craft. She generally writes quickly and freely, especially during the middle of the night, not worrying about revision, her writer's alchemy turning focused observations of daily life into stories that represent a working through of her own emotions. 'There's a connection between my mind and my fingers,' she says (28 May 1998). When she's writing regularly, stories flow out through her arm, and there's a living relationship with the paper that would not exist, she believes, if she typed on a computer screen. This method of writing may look onerous, but it is suitable to her circumstances and absolutely essential to keeping her productivity flowing. Like Buchi Emecheta, whose most productive years were those in which she was a single mother of five young children, Darko has found that the necessity of squeezing writing in among other responsibilities is a motivating and focusing factor in itself.[4]

Darko carries a small notebook with her at all times, in which she writes down ideas and scenes prompted by what she sees every day. This habit of observing, overhearing, recording, and remembering typifies most writers and it is inseparable from the writing process itself. Darko explains: 'I write little things, and when I finally decide on a story line, they're there. As I'm writing a story, I also collect ideas. They're not separate processes for me' (13 July 1999).

For most African women writers, there is no 'room of one's own'. Darko keeps a small table in the living room in full view of her family during the day, with a 'do not touch' sign on her papers. It is impossible to keep her notes private. Every aspect of her book and her writing life is either in the family living space or her office space. As she says,

> I'm a mother, a wife, and I live in this kind of situation here and I write. Even the whole environment here, it's kind of inorderly and it's kind of a bit hectic, yeah? And somehow you get used to this kind of environment, and it sort of begins to have an impact on your creativity (3 December 1999).

The impact is that Darko describes her writing process as 'just putting down pieces', which get smoothed into a whole text when the urge comes to her. The concept of piecework – assembling disparate units, crafting a whole from little bits – is perhaps more characteristic of women writers who have only bits of time to devote to their craft. Likewise in her material world, Darko must make do with a kind of patchwork. The scarcity and high cost of paper, reliable pens, and typewriter ribbon is a problem in West Africa. Darko ran out of ribbon for her Smith-Corona typewriter during a time in Ghana when no ribbons were being imported, so she had to finish the last 220 pages of one of her manuscripts in longhand. 'People have no idea what African writers go through to get what others can take for granted. The things you do just so you can afford paper and postage stamps! And your own people think you're crazy,' she exclaimed (4 August 2000).

There is another lack that has a profound effect on Darko and those like her: the connection with other writers. Most women I interviewed were unaware of other women writing on the continent. Access to new novels by African women is extremely limited, and the works of earlier writers are not always available either. Given the significance of mothers and elders as mentors in African cultures, being unable to place oneself in a line of women writers seems particularly damaging to a writer's sense of self. Emerging women writers in this region suffer from the local lack of writing groups, bookstores, local publishers, and conferences. They find the writing process even more solitary and unsupported than it is by nature.

Darko's independent nature has helped her cope. She credits no one particular person with helping her on her way, nor has any writer given her writing advice. Fiercely self-reliant and sure of her narrative gift, without 'anxiety of influence', she sees herself as one who forges ahead without the need or time for guidance. She has recently met several of the 'matriarchs' of African women writers – Aminata Sow Fall, Ama Ata Aidoo, and Buchi Emecheta, for example – and Aidoo, in particular, has offered encouragement.

> What I really appreciate about Ama Ata Aidoo, is that although she's at a very different level from me, she doesn't hold back support. She came to my book launch, which really meant a lot. I learned later from my husband that she even warned him, 'If you give her any problems that cause her to stop writing, you'll have to answer to me!' People told me she's too saucy, but I don't care. She's been very generous (3 June 1999).

What value does talking about the process of writing have? Given how little time is free in a Ghanaian woman's day, is it fair to say that talking about writing decreases the time available for writing itself? As Darko herself said once, when invited to a writer's conference: 'It's four days! My God! Look at all the pages I'd miss!' (19 January 2001). Still, I would argue that talking about writing serves a valuable function for women writers in particular. It heightens awareness of the craft and legitimises their participation in the process. Especially for unknown writers or unpublished writers, discussing the process may be the only way to link themselves to a developing literary tradition. To talk process is to join a culture of writing and reading. That writing and reading culture, especially because it is not an explicit one in Ghana, may seem hidden from the budding writer.

But what happens when that talk takes place outside one's own culture? Darko had an opportunity to find out when she won a fellowship to spend six months writing in Stuttgart, Germany, in 1999. Her creative connection to Germany is profound, so she looked forward to the return. Things worked out rather differently than she expected, however, since she actually found it difficult to write during her time at the Akademie Schloss Solitude. Out of her normal context, without the pressures of having to salvage a few hours from her other responsibilities, it was a challenge to set up a writing schedule that worked for her. She was surprised to find that the thing she had been longing for – solitude and freedom from responsibilities – were so unfamiliar that her writing did not flow as it had. 'I was suffering some blockages. I mean, nothing was coming, in the initial stages, at least. I think everything was just too perfect!' (3 June 1999). She eventually decided that the situation at home in Ghana would be more conducive to the psychic state she needed to write.

> I went through total mental blackouts at first in Germany, where no thoughts would come. I was living in a small studio and I thought it was because the walls were bare, so I hung pictures. But still nothing happened. I was alone, but I need hectic to jolt me . . . I'm going back to the hectic (3 June 1999).

On the other hand, when Darko won sponsorship for the prestigious Iowa International Writers' workshop, she found an opportunity to get critical feedback from other writers on her new manuscript. She published the first chapter of *Faceless* on the workshop's internet homepage. As much as solitude, writers need connection with other writers to develop their talents.

So there are many factors that make an African woman's development as a writer challenging and her chances of success slim. She is required to steal time for her practice from a life that is crowded with family obligations and a hectic work schedule. She is isolated from other women engaged in writing and reading. She works under conditions of material deprivation: paper, pens, even electricity are unreliable or completely unavailable. She gets little feedback from her readership, most of which is outside her own country. She may even be forced to live and write away from her home culture in order to find more favourable material and psychic conditions and fewer time constraints. But then she will have to cope with the additional challenges of adjusting to a foreign culture. Still, she writes. As Darko and others like her have demonstrated for over seventy years, it is still possible, and desirable, to craft a writing life in Africa.

## THE BOOK MAKES THE WRITER

Writing alone does not automatically cause one to 'become' a writer in one's own mind or anyone else's. Only publication and a readership can do that. Wherever words in print are valorised, the makers of those words are themselves made in the act of publication. According to many writers, only the material object, the published book – not the act of writing or being read by others – entitles one to be called a 'real' writer. The book, the tangible evidence of the craft – with cover, pages, typeface, and an assigned place on a bookstore shelf – is a commodity to be bought and sold. It exists as a result of activities that are generally quite removed from the writer herself. Publishers control the practical aspects of making a book and therefore have great symbolic control over the writer. By buying, shaping and marketing the writer's words, they validate her literary worth. By investing in her continued production, they ensure that she has a literary future.

The stamp of approval by an entity that can grant authority to speak – and can also create a public place in which to speak – is particularly important to women, who are generally writing from a position outside official power structures. But this approval comes at a price. The publisher and the writer often exist in a relationship that bears an uncomfortable resemblance to that of an imperial power and its colony – the publisher extracting the natural resources from the writer at a beneficial price, then manufacturing the finished product and selling it for a profit, of which only a tiny portion goes back to the writer. On the writer's side, there is a tension between relief at being recognised and resentment at being exploited. It may be an inevitable part of the writer-publisher relationship, especially in the post-colonial context.

Three special publication difficulties face writers like Amma Darko. First, the geographic and cultural distance from Western publishers of African literature puts the writer at a disadvantage in gaining access to editors and agents, negotiating royalties, and marketing her own work on reading tours. Secondly, the inherent imbalance of power between author and publisher is exacerbated when the most successful and prestigious publishers are multinational corporations based in former imperial nations. The third difficulty arises if the writer turns to indigenous publishing firms to produce her work. In this case, she must contend with the realities of publishing in post-colonial Africa: small, under-capitalised houses; expensive materials in an inflationary economy; underpaid staff; printing irregularities; cultural expectations that the author herself should subsidise publication; and lack of means of wide distribution, which means that her work may be difficult to find and soon go out of print. The publishing chronology of Darko's novels illustrates these three challenges.

Darko's first published novel, *Beyond the Horizon*, was originally written in English, but was published first in German in 1991 because the manuscript itself was circulating in Germany. Through a roundabout process no one can precisely identify, the manuscript came to the attention of a woman film-maker in Berlin who wanted to obtain movie rights and film the work. Though the film was never made, contacts at the Protestant Centre for Third World Cinema in Stuttgart began actively seeking publishers for the book version. Jorg Hunger, of Schmetterling Verlag, agreed to publish the work in translation, believing that German people should hear Darko's story. The moment was right. Shortly after the novel appeared, a German book association began a three-year campaign called 'Afrikanissimo' to organise readings of African literature, and the work had a ready-made forum. The first print run was sold out within three months, and a second edition came out in 1994, before it had yet appeared in English. Schmetterling, in effect, became Darko's agent, and it was through this German publisher that her manuscript came to the attention of Heinemann, who published the work in 1995. Darko had little control over the process.

One of the strengths of this novel is its poignant depiction of the pressure on those who are abroad – 'beyond the horizon' – to send money home no matter how they earn it. Darko's pity for immigrants, tied by family obligations to send money home, is deeply felt. There seems to be no escape; money and material goods from Europe prove the 'been-to' has been successful and brought honour to the family at home.[5] Indeed, the dream of a new life has not been attained but sold off, as the German title *Der Verkaufte Traum*, indicates. But because the novel was first published in German, it was read first not by the audience who might have profited most from its sad lesson but by those who were already aware of the situation from the outside. The novel was not available in English for several years. Even after it appeared in Heinemann's African Writers' Series, it was difficult to find in Accra, where young girls with dreams of their own future journeys abroad might take heed of its warning.

Darko's second published work, *Webs* (*Spinwebben* in German), came out in German in 1996, and it has not yet been published in English. This rambling story of an 'African daughter' is made up partly of Darko's own experiences and partly those of her friends, interspersed with commentary on Ghana's political history – a kind of coming-of-age tale for the girl and the nation, both having gone through uncertain times in their search for identity and a sense of purpose. The novel takes a look at the life of a different kind of African woman: one who is educated and who has had a very different experience in her encounter with Europe from that portrayed in *Beyond the Horizon*. Darko calls *Webs* her text of 'self-discovery', reflecting on the impact of colonialism on the daily life and mentality of Ghanaians. While the narrator should not be taken literally to be the author, she has much in common with Darko's ambitious spirit and is willing to pay the price of straddling two cultures. The explicit intersections with political life in Ghana after Independence are unusual in a novel about a woman's life and make a worthwhile contribution to the field of women's writing. Indeed, a section from this work has been submitted for inclusion in the forthcoming West African volume in the *Women Writing Africa* project of the Feminist Press.

By the time of Darko's third work, publication in English had in a sense caught up with publication in German. In fact, *The Housemaid* appeared in English in1998, slightly before the German version. It is representative of Darko's conversational and satirical style as a storyteller who is particularly concerned with the roles of family and authority figures in crafting the lives of women. In this story of a small maid embroiled in a national scandal over an abandoned dead baby, Darko takes on the sensitive topic of witchcraft and its pervasiveness in all levels of society. She does so with wry humour rather than outraged condemnation. Witchcraft is blamed, and women with it, for many things that go wrong in Ghanaian society. But in fact every episode in the book revolves around human deceit and manipulation; every interaction between people is based on the material gain each party has anticipated from it. The rituals of negotiation and manipulation of societal jealousy give an insight into cultural problems Darko bravely exposes. Exploitation in all its permutations – and the consequent pervasive corruption of relationships in Ghanaian society – is reflected in the layered structure of the story, which shifts time and place and gradually unpeels itself rather than spinning out in a straightforward linear narrative. This spiralling and overlapping pattern of events and perspectives reinforces the sense of Ghanaian society as a web of interconnected people and actions. In the network of women reaching from village to city and radiating throughout Ghana, individual stories are less significant than their roles in a larger social context in which women are victimised but also are responsible for victimising each other. By this time Darko had begun to develop a reputation, at least in Germany, as a committed social critic, unafraid to depict homegrown social problems.

German publications overall provide a fuller picture of the scope of Darko's talents. The German edition of *The Housemaid* included a short story (*In Excess*) about the feelings of a second wife upon the arrival of a third wife in the home. Schmetterling also published Darko's fourth novel, *A Cross of a Kind* (*Verirrtes Herz* in German) in 2000, and that work has never been published in English. The novel is about the trials of a young girl who must sell cassava balls at the train station in order to pay for her brothers' education and help support her family. The bitterness she feels at her second-class status is increased when her society shuns her after she is raped. Her brothers' successful and happy lives and her own lack of education rankle her so deeply that she engages in vengeful manipulations and accusations of witchcraft.

A fourth work of Darko's that is not available in English is a short story written for a 2001 anthology compiled by the German office of Amnesty International. The anthology, called *Aller Menschen Würde* (*Everyone's Dignity*), includes contributions from such well-known writers as Nadine Gordimer. Darko's *Colour Palaver* is drawn from an experience she had in Germany.[6] An African woman rebukes a German man for assuming that she is a prostitute. She muses about the significance of being black in Germany and the destructive cycle of economic interactions between Africa and the West. She remembers overhearing a conversation about the 'colour of poverty' between two young men in a Ghanaian bar hawking tapes of so-called 'Burger highlife' music, an adaptation of indigenous West African music composed by Ghanaians living in Hamburg and then imported back into Ghana. The cycle of exporting raw materials at low prices and importing finished goods at high prices perpetuates Africa's position at the losing end of the commercial exchange, or palaver, with Europe. The racist insult to one woman becomes part of a larger discourse on money and colour. In its series of questions and conflicts with no easy answer, the work contains stylistic traits prominent elsewhere in Darko's work: shifting locations, open-endedness, overheard conversations, bits of slang, and finally the narrator's reflection that individual experiences have wider political implications.

By the time of her most recent novel, *Faceless*, published in both English and German in 2003, Amma Darko had made a significant change in her publishing practices. Even before Heinemann discontinued the African Writers' Series, Darko determined to shift her allegiance to a local publisher, Sub-Saharan in Accra, which also publishes the works of Ama Ata Aidoo. This represented a daring move, as she herself recognised, one that might limit her growing reputation. 'Many people want to play it safe. Most creative writers are published outside' (3 June 1999). With the largest output of African fiction coming from prestigious multinational firms like Heinemann, Longman, and Macmillan that are based outside Africa, African writers can reach more people, garner a greater reputation, and earn more money by being published by a Western press, thereby perpetuating the sense that 'business' of African literature takes place outside the continent. Though the African branches of Western publishers have been indigenised to some extent, the houses are still fundamentally oriented toward a Western market, where the largest audience exists. The scarcity of well-funded African publishers has meant that publishers outside the continent have determined what will be presented to the African public as their own literature.

Thus there are two contexts in which those works are marketed and consumed – home and away – with different literacy rates, numbers of bookstores and public libraries, roles of literature in the country's cultural life, and populations that are or are not able and willing to read the works. This duality of creation and reception contexts has a fragmenting impact on all postcolonial writers, but particularly on women, since their rates of literacy, access to higher education, and validated cultural production have been more sharply limited than men's. Their participation in the process at every level is therefore even more fragmented.

Darko's largest audience was in Germany, but she recognised the need to connect with her potential readers at home. Staking the entire process of publishing, marketing and sales of her novels in English on a small local publisher was a risk. The situation in Ghana is not particularly promising.

Publishers are under-capitalised. Bookstores tend to be small, crowded, under-supplied. When books are expensive, in order to recoup the publisher's expenses, the general public cannot buy them. When supply networks throughout the continent or to the West are unreliable, readers elsewhere may not even know of a book's existence. It took a leap of faith in herself, her audience, and her country to turn her back on Heinemann. But her efforts to support local enterprise and get her work out to a local public have been rewarded against all expectations.

There are several reasons for this. First of all, there are changes occurring in the local publishing scene. In contrast to the 1960s and 1970s, when European publishers retained majority shares in publishing corporations and held powerful appointments as technical advisors, today locals currently own and operate branches of multinational publishing companies, like Heinemann East Africa, and Longman's Caribbean, for example. Secondly, there has been a growth in the number of successful indigenous publishers, who must invest in their writers to contribute to their own reputation, which leads to greater competition and increasing professionalism of those enterprises. Thirdly, Darko's novels have been gaining more attention in English-speaking critical circles. Well-known poet and professor Kofi Anyidoho taught *Beyond the Horizon* at the University of Ghana at Legon and wrote the introduction to *Faceless*. *Horizon* and *Housemaid* have both been recommended as examination texts in Ghana.

Considering the overlapping circles of local and foreign publishing and critical influence, one can see that being known first as a German writer may not have been to Darko's disadvantage after all. Schmetterling has made sure that Germans have access to all her works and sponsored annual reading tours, helping to position Darko in the West as the politically astute and committed writer she is. The German support brought in support from Heinemann and other publishers in Europe. *Beyond the Horizon* has begun appearing on university syllabi in the USA, Europe, and Africa. Therefore students in places as far-flung as New Jersey, Texas, Italy, Germany, Ghana, and Togo are exposed to her work and want to know more. Critical papers on Darko have begun appearing at conferences. Through an arrangement with African Books Collective, Sub-Saharan has been able to provide her latest work, *Faceless,* efficiently to readers abroad. If Darko had been published first in Ghana back in the early 1990s, she might not have found such an engaged readership or such a supportive publisher.

## RECOGNITION BY AFRICAN READERS

Over thirty years ago, Chinua Achebe concluded that Africans did not generally have the habit of reading for pleasure.[9] But times are changing, and Achebe's view may need updating. Despite slow progress, it seems that educators and journalists are clearly concerned with helping to develop a reading culture in Ghana, and elsewhere in West Africa, today. Book clubs for children are sponsored by local publishers like Afram, and daily newspaper columns print book reviews and interview writers on their works and on reading practices.

Still, the development of Darko's local audience will depend on further changes in societal conditions and attitudes. Women writers have no chance of developing a local readership if they live in societies where women have no leisure time and cultural values militate against privacy. As Darko has said: 'What time does the Ghanaian woman have to read? [In Germany] I can read on the bus; I can't imagine myself reading on the *tro-tro!*' (3 June 1999). Nonetheless, despite the claim that people do not read, there is evidence that many actually do. Romance novels are popular with educated professional men and women, university students, and teachers, effectively blurring the line in the public's eye between 'popular' and 'serious' fiction. Two Series ('Pacesetter' by Macmillan and 'Heartbeats' by Heinemann) are aimed at a growing young, university-educated, and affluent market that wants a good, fast-paced romance story in a modern African setting. Clearly, reading for pleasure is going on. Prior to the existence of these African-oriented series, the 'Mills and Boon' series of romance novels were also extremely popular in English-speaking West Africa.[8] Darko, like many of her urban professional counterparts throughout West Africa, reads primarily popular bestsellers from the West, though in recent years she has become more interested in African fiction from around the continent.

The challenge for an emerging writer seeking to find an audience is to create works that have broad general appeal and are not restricted to the university classroom. Darko's work can do that because of its moral message, humour, witty dialogue, and lack of abstraction, making it easily accessible to any reader. She deals with African problems in a forthright way, daring to take on the problems that cultural traditions create. For readers in the West – both in the classroom and on the street – her novels portray the contemporary urban African scene with specific detail and ironic humour, in a way that does not require an extensive knowledge of the African history and culture for an outsider to understand.

Micere Mugo has claimed: 'Any writer who is not recognised in her own village by ordinary people is not worthy of being called a writer.'[9] But how can a writer be known in her own village, or even her own country, if her books are not available there or if people do not read? Access to books must precede the development of a reading habit. If books are not available in Africa, then local audiences are unaware of them and do not request them. Even where book titles are known, the difficulty and expense of obtaining them, along with the inadequacies of the library system – there are only sixty public libraries in all of

Ghana to serve a literate population of 18 million – means that in effect there is no affordable way for most Ghanaians to know and keep up with the literature of their own country except through school examination texts. This means that only the most educated will read, and only those in academia will keep up with literature after university. The end result is the uniquely post-colonial rupture of what once was a more dialogic relationship between creator and audience reinforced by Africa's oral narrative tradition. The circle of supply and demand seems to perpetuate the imbalance.

Even in the West, there seems to be a narrower pipeline to readers than there was formerly. Niyi Osundare writes:

> ...one thing is sure, the period in which Achebe and Soyinka launched themselves on to the literary scene was saner and kinder than the one in which their successors are presently trapped. Whereas their works received enthusiastic attention from publishers and were distributed all over the world, overseas publishers now see African literature as a bad risk, while local ones only manage to bring out a few titles over a long period.[10]

The discontinuation of the African Writers' Series in 2002 seems to prove his point. It is in this context that the present generation of emerging writers struggles for recognition. Neither adequately recognised at home nor as prized abroad as in former times, they are especially removed from their readers. Amma Darko represents an interesting case of an emerging writer whose reputation was made first in translation and then in English by a prestigious series published in London, whose works have been quickly translated into other languages, and whose future success in English is now dependent on a local Ghanaian publisher and its ability to distribute her books at home and abroad.

As a published writer in a country with an emerging readership, Darko stands on the cusp of this change in the reading habits in Ghana. To know one's own literary tradition and see oneself there, and to recognise connections with other literatures, is as significant for developing readers as it is for writers. A gradually growing and changing readership both at home and abroad will have a profound effect on what is available to be read in the future in West Africa. Times are changing, and Amma Darko is representative of those changes. There is greater tolerance in West Africa today for using literature (either as a writer or a reader) to challenge some traditional cultural expectations. In fact, perhaps more than in many societies, West Africa promotes literature as a social guide, giving credibility to that challenge.

The personal is truly political in Darko's writing. Her educational purpose, prominent in all her work, is to remind readers of the relationship of their responsibility toward others who are victims of their societies. Getting that message to African readers is probably Darko's most compelling goal as a writer at this point in her life. Her fiction makes one think about the condition of Africans in Europe, the social machinations of different classes all trying to get ahead, or the impact of a large societal issue on the individual. Redemptive possibilities exist, even for those in desperate circumstances. By the end of *Beyond the Horizon*, the narrator knows she will provide a better life for her children than she has had. *The Housemaid* closes with laughter mixed with tears to lighten the burden of self-knowledge and self-reform. *Faceless* closes with an epilogue that speaks to the persistence of tragedy and social crisis in the midst of the individual's mundane daily concerns. Even in a society supposedly without a 'reading habit', a space is gradually being opened for the general appeal of literature firmly embedded in the everyday but also rising above the mundane.

But it is important to acknowledge that things are difficult today for new African women writers. Political and economic factors, plus a general lowering of educational standards that have followed tough economic times, mean that the general readership is engaged in a constant struggle to get ahead or stay afloat. There seems to be less of the energy and exuberance that sustained writers and readers in early post-Independence days. So despite the fact that there are more indigenous publishers and higher literacy rates today, this is still a precarious time for women readers and writers in Ghana. Women readers are there, and they must be provided with more fiction that speaks to their own condition. More Ghanaian women are writing than people realise. My own study identified over 30 women fiction writers in Ghana (and about 100 in all of English-speaking West Africa) who had published at least one novel or collection of short stories by the year 2000. There are many more today. But they lack formal means of sustaining themselves and must develop their own networks in order to connect with others and be heard. They must think beyond their current living realities, and beyond what has been presented as literary reality, to write new stories that speak to today's readership.

Texts and reading are points in a continuous circle of artistic production and reception, and they operate upon each other in ways that can either enable creation or shut it off. The published book itself is both product and producer of a reading dynamic. And the act of reading is a kind of re-creation both of the text and of literary expectations for the next text. Therefore, critical interpretations must be considered in the light of the cultural contexts from which texts emerge, as well as the tropes that govern stories and storytellers. Especially in a region like West Africa with a relatively young novelistic tradition (though a long oral narrative tradition), it may be impossible to separate readings of a book from reading expectations created by a book. The law of supply and demand seems to work this way: what is available to be read determines in large measure what can be written. It is in everyone's interest to sustain the circle through encouraging new writers, local publishing, reading groups, and critical attention to new works.

Amma Darko's experience typifies a host of contemporary issues for today's African woman writer: inadequate supply and distribution of what has been written, struggle to gain a readership in her own country, lack of awareness of the women writers who preceded her, lack of critical attention at home and in the West. As the author of three published works in English, she might expect to be more widely known. But despite the growing numbers of women writers from this region, there seems to be less known about this new generation. Still, they are neither silent nor invisible. Amma Darko is writing her way forward, expanding the range and reach of Ghanaian fiction. She and other women writers like her should be spared the neglect that plagued their literary foremothers.

There is a popular Akan proverb that speaks to the complex relationship of writer and reader: 'The one who cuts the path can't tell if it's crooked. Only those who come behind can know.'[11] Darko stays focused on her goal and continues, making small corrections but never stopping as she writes her way forward to good stories that ring true to her experience. It is the responsibility of the rest of us to comment on her path and acknowledge the difficulties of cutting it.

# Monica Bungaro

## Victims and/or Victimisers? Women's De(Con)structive Power in *The Housemaid*

### THE DIALECTIC NATURE OF AFRICAN WOMEN'S DISCOURSE

The novels of the 1990s offer a new gaze turned to the future, actively reflecting on the elements necessary for a transformation of African society and a re-evaluation of woman's status within that society. As a symbol of this creative approach, today's African women's texts exploit multiple subject positions as a textual strategy for challenging the marginal status allocated to them in dominant discourses. Rather than viewing the marginal condition of African women as the cause for reiterations of their victimhood, which then would cement them into this role, writers describe this marginalisation in ways that stress fluidity and movement. African women's marginal positionality implies the existence of stable imperial centres and states which can only be written back to or subverted by more dialogical models of subjectivity able to question oppositional binaries.

Obioma Nnaemeka states that 'one must focus upon the ambiguous interstices of the binaries where woman is both benevolent and malevolent with powers that are healing and lethal' (*The Politics of Mothering*, 1997: 2). This dialogic of difference and dialectic of identity characterises both African women's subjectivity and African women's discourse. As African women writers are struggling to make themselves visible and their voices heard inside and outside the continent by creating new locations and alternative scenarios to the ruling hegemonies, they are breaking out of the dominant political, economic, cultural conceptions of gender and are problematising their identities and subject positions. By freeing herself from simplistic dualisms and dichotomised paradigms that try to encapsulate her composite self and experience in all-encompassing and convenient definitions, the African woman writer is increasingly inventing and using strategies that express critical dissent from dominant narratives.

In other words, by identifying places where shifting and multi-layered identities are forged out of the debris of corroded, formerly homogeneous identities, she is able to write, as Rachel Du Plessis would say, 'beyond the ending':

> 'Writing beyond the ending means not repeating your words and following your methods but... finding new words and creating new methods. It

produces a narrative that denies or reconstructs seductive patterns of feelings that are culturally mandated, internally policed, hegemonically poised.' (1985: 5)

Writing, in this sense, acts as an effective weapon in counteracting the dominance of male mythologies; it is an act engaged not only in formulating alternatives but also in accurately recording what is, in fact, already there. The African woman writer is not only involved in making herself heard, in changing the architecture of male-centred ideologies and languages but also in discovering new forms and languages to express her experience, an experience that may as well incorporate extremes, thus transgressing and displacing acquired notions of femaleness.

The ability to master language and create her version of the story with constant negotiations along the winner-loser demarcation line is typical of Amma Darko. The portrayal of credible female characters is symbolic of and intricately related to the African woman's dawning understanding of herself, who she is, what she can do, what she wants to be and of both her destructive and deconstructive power. Darko's novels offer updated insights into women's predicament in fast-changing and increasingly unstable post-colonial environments and contexts where women are simultaneously victims and accomplices of/with the on-going system.

In the general atmosphere of corruption and exploitation typical of most post-colonial African societies, any distinction between victims and victimisers, abusers and abused becomes blurred. In *The Housemaid,* fixed notions of maternity, motherhood, manhood and womanhood are altered, and alternate ideas of femaleness and motherhood are introduced, sometimes in their extreme form. As a consequence, Darko highlights the idea that victims must accept some of the responsibility for their victimisation especially when they foolishly agree to participate in the exploitation of other women by permitting themselves to be dominated.

*The Housemaid* therefore calls for a reassessment of female and male status and of the image of the traditional bonding between mother and child. Confirmation of this comes from the following points developed in the narrative: daughters in revolt against mothers, the daughter's exploitation by the mother and the daughter's perception of that exploitation, the mother's inability to provide comfort and support to the daughter, the conflict between generations (mother-daughter-grandmother with the mother and grandmother as two diametrically opposite forces) and absent, weak and exploitative fathers. Stereotypical images of the mother (and grandmother) figure as carrier of life and eternal nurturer, of fathers and husbands as tyrannical and oppressive, and of daughters as obedient and submissive are subverted, and cultural practices are often viewed as abuse. By challenging constructions of womanhood, the novel demonstrates how new areas of generational and gender conflict have opened up in modern society.

African women writers have historically interrogated patriarchy and their stories are the expression of social dissidence. These stories are told in the context of a changing world, a world in which being black, female and poor may have catastrophic consequences. Feminists today have much to say about the collective victimisation of women by patriarchal societies as well as the victimisation of individuals in the form of rape, spousal abuse and spiritual and psychological oppression. But few feminists have commented upon woman-on-woman violence and abuse. Like Aidoo before her, Darko explodes gender configurations that automatically assign victimhood to females by focusing on the multiple subjectivity inherent in female personhood. In fact, she ruptures the oppressor/victim dichotomy characteristic of liberal feminist theorising of motherhood and femaleness in general, by demonstrating 'that agency and victimhood are not mutually exclusive...[for] victims are also agents who can change their lives and affect other lives in radical ways' (*Nnaemeka*, 1997: 3).

The questioning of norms of masculinity, femininity and maternity is at the centre of African women's agenda. Women writers today are putting their cards on the table as they are re-conceptualising femaleness, pointing out both its regenerative as well as its destructive potential. Rather than idealise womanhood in order to exonerate it, Darko's unbiased awareness of the situation of women and her determination to reveal painful truths, to name the disease, are a first step towards curing it.

## AGENCY AND VICTIMHOOD IN THE HOUSEMAID

*The Housemaid*, has a complex structure that testifies to Darko's, and, more generally, to younger women writers' willingness and ability to refine the basic tools of the genre by making the plot more complicated and the narration polyphonic, that is, by using multiple voices that echo and reply to each other and thus create an effect of mirroring and counter-mirroring for readers. Most of the tales that compose the articulated fabric of the novel are told in a humorous vein that at times conflates into an ironic oblique narration. The novel's myriad subtle rhetorical strategies and its scathing and often cutting irony, offer an alternative to dramatic and/or social realist scripts.

*The Housemaid*'s plot is internally sustained by a contrastive analysis based on the representation of generational and gender-aligned tensions that run through the novel and make their appearance in it from the beginning. Intertwined with them, is the novel's ambiguous engagement with an acute awareness of the inequalities of present-day Ghana. From the very beginning of the novel, the reader is button-holed by an insistent narrator with a clear message, one that picks up certain characteristics of the refrains recited by Ama Ata Aidoo.

Opening the book we read: 'In Ghana if you want to come into the world as a she, acquire the habit of praying and master it. Because you will need it, desperately, as old age pursues you and mother nature's hand approaches you with a wry smile, paint and brush at the ready, to daub you with wrinkles' (1). The opening of the novel makes no secret of the author's attitude to gender issues, a point confirmed by a direct, poignant and sarcastic style that establishes the tone of the whole novel from its beginning. As Darko herself affirms:

> 'Though some change has occurred in today's Ghana as to the relationship between men and women due to women's easier access to education and financial resources, even in families where women themselves are pursuing successful careers, they are still expected to arrange the childcare, do the bulk of the domestic work and all the domestic planning. From this point of view, nothing has changed. I can do my job, dedicate myself to writing, still when I come back home, I am no longer a worker or a writer. I am a wife and a mother' (Bungaro 2000).

According to the author, therefore, gender still makes a difference. It is in itself a generator of inequalities, it is an indelible mark. In this sense, Darko's opening does not simply bear testimony to a conventionally accepted reality, but through its biting irony intends to shake the readership, especially the women, and remind them of the risks and impediments inherent in their gender and their position as women in an African context.

Not surprisingly then, *The Housemaid*'s world is a world composed primarily of women and in which men intervene only as passing characters, official or transitory lovers, drunken or weak fathers, and/or oppressors. As the story unfolds it becomes clear that seven different women play their part in the drama represented: Tika, Teacher, Efia, Efia's mother and grandmother, Akua, and Bibio.

Darko employs an extended flashback to provide a structure for her book. She moves from the discovery of the body of a dead baby to investigate the ambitions, frustrations and schemes by which Efia is brought to give birth to a still-born child whose body she then tries to conceal. The focus in all this is very much on the role of women, but not in an unbiased manner. The writer is fully aware of a tendency to brand unfortunate women witches, though she herself creates some desperately twisted, evil matrons. Foremost among these, is Efia's grandmother, who, quite cantankerous by nature, and motivated by resentment, greed and envy, encourages the girl, with the help of Efia's mother, to become pregnant while working as a house-maid for Tika, a wealthy businesswoman. The plan is that Efia should then name one of her madam's business partners, one of those who regularly 'discuss business' with Tika in her bedroom, as the father of her unborn child. This wicked manipulation of a young woman is eventually uncovered by Tika with the help of her intellectual friend, Teacher, a woman who, because of her quality status and her manners, is usually asked by other women from Accra to search in the nearby villages for trustworthy and hardworking housemaids. When the three women's plan to get hold of Tika's wealth is discovered, Efia is cast out. Pregnant, alone and desperate, she hides in the house of Akua, another prostitute living in the city. She then gives birth and conceals the body of her still-born child in a rubbish dump, after attempting in vain to bring the dead body to her village for a ritual ceremony that, in her mind, could prevent Tika's curse from affecting her and her family. The little corpse is subsequently found by two boy scavengers, Bibio's brothers, who are searching the rubbish dump for anything that may be useful. The circle then is completed.

The intricate web of deceit and relationships lends itself to multiple interpretations. One thing in the novel seems quite clear, though. There is no room for bipolar perspectives, good or evil, healer or destroyer, abuser or abused. As a mirror of society where confusion and corruption reign, men and women in the novel appear simultaneously victims of the system and victimisers, either consciously or unconsciously. They use and are used, they exploit and are exploited. In this way, Darko provocatively shows that greed and lust are not gender-specific, that women too can be oppressed as well as oppressors. Though gender still matters, gender conflicts in the novel never override or obscure class conflicts. Darko's point is that both class and gender stratification contribute to the chaos characterising modern Ghana and often force the desperate individual, either man or woman, to search for questionable alternatives.

The main relationship in the novel is between mother and daughter, and in two out of three mother-daughter dyads, Bibio and Mami Korkor, Efia and her mother, Tika and Sekyiwa, either the mother or the daughter functions as a prostitute, Efia, Tika and Sekyiwa. Common to each of these dyads is the daughter's repulsion towards the mother (though less evident in Efia's case) and the daughters' role as victims of their mothers' greed and/or mistakes. The relation is played out in terms of power and domination, the mother portrayed as heartless, cold and calculating (Sekyiwa and Efia's mother and grandmother), authoritarian (Efia's mother and grandmother), or weak and powerless (Mami Korkor). Men, on the other hand, appear as either victims of women's abuse and manipulation (Tika's father and Nsorhe) or exploiters of women's bodies and minds (Efia's father). However, a closer look at the novel reveals a more subtle strategy of characterisation.

The idea of daughters who do not want to become like their mothers, but who inevitably do so is a leitmotif in *The Housemaid*. Darko's novel, among other things, raises the question of a daughter's development in relation to the mother's life. If the mother becomes a willing victim of the system by exposing her body to abuse and exploitation, then the children will bear the consequences. Mami

Korkor's inability to put an end to a relationship with a man who has impregnated her several times without offering any financial support has caused Bibio and her brothers' misery. Women's inability to challenge patriarchal forms of repression results in their children being forced to pay for the mother's mistakes. In this sense, Mami Korkor daily enhances her marginal status by accepting an irresponsible lover and multiple pregnancies without offering any resistance. Her actions, or rather her inaction, condemn her daughter, Bibio, to victim status too. The mother's victimisation not only humiliates the mother, it mutilates the daughter who has no valid gender model to cling onto. According to Vivien Nice: 'In a nuclear family where mother carries the work and responsibility of caring without the power, we may wonder why our mothers are such martyrs to the needs of others and feel angry with her that she does not offer us a better model of independence and assertiveness' (1992: 68).

Bibio rejects the idea of being a mini-version of Mami Korkor, as she finds in her no acceptable model of womanhood. The daughter then attacks the mother as the tool of patriarchy, accusing her of colluding with the same power structures she is supposed to challenge. Bibio's hostile attitude towards her mother finds its main reason in her rejection of a life she is condemned to live because of her mother's mistakes. She feels rage at her mother's powerlessness because of her intense identification. As a result of Bibio's growing anger at her mother for having turned her into an adult at the age of eight and for the miserable life she has been condemned to live, combined with the mother's defensive attitude, mother and daughter become trapped into woman-on-woman abuse. In confronting her mother, Bibio adopts the double role of judge and aggressor: 'You should have sent me to school to learn some manners. But since you let me stay home to play mother to you and your friend's sons where else can I learn my manners but in the streets?' (11). If the daughter verbally insults the mother, the mother is initially passive, unable to deny the evidence. It is clear that Mami Korkor feels guilty for failing to meet her daughter's needs: 'Her daughter was growing on the wrong side of the tracks. But how could she change things? She had to hawk fish from dawn to dusk to earn just enough to feed herself and her four children' (11). Frustrated by her daughter's continuous attacks, Mami Korkor too starts insulting Bibio, thus creating a chain of abuse that leads to non-communication: 'Why didn't an idea like this occur to me at your birth? It would have spared me the pain of having to live with your insolence now?' (99–100). Non-communication is both the consequence and the symbolic expression of their paralysing conditions.

Though Mami Korkor is shown to offer her daughter no acceptable model of womanhood and motherhood, Darko also seems to focus on the forces acting upon the mother. What the daughter fails to see then is the social system operating at her mother's expense. As Adrienne Rich asserts: 'It is easier by far to hate and reject a mother outright than to see beyond her to the forces acting upon her' (*Of Woman Born* 1977: 235). The mother-daughter predicament is aggravated by their economic status. Poverty, here, contributes to the deterioration of an already crippled relationship. By refusing to accept the mother's position and mirror image, Bibio is not only revolting against her mother, she is revolting against society's exploitation of women, though as Gay Wilentz reminds us: 'women too often uphold practices that proscribe their choices and rights as women' (2000: 44) .

The conditions of life have meant for many poor African women like Mami Korkor that little maternal energy remains at the end of the day since sheer physical survival needs to be guaranteed before all else. In the conditions of poverty and male absence, the mother fulfils the provider role and Bibio as the eldest and only daughter comes next in the line of 'natural providers'. *The Housemaid* shows that the mother assumes the father's role but not necessarily the power and dominance associated with it. Father figures are either absent or unreliable and the woman is by force responsible for childbearing, child caring and house-keeping. As Patricia Mohammed affirms: 'The centrality of women in their capacity as mothers does not necessarily translate into similar institutional or ideological centrality' (*Gendered Realities: Essays in Caribbean Feminist Thoughts* 2001: 24).

Darko's critique does not seem to be directed at Mami Korkor's inability to take better care of her daughter, but rather at society's failure to guarantee a decent life for its members, especially for women, who appear to be still subordinated and subjugated in most contemporary societies. Darko's biting remarks in the novel are meant to uncover the ineffectiveness of legislation and social services in dealing with the growing problem of single mothers and employment in Africa. She focuses on the instability and collapse of a family structure, in which a woman abandoned by a man, has to confront on her own the financial burden of a family. It is no surprise then that the survival of the family in such circumstances also depends on child labour. To speak of mother-daughter relations in these terms is therefore to attack the patriarchal and neo-colonial structures of present-day Ghana and to demonstrate the writer's participation in an act of radical revolt.

Chapter Two of the novel introduces Tika, the main female character, whose story is gradually revealed through a movement backwards into her past life, which lacks a chronological and linear trajectory and is realised through an alternation between omniscient and internal focalisation, the use of either free-indirect speech ('she swore to herself "never again"', 17) and psycho-narration ('she had invested so much of herself in this love', 17).

When the reader meets Tika for the first time, s/he is told that she is 'single and childless at the ripe old age of 35' (17), she lives only with Efia, her housemaid, in a two-room estate house and travels all over Africa 'to scout for goods to sell in Ghana' (17). The fact that the first few hints at Tika's love affair with her classmate Owuraku are immediately followed by a flood of memories of her mother convinces the reader that the main focus of attention is neither on Tika's business life nor on her relationship with her boyfriend, but on her mother who represents a turning point in Tika's future choices as a woman. Sekyiwa is what male writers have usually defined as a fallen woman. She is illiterate, unscrupulous and deceiving. At the age of 22, she began an affair with a rich married man whose wife is barren. She gets pregnant and makes sure the good-natured man leaves his wife, and sets her up in business. She thus becomes 'one of the wealthy market mammies' (18). But as soon as 'her husband's libido' (18) wanes away she turns to other men. Little Tika begins to witness fights and arguments between her parents with her mother insulting her father ('what life is there with a dead penis?' 18) and her father imploring, pleading and weeping. Tika's father becomes then a victim of Sekyiwa's abuse, until one day, after a failed attempt of reconciliation with his first wife, he dies.

From this point in the novel, Tika takes on a double role in the narrative. As the daughter of a totally illiterate, unscrupulous and money-oriented woman, Tika is the victim of her mother's greed. In a society still economically dependent on foreign aid for survival, like most African post-colonial countries, money is worshipped by many above principles and values. Materialistic instincts are shown to prevail over dignity and morals. An economic attitude characterises most of Darko's figures in the novel. Sekyiwa is obsessed with money and teaches Tika to value it over everything else. Through her mother, Tika learns to use her appeal to seduce men and secure financial support. Sekyiwa and Tika's manner of acquiring wealth by using their 'bottom power' (Nwapa, 1981: 126) compromises their moral integrity.

Until now, in African literature, the mother had been cast as 'the guardian of tradition', especially for the daughter. In this novel, instead, social success and appearances are the only legacy Sekyiwa passes down to Tika. Darko's 'truth' subverts stereotypical notions about motherhood and womanhood that prove one-sided and unacceptable and presents motherhood, femininity and masculinity as multi-faceted essences, which might incorporate excesses.

The father's vulnerability and weakness allow a shift of power from father to mother. This imbalance between her mother's omnipotence and her father's absolute powerlessness has devastating effects on Tika's psyche and future choices. The father's passivity and lack of authority allow Sekyiwa to exercise her power and influence on her daughter without finding any resistance. In this sense, paradoxically, Tika's father can be viewed as victimiser. From being victim of his second wife, he becomes complicit in the victimisation of his daughter, since he is not able to provide Tika with protection and comfort in moments of crisis. Though not absent physically, Tika's father is psychologically absent and emotionally unavailable. Unable to defend himself against Sekyiwa's continuous attacks, he cannot provide a valuable role model. The mother's dominance and example have a profound impact on Tika's future behaviour. Moreover, Darko's passing comment on the father's past behaviour when 'he jilted his first wife for Sekyiwa' (36) strongly contrasts with the victim-status he has gained early in the novel. Darko, in this respect, clearly throws the reader off balance, as no clear-cut definitions are offered in terms of who victimises and who is the victim in the novel.

Usually readers have been confronted with despotic fathers and abusive husbands in much African literature. But Darko here is not simply creating a role reversal: Tika's father is the one represented as a weak, sensitive, accommodating husband and loving father compared to his self-centred, money and sex-oriented wife. The author also suggests that men too can be simultaneously abusers and abused, and that oppression is not necessarily a male prerogative. It is a human prerogative.

Tika too is a double-faced character. Following in her mother's footsteps, she considers the female body for its value as merchandise. If the mother offers the model of prostitution and the marketed body as a basic approach to life, Tika accepts that model without questioning it and exposes herself and her body to exploitation. Motivated by money and greed, Sekyiwa is unable to fulfil traditional duties of maternity. So is Tika. Though the status of the prostitute-mother plays a key role for the daughter, who is presented with the image of woman's inevitable degradation, still the doubt about Tika's choice remains. Could she have taken a different direction from her mother's? Refusing the mother's path would imply a new awareness on the daughter's part, an awareness that would lead to a movement of revolt, not only against the mother but also against the entire community. Unable to challenge her environment and what her mother represents, Tika follows in her mother's footsteps. Obsessed with proving her success to Owuraku, Tika invests all her energy in her business, even her dignity, as she takes up lover after lover behind her boyfriend's back. Though a victim of Sekyiwa's greed, Tika, by her choosing, turns into an unscrupulous business woman who, by using as much as getting used by men, colludes with a system of exploitation that feeds itself on gender and class inequities and imbalances.

Nevertheless, sarcastic narrative comments about a woman getting into business, where, along with the difficulty of making profits, she also has to conform to a system based on cash bribes and sexual favours if she wants to survive, serve to indicate a more subtle and intricate web of oppression. Darko is not justifying Tika's choices but is presenting mitigating factors by inserting women's lives and decisions in the more complex context of economic and social instability that characterises contemporary Ghana. Lack of education and training, and sometimes the allure of making easy money, give women little choice and place them at a considerable disadvantage (Little, 1975: 30).

The disapproval of Tika's belief in the power of money ('Money is the power. Not books'. . . 24), is immediately preceded by a sudden incursion into

Owuraku's quite distinctive perception that 'money was good, but not at any price' (24). That is the lesson Tika has not learnt yet. Because she seizes every possible opportunity to make money even when that implies lying to the one she loves, Tika's delineation as a 'good' character, victim of her mother's schemes and insatiable greed, vacillates. Another blow to the reader's potential justification of Tika's conduct as a result of the mothers' influence, comes when, after breaking with Owuraku, who in the meantime has been informed of her flirtations with other men, Tika becomes pregnant by one of the married men she sleeps with and, despite the man's marriage proposal, decides on an abortion.

Though her mother desperately tries to talk her out of it: 'Tika, please, I urge you, keep this pregnancy [...]. I am desperate for a grandchild. Please reconsider aborting this baby. I beg you...' (27), Tika refuses to bring a baby into the world, as she fears it may become like her mother and herself and reproduce the same sort of relationship she is trying to win free of: 'I won't keep this pregnancy. What if he grows to be to me what I have become to you?' (27).

Tika is therefore an ambivalent character: she is cunning (she easily uncovers Efia's and her family's plan to get hold of her wealth), determined (she is successful in her business, she leaves her mother's house) and professional in her work as a goods seller. But what is assumed to be her agency is questionable. On the one hand, Tika can be acclaimed because she is active and venturesome. Such a reading however overstates her assertiveness by equating agency with success and mobility, when very often the novel highlights the operation of the influence of and vengeance toward Tika's mother and emphasises Tika's passivity in certain circumstances; for example, when she promptly accepts Sekyiwa's proposal to set her up in business as an easy way to buy her forgiveness.

Once again in the text, Darko does away with compartmentalised notions of identity and problematises her female characters by portraying them as credible human beings, as simultaneously creators and destroyers, healers and deceivers, powerful and powerless. Though, on one side, Sekyiwa is depicted as contradicting any ideas related to 'good mothering', since she is unable to fulfil her maternal role in providing sufficient love and a decent upbringing for her daughter, on the other side, she does not see abortion as the solution to women's problems. Though her desperate need for a grandchild sounds like a selfish request to make up for the pain she has caused Tika and her father over the years, Sekyiwa's attempt to talk her daughter out of her decision to abort has the effect of partly redeeming the character from the all-round portrayal of evil matron the reader has been given so far. A change in her attitude towards life is clearly discernible soon after Tika's abortion: 'Why work so hard and save, save, save? Who am I doing this for?' (38).

It is not clear whether Sekyiwa is able to discern what is beneficial for her daughter's future, independent of whatever may be beneficial to herself or whether she is concerned with models of respectability and reputation that come with the status of 'mother' and 'grandmother'. Even in a society that is experimenting with woman's emancipation, professional success and wealth are not enough to justify a childless existence (Ngcobo, 1988). Tika's choice of aborting the baby is questionable, not because she apparently shows no innate physiological need to have a baby but because her rejection of motherhood seems to be based on the rejection of her mother's authority and emotional abuse rather than of society's expectations: 'What if he grows to be to me what I have become to you?' (27). Rather than running away from the responsibility of having a child, she seems to be running away from her mother, haunted by the fear of replicating the mother-daughter relationship she has experienced so far. Abortion as a woman's choice seems to be validated in many contemporary African women's novels. In this case, although Tika's decision is not gratuitous, her motivation for abortion seems less justifiable in terms of other viable possibilities offered to the character.

More importantly, on no occasion does Tika reflect on her abortion, once she has got through it and the only marks she bears seem to be physical (her womb has been removed) rather than psychological. In one sense, arguably, the victim of maternal abuse and control has turned into a limited, fragmented, dislocated and handicapped individual (Haney 1996). Tika's inability to valorise the womb as a site of connectedness, of solidarity and social kinship that can protect women from patriarchal assaults represents one of her major failures. Darko shows that some women choose to be engaged in abortion rather than be party to breeding human beings who are fated to be victims. Tika's imagining herself as a mother whose maternal agency is wrestled from her through the victimisation of her children (exactly what her mother did to her), redefines motherhood to entail non-production. In other words, Tika is afraid of becoming a victimiser of her children, a replica of her abusive mother. Tika's childlessness then is to be attributed to the restlessness of her soul. Once again, Darko bluntly shows that the positions of victim and victimiser not only can coexist but are also inexplicably and/or contradictorily intertwined and interconnected.

Another example of the impossibility of defining Darko's characters in the novel along the lines of mere victims of oppression and unfortunate circumstances, is Efia. Efia is the housemaid of the title, who, with the sinister help of her mother and grandmother, tries to deceive Tika by getting pregnant in order to make a claim for Tika's protection and later for her money. Much of the novel's plot revolves around the mother and grandmother's plan to put their hands on Tika's wealth. Emotional abuse is at the core of the mother-daughter-grandmother's relationship in the text. The grandmother is the one who takes over and adopts a position of control. She constantly silences her daughter, by exercising the authority that society gives old women as repositories of wisdom. Research indicates that in West African societies, the elders are honoured and command immense respect (Oppong 1983). However, in the novel, the grandmother figure, a tie to the past and a symbol of resourcefulness and wisdom, the guardian of a certain order, has disappeared to be replaced by a voracious, evil and domineering matron whose only motivation in life is money.

If ambiguity does not seem to characterise Efia's grandmother's thoughts and actions (she never shows signs of repentance in the novel), ambivalence dominates the portrayal of Efia and her mother. Though Efia's mother does not oppose the grandmother's sinister plan to get hold of Tika's money by using Efia's naivety and charm, she initially, though mildly, questions the grandmother's initiative: 'But, you do know what you're doing mother, or?' (47). Though the novel offers no insight into mother-daughter past relationships, the grandmother's authoritarian and controlling attitude towards her daughter and granddaughter hints at a highly repressive family economy. The grandmother manifests calculating logic, action and destructive power. She functions as an agent of dehumanisation; she diminishes human agency through exploitation and her victims (Efia and Efia's mother) apparently manifest the qualities associated with passivity and powerlessness.

Such a reading will see Efia's mother's involvement in her daughter's exploitation as a result of her inability to challenge her own mother's indomitable presence. Encountering little opposition from her daughter, the grandmother seizes control of Efia's mother and the daughter in turn seizes control of Efia, thus creating a chain of oppression. The grandmother has learnt the art of survival which, for her, depends on how skilfully a woman can manipulate circumstances to her advantage, and though ineffective in the end, her plan causes the destruction of her granddaughter.

Efia's mother, on the other hand, foolishly agrees to her mother's and husband's plan, and, in this respect, she can be viewed as both victim and victimiser. Unable to defy her mother's authority and power over the family, she becomes a willing victim of her manipulations and as a consequence, she turns into a victimiser of her daughter, Efia. By lacking self-awareness and perception and by succumbing to the temptation offered by money, Efia's mother ultimately puts herself and her daughter at the mercy of unworthy individuals who victimise them both. She is trapped, unable and unwilling to assert her agency for change. And even her attempts to question her mother's actions by defending Efia when things start going wrong prove in vain. By permitting herself to be dominated by her husband and mother, she has little by little authorised them to exercise absolute power over herself and Efia, as the following example demonstrates:

> 'But couldn't your daughter have chosen better men?'
> 'I don't recall us having advised her on that, mother.'
> The old lady frowned suspiciously. 'Are you being sarcastic with me?'

'No mother'; haltingly, 'it's just that I think we shouldn't forget that everything she did was your idea.' (74)

The responsibility to safeguard her own daughter is here replaced by the mother's complicity in exploiting the daughter's naivety and appearance. Victim of the grandmother's scheming in a suffocating and constraining family environment, Efia's mother lets the old woman use her as an intermediary between Tika and Efia. In so doing, she then functions as both the instrument of her own mother's greed and the agent of oppression of her only daughter. Mother and grandmother then participate actively in oppressive practices and become instruments of oppression by subscribing to ideologies of dominance.

Although Efia's mother shows good intentions in the beginning, she then quickly succumbs to her husband's and mother's will. Efia's mother's inability to challenge both her husband's and mother's authority results in an overt exploitation of Efia. By becoming an accomplice of her husband's and mother's scheming, she actively perpetuates oppression and condemns Efia to silence and subjugation. In this sense, she becomes party to the appropriation of female agency for the ultimate furtherance of patriarchy and gender oppression. As Naana Banyia Horne affirms: 'Gender oppression persists because of the support some women lend to the victimisation of other women' (*The Politics of Mothering: Multiple Subjectivity and Gendered Discourse in Aidoo's Plays* 1999: 321). In the end, then, Efia's mother becomes one of the strongest proponents of gender oppression through her support of her mother's and husband's struggle to dominate and exploit Efia and her character acquires validation within the masculinist context of domestication of the female.

Darko here makes evident that victims are not always passive; for they often stave off victimisation of their person by becoming co-opted into oppressive actions. In this respect, it is not a coincidence that Efia's mother is not only the object of her mother's ironic comments and insults, but she is also the willing victim of her good-for-nothing-but-drink husband whose actions she seems to justify on several occasions. Once enemies, Efia's father and grandmother become best friends when he comes up with the idea of putting their hands on Tika's money by using Efia. When things start falling apart, Efia's mother defends her husband from the grandmother's accusations and proposes he pours libation to the gods to win their favour. Interestingly enough, Efia's mother takes her husband's side, hoping that his male authority in the family would keep her mother's authority contained when she starts insulting her and Efia for all that went wrong: 'My husband will deal with you', she inwardly consoled herself' (92). Efia's father, however, is all but a caring and loving father and husband:

'What are we getting out of our daughter's going to the city to serve somebody?' '... Didn't we take care of her up to this stage?...'

'That was our responsibility.'

'You prepared well for a confrontation, eh?' (Efia's father and mother, 44).

Irony and humour converge and abound as Darko weaves a tale of deceit and greed: a tale where Efia's mother and grandmother are clearly represented as part of patriarchy and although ineffective in their roles they too prop up the system. In exposing the insidiousness of some women's actions in society, the novel stresses the betrayal and the pressure of woman-on-woman abuse. Darko shows how the oppression of women is not simply a masculinist flaw as some feminist analyses claim, but that it also entails woman-on-woman violence, often the outcome of institutionalised, hierarchical spaces where women are both victims and collaborators in an unequal system.

At first glance, other female characters, like Akua and Efia, seem to fall into well-explored categories of victims and schemers, being representative of the rural girls who leave the village (Kataso) hoping for a better life in the city and end up being respectively a prostitute and a disgraced maid. However, once again, Darko warns us against a Manichean binary logic that privileges a demarcation line between good and evil, nature and mind, female and male traits, by hinting at contradictory and overlapping subject positions that simultaneously incorporate multiple differentials and layers of existence. In this sense, Darko can be seen as theorising the multiple subjectivity and agency that inform human interaction within a gendered and class-stratified context of existence.

To the reader, Efia appears to passively accept any decisions made by her mother and grandmother without questioning their reasons. Poor and uneducated, like her mother and grandmother, she seems to perfectly reproduce a chain of female self-subjugation and oppression. As much as her mother is unable to effectively oppose her grandmother's decisions to protect the weak and keep the victimisers at bay, Efia is unable, and to some extent unwilling, to put up any resistance to her mother and grandmother's authority. Given the highly-rated position that elderly women occupy in most African societies, it is not surprising that a young daughter like Efia refuses to openly confront the elders, opposing both her mother and grandmother's will in order to take a different direction. Confirmation of Efia's total obedience to both her mother and grandmother comes from her silence in the most salient scenes of the novel. Significantly, no serious family deliberation takes place without Efia's grandmother being present and in most conversations about the plan, Efia is mute. When the grandmother and the mother confront Tika about Efia's pregnancy, Efia is only able to stutter: 'It... it... was... Mr... er... Nsorhwe' (80). Even when her grandmother insults Efia for letting them choose Nsorwhe as the man who made her pregnant, she falls silent and accepts victimisation: 'You fool, fool, fool! Why of all your whore of a madam's lovers did you let us choose this little, ugly, square-headed man? You fool a thousand times over' (91). Efia, is then silenced by the text itself. The grandmother, the mother and her father speak for her for most of the novel. Efia is almost completely de-textualised but for a few words/phrases that directly escape her mouth and these in the form of questions, such as: 'What if Auntie Teacher tries to force me to speak?' (67), or 'Will you let her do it? Send me back?' (76). When it comes to money though, Efia shows no hesitation. She not only cunningly hides her lovers from Tika but also, fearing ridicule for returning to Kataso for the yam festival empty-handed and pregnant, she steals Tika's money.

In *The Housemaid* money then seems to justify reciprocal female exploitation, and in the process the women all simultaneously function as both victims and victimisers of one another. Efia in this respect is as much a victim of her mother and grandmother's manipulation as a victimiser of Tika and of the unborn baby she gets rid of in the rubbish dump. By adopting a matrifocal structure, Darko shows how the mother-daughter relation here assumes a new frightening dimension: the mother is no longer a source of support but a source of oppression. The girl's youth and her body become instrumental to the grandmother's and mother's plan of acquiring wealth through deceit and manipulation. The mother is shown to betray the institutionalised notion of maternal love and devotion. Until now, in both Western and African societies, we were always assured that maternal love was inherent in every woman. Darko courageously points out that maternal love should not be necessarily thought of as existing naturally. In the case of African women, very few writers have dared consider such a possibility.

Also, the presence of authorial condemnation of Efia and her family's conduct through ironic comments implies that Darko is critical of women's eagerness to become economically independent by using any possible means at their disposal. Economic, cultural and social transformations have deeply affected the lives and experiences of African women, prompting tensions and conflicts between generations and in the family. For many women living in the villages, life seems more prosperous in the city and the allure of greener pastures is powerful. Imbalances in distribution mean that Akua and Efia make or take opportunities to leave Kataso, their village in the eastern hills, which has 'no flowing water, no electricity, no entertainment centre, nothing' (29), for the cities. The attractions of greener pastures, whether at Kumasi railway station or in service to a wealthy businesswoman in Accra, are all too obvious to village children. Akua's journey from Kataso to Kumasi in search of a better life is briefly described in Chapter Three. Having no money to pay the truck driver to go to the city, Akua readily prostitutes herself in return for a lift. Just very few lines are devoted to the scene. All we know is that 'Akua liked it' (31). Through this passing statement, Darko is cleverly hinting at the way Akua is not ashamed of what she has done. On the contrary, Akua seems to consider sexual favours as a common strategy for getting what she wants. If the very first few lines introducing Akua offer the reader a negative image of the character, Darko promptly corrects that image by providing the reader with relevant background information about how difficult it is for a woman to survive in the city: 'Life as a porter in Kumasi was not what a normal person would call living. It was survival [. . . ]. Like her mates, Akua had no regular home. They all lived in unfinished buildings [. . . ]. Thanks to bribes of cash and sex, workers at the building sites regularly tipped them on the next place available for occupation' (32). In the city then, the young, inexperienced girl may require not only economic opportunities but also physical protection.

As Kenneth Little observed that: 'The urban economy does not provide women as a whole with the safeguard and security they traditionally enjoy in most rural systems' (*African Women in Town,* 1973: 29). In the urban situation, illiterate women need men. Consequently, sex often provides in itself the primary basis for mutually convenient arrangements between individual women and men. Darko focuses attention on the reality that movement to town for a young female may start as an adventure, but it is often made with the conscious intention of a means to an end conceived of in monetary terms and perhaps with the idea of acquiring some prestige on returning home. The degrading conditions under which Akua lives in the city still qualify her 'as one of the soon-to-be envied – a returnee' (33).

If Akua's decision to leave home for the city seems too obvious, Darko also provocatively points out that the expectations the family back home has are so high that 'If she was going to satisfy her people back home, then God knows, she needed every cedi' (32). The woman goes home when she has the money she came to town for. Life in Kumasi is not what Akua had imagined, but from her point of view the squalor of an Accra slum is nevertheless better than life in the village. The giving and taking of backhanders is an inevitable and unavoidable part of the effort to survive. As John Caldwell explains:

> 'Rural-urban migration is more than anything a search for money and indirectly for the things that money can buy, and that can be more easily acquired in the town. The town imposes new social and economic conditions upon the migrant and may in time accustom him to these conditions'. (*African Rural-Urban Migration: The Movement to Ghana's Towns*: 1968: 171).

As a result, Akua is willing to endure all the limitations and frustrations of living on a building site and of accepting anything that comes her way if that means proudly returning home for the festival. Going back home empty-handed would be shameful and unbearable.

Darko seems to imply here that the community's expectations often place women in a very difficult predicament by pressuring them to conform to certain standards. The girl who leaves the village for the city is expected to find fortune and to help other members of the family by sending money and goods back to the village. Darko shows that for many women life in the city is a continual fight for survival, and poor and uneducated women are more prone to adapt themselves to patriarchal and oppressive mechanisms having nowhere else to go. For these women a hard life in the city is always better than returning to the village empty-handed. Darko's point here is that whether in the city or in the rural areas around Accra, women should be able to fight against squalor and economic instability without being 'forced' by the system to give up their dignity.

Darko's bluntness and frankness in naming and exposing the malaise of her society makes her one of the most militant writers on the contemporary African literary scene. Though the centre of attention in her novel is directed at the exposure of the enslavement of women by a gender-biased regime, Darko realises that women's histories and experiences cannot be understood by referring to an abstract ideal of feminist consciousness, but can only be addressed by considering the complex interplay between the social and material conditions affecting women's lives.

If one were to evaluate the characters in *The Housemaid* on the basis of these three elements – morals, autonomy and emotional strength – then Teacher would certainly come out as the most successful of the female figures. Teacher possesses the qualities of independence, fortitude and emotional strength which enable her to succeed in her job as a teacher in Accra. She is respected for her ability in recruiting girls from the villages and situating them with well-off families in the city. Teacher is the one who supports Tika when she is in hospital aborting her child, and the one who advises her on Efia and her family. One can actually see her as having charted her way through society, by completing her education and gaining professional training and then by acquiring the kind of emancipation and independence she needs. Darko, however, seems to implicitly point out that Teacher's stainless conduct and success in life is partly due to her upbringing in a good, well-off family who adopted her and then sent her to school.

Tika's background is not as sound as Teacher's is, and Tika's choices in life have been more the result of her antagonism to her mother than the outcome of a wicked, self-centred, money-oriented mind. This idea is confirmed by choices made by the author on the stylistic and narrative levels. Tika's character is hardly ever the target of Darko's cutting remarks and devastating irony. Furthermore, among a plethora of female characters, Tika is the most rounded and convincing and the novel is mostly focalised through her. Despite her arguable choices, Tika seems, in Darko's presentation, a largely positive character, not only because of her ability to embark on an independent income-generating activity (as a goods seller) but especially because the emotional turbulence she has gone through eventually makes her a more understanding human being. She is able to forgive when it comes to Efia, because she realises that 'She was as much a victim of her people's manipulation as I was' (105).

At the very end of the novel, the dyadic conversation occurring between Teacher and Tika at the very end of the story confirms Darko's professional skill in matching literary grace with veracity of characterisation.

> 'Tika about your mother... She is not a woman of means anymore, you know. She is growing old as well. And you, her only child, have also abandoned her. You know what that can lead to, or? Why not go and look for her?'
> 'Who says she would want to patch things up now? She was ready once, when I wasn't. Would she be now, just because I am?'
> 'Are you? If you are then try.'
> And she burst out laughing and crying at the same time. Teacher joined in. And, together, they laughed and cried; laughing and crying away their pain, their disappointment, their anger, their fear. And laughing with hope (106–7).

The hurts and disappointments of a lifetime hung heavily in the silence between mother and daughter, as this passage demonstrates. However, the structural openness at the end of the text allows for a possibility of change that preserves hope; hope for a future reconciliation between mother and daughter, and, on a larger scale, for a partnership between women (the last image of Teacher and Tika's sharing laughter and tears seems to evoke it) in an economically unstable and male-oriented society. Darko's novel closes then on a positive note with regard to female bonding. It hints at the fact that, in spite of all the odds, the loneliness, the appalling conditions, women do have one remaining safe-nest: themselves. The solidarity between Teacher and Tika at a time of desperate need or crisis is one of the factors that helps to ensure their survival. Female bonding is not the solution to women's problems in society but it often helps them to recognise, through dialogue and confrontation, the signs of their oppression in order to react against them. The structural openness of *The Housemaid* responds both to the realisation that a sense of things to come cannot be completely blocked out and to the willingness to give a positive reading about what might happen from now on. Endings are not arrested in a difficult and frozen 'now': belief in an ongoing, unfolding and promising destiny is strongly present, and this in turn, broadens the possibilities for stylistic and thematic risk-taking, as well as for a risky making of predictions. Works written by the younger generation of African women authors are open-ended because the quest for female identity and its full realisation in a multi-faceted, oppressive society seems to be a soap-opera, endless but always advancing.

However critical of the complicity of women with patriarchal standards and ideologies she may be, Darko deploys interpellative tactics that constitute a systematic provocation, in the form of specifically disruptive formal and rhetorical elements, such as an ironic undercutting of statements or ideas, hoping to thereby incite the radicalisation of her readers, especially the women. This aspect of provocation through humour and sarcasm is not simply limited to the vision of a corrupt, vicious and masculinist world that one wishes to accuse or flee. Instead Darko's writing evokes the possibility of a better world, and in this evocation is its force, as the moving image of hope that closes the novel confirms: 'Tika bursts out laughing and crying out at the same time. Teacher, joined in. And together they laughed and cried... And laughing with hope' (107). At bottom, therefore, Darko's humorous vein corresponds to a 'token of spiritual survival' (Trump 1988: 34 ).

## CONCLUSION

Darko's rhetoric of realism conceals certain ironies and is a strategy of narration which presents women in shifting, changeable positions as a way of countering their static definitions in a patriarchal society, though the protagonists' actions and choices mostly shift in relation to a pragmatic sense of their own needs as persons and as women. In this sense, Akua and Efia's aspirations and particularly their economic opportunities are shown to be influenced by the gender rules and expectations of their own communities. The world of such women thus becomes the site of some of Darko's most biting and devastating ironies. At one level, the irony is directed against superstition and the myths of elderly widows, who are believed to be living in the woods and devouring children and who are labelled as witches. At another level, it is directed against the economic inequalities and instabilities of a fast-changing society where money is worshipped above everything else, often at the expense of dignity, so that deceit, cash bribes and sexual exchanges are on the everyday agenda in both the rural and the city world. At yet another crucial level, the novel's irony is directed towards those women complicit with the ongoing system and also towards pre-packaged concepts of manhood and womanhood. The ironic thrust of the text does not allow for any romanticisation or idealisation of women. Women are human actors in a world shared by men and not passive reactors in a man's world. Darko also illuminates the perception that character traits are not gender specific: most of the men in the novel are sensitive and fragile like Tika's father, gullible and honest like Nsorhwe, the man falsely accused of getting Efia pregnant, or good-for-nothing-but-drink, like Efia's father. Darko's technique is deflationary towards men as much as towards women, male caricatures in fact are not opposed to exemplary female characters. It is as if men and women were confused figures in an equally muddled society, though gender still makes a difference, as women still have to make a greater effort to fulfil themselves. However debatable the position of most of Darko's female characters in society is, these women are portrayed as vital and viable human beings, not as appendages or peripheral beings in a world dominated by towering male protagonists.

Darko therefore succeeds in relaying her messages by means of a searing irony. By adopting a satirical tone, she tries to awaken female sensibility to sexual inequality and prejudices against women in society. More importantly, Darko urges readers and critics to take another look at the text in order to see how violence is not a male but a human problem, how African literary texts can speak simultaneously about the victimhood and power of women. Though Darko is particularly aware of some women's collaboration in an equal system, she also demonstrates that women's histories and experiences can only be understood by considering the complex interplay between the social and material conditions affecting their lives. Darko is not justifying her female characters' choices but is presenting a credible picture of women's predicament by inserting women's lives and decisions in the more complex context of gender and class stratification that characterises present-day Ghana. The increasing importance that economic factors have assumed in Ghana and in many other post-colonial African societies means that more and more women perceive an opportunity of improving their status. However, Darko demonstrates that the allure of making easy money in a largely corrupt and chaotic environment further contributes to women's profound alienation and powerlessness in society and, in some cases, leads to their destruction.

# Sean P. O'Connell and Vincent Odamtten

## *Licit Desires, Alien Bodies and the Economics of Invisibility in Amma Darko's* Beyond the Horizon *and Stephen Frears'* Dirty Pretty Things

*'Why haven't I seen you people before?'*
*'We're the people you never see.'*
from the last moments of *Dirty Pretty Things*

In Western countries, the construction of *nationality* has, in the aftermath of formal decolonisation, become a more problematic category of being. No longer is it implicitly equated with a specific ethnicity or even a so-called common origin, tradition and /or language. For, the subjects of the erstwhile empires of the late nineteenth and early twentieth centuries have now returned to the former metropolitan centres, bringing with them more than a splash of colour or exoticism. And yet Western states by various instruments of coercion make the acquisition of *nationality* and the corresponding status of 'citizenship', (itself characterised historically by a bureaucratic balance of race and immigration policy) the means by which the former colonised subject moves from the non-being of alien worker to the human, politically recognised, consumer-producer. As a result of this balance, citizens and legal residents of Western nations have traditionally been defined in a normative ethnic-racial opposition to the *non*-citizen and/or undocumented *aliens*.

Although the era of overt racial discrimination in immigration quotas and policies may have dissipated, contemporary globalisation and decolonisation phenomena have contributed to the rise of an invisible underclass of society that is largely undocumented and racialised.[1] Implicit links have come to exist between citizenship, race and the human that have largely been ignored by dominant Western culture, even though the arena for this linkage is within the West itself. In the context of such cultural occlusion, novelist Amma Darko and film-maker Stephen Frears have created two compelling narratives that offer chilling insights into the lives led by undocumented, non-white immigrants in Western democracies. The novelist and film-maker develop our sense of the presence of the people 'who aren't there', challenging the social process which seeks to render simultaneously invisible and serviceable the physical bodies of the illegal or undocumented alien.

Amma Darko's novel *Beyond the Horizon* is distinctly different in its primary thesis from Stephen Frears' film *Dirty Pretty Things*. Whereas *Beyond the Horizon* is primarily a coming-of-age narrative about a young woman transplanted from her village in Africa to urban Germany, *Dirty Pretty Things* principally examines the distressing circumstances of immigrants living in contemporary London 'without papers'. One cannot ignore the parallel experiences of the main characters in both of these narratives when they find themselves living illegally in lands devastatingly foreign to them. Nevertheless, issues of gender, educational background and the ethical frameworks of the principal protagonists in each treatment distinguish them from one another. It is no coincidence that these 'illegals' are employed in positions that most documented citizens would deem intolerably humiliating. Given the demeaning occupations these *alien* characters accept, we may then be puzzled by their motivations, the licit desires, that seem to propel them into this netherworld. Indeed, in both of these narratives, the link between citizenship and humanness is increasingly solidified as the stories progress, while illegal alien status quickly becomes equated with the subhuman non-person and the body, as a whole or in parts, as saleable goods.

## CLASH OF CULTURES

One of the central questions that both Darko and Frears examine in their respective works is to what degree is citizenship (or legal residency) valued by illegal immigrants. How much of oneself is an undocumented immigrant willing to exploit in order to remain in the host[2] country? The answer is different for Darko's and Frears' characters, but ultimately each protagonist is willing to put his or her life, reputation and personal integrity at risk in order to 'acquire' the documentation that would theoretically afford them all of the rights and privileges that the documented citizen so-often takes for granted. Moreover, both works emphasise that part or all of the physical body may even have to be surrendered to the appetites of the dominant cultural class in order to purchase the dubious privilege of a continued presence in the host country. Though unfortunately we may be inclined to take for granted the prostitution into which Mara of *Beyond the Horizon* is entrapped as part and parcel of a widespread and purportedly 'inevitable' connection between illegal immigration and the traffic in women as a commodity, the trade in vital organs at the centre of *Dirty Pretty Things* may still have the capacity to shock the viewer.

Throughout *Beyond the Horizon*, Darko's protagonist, Mara, finds herself in morally ambiguous positions and is given the task of making profound 'choices' about the direction of her life. In this case, she makes decisions usually motivated by licit desires. However, they are executed in the borderlands between legality and illegality. Thus the temporal and spatial locations and the socio-political contexts of such acts make problematical the consequences of otherwise very understandable and human desires. At the beginning of the novel, Mara is sitting in front of a mirror in her chamber at the German brothel where she is employed. She takes the reader on a journey that begins chronologically in a remote Ghanaian village, Naka. Her life is disrupted when her father arranges for her to marry a man from a neighbouring village. Her new husband, Akobi, uproots her from a rural setting and transplants her to Accra, the capital city. There, Mara is abused and raped by her insecure husband who is obsessed with acquiring wealth and living a Western lifestyle.

Like Mara, Akobi is driven by licit desires. However the privilege afforded by his gender, coupled with his lack of understanding of how such desires might unfold in the neocolonial context of the world in which they live, make his actions all the more disastrous. Akobi eventually immigrates to Germany where he marries Gitte, a German woman, in order to acquire citizenship and enter that inner circle of the 'human'. Happily secure in his new status, he then proceeds to procure Comfort, a Ghanaian woman who had once rejected him, as a mistress. In order to finance this new life, he *imports* Mara by an illegal and illicit route to Germany with the intention of selling her into prostitution. Although it might be argued that Mara initially accepts a life of prostitution because she is following the dictates of the traditional African wife's duty to obey her husband's wishes, this ignores the reality of her coercion. The testimony of her narrative confirms that she acknowledges a sense of guilt, since she is certainly violating the values she learnt as a child in the village of Naka. Nonetheless, her isolation in a foreign culture and a degree of innocence on her part contributes to her disastrous circumstances. While imprisoned as a prostitute, Mara befriends the wife of her first pimp who, in a show of female solidarity, arranges for Mara to escape not to freedom, but to another, more tolerant, pimp, which will only confirm her in a virtual lifetime of prostitution in another brothel. Mara accepts, and the chronology of her personal narrative ends where the novel begins.

This narrative turning on itself, captured metaphorically in the opening pages of Darko's novel, by the use of the oval mirror and a play on reflections, finds its visual echo in Stephen Frears' somewhat romanticised neo-*noir* tale, *Dirty Pretty Things*, set in the rich multicultural urban landscape of post-colonial London. The sense of oppression and claustrophobia, expressed in Darko's novel by the tiny room from which Mara speaks to us, finds its equivalent with Frears' close-ups and dark shots. Both works suggest simultaneously an intimate familiarity and a sense of alienation and anonymity. Indeed its publicists described the film as:

> a harrowing tale of struggle and survival for two immigrants who learn that everything is for sale in London's secret underworld! Part of an invisible

> working class, Nigerian exile Okwe and Turkish chambermaid Senay toil at a west London hotel (The Baltic Hotel) that is full of illegal activity. Then late one night Okwe makes a shocking discovery, which creates an impossible dilemma and tests the limits of all they know![3]

Despite a degree of hyperbole, the description frames the way the viewer is expected to interpret the action. In short, it expresses an ideological perspective that ultimately underscores the dominant society's view of the legality or otherwise of flows of people and goods across international boarders.

Okwe, a pathologist and once respected doctor, is compelled to flee Nigeria when he is framed for the murder of his wife. Unlike Mara, his Western education and life experiences (he has been to America as a student and returned to Nigeria) provide Okwe with a substantial practical understanding of 'the way the world works', yet his circumstances compel him to suppress his true identity. He may appear as naïve as Mara and Senay at times, but this façade can only be maintained for so long, and cracks begin to appear. He is obsessive about working, and chews 'khat', a stimulant, to avoid sleeping, perhaps to avoid his nightmares. Just as Mara's village training fails to give her protection from the demanding horrors of the Western world, so Senay's faith is no protection against the unbridled libidos of males who prey on her in her status as an unprotected female. What is significant about all three characters, however, is that they initially cling to the moral and ethical codes of behaviour with which they grew up. Yet, each is forced to jettison parts of their past, either literally or symbolically, in order to survive in the new environments to which each has been drawn.

Okwe's professional specialisation, his expertise in the diagnosis and interpretation of the changes produced by disease in the body, is in sharp contrast to his uncertain ability to read the motivations and feelings of those around him. His friend and chess partner, Guo Yi, a morgue attendant, has to practically scream in his face that Senay is in love with him before Okwe realizes the truth. In trying to stay out of trouble, away from the watchful eyes of the authorities, moreover, he leaves himself vulnerable to the machinations of Juan, a.k.a. 'Sneaky', the sleazy hotel manager who runs an illegal organ harvesting business out of the hotel. Juan blackmails Okwe into using his skills as a doctor to help the donors, who are primarily undocumented aliens, exchange their organs for papers and passports that will transform their status to legal citizenship and paradoxically allow them to feel fully human. Okwe backs himself into a corner from which the only escape is a morally dubious compromise. He quickly falls a victim to political and socio-economic forces he only partially understands and over which he absolutely has no control.

Senay is in London occupying an indeterminate state between legality and illegality, waiting for the finalisation of her papers. As a Turkish refugee with little in the way of marketable skills, she is obvious prey for denizens of the underworld. While in this legal limbo she shares her small flat with fellow traveller, Okwe. Her dream is to escape the old world and find paradise in New York, where she would live with her cousin under the assumed name of Isabella. The romantic tension that is generated by this 'domestic' arrangement in the apartment is exquisitely played out, slowly unfolding in contrapuntal synchrony with the disclosure of the illegal organ trading that draws the main characters together. Like Darko's protagonist, Senay can be characterised as an innocent and naive player, 'a greenhorn' (as Mama Kiosk describes Mara in *Beyond the Horizon*).[4] Yet, both women have an inner core of strength and resilience. How else would they have survived the torments that daily plague their lives?

Although provided with temporary papers, a route to citizenship, Senay is forbidden to work. Basic survival skills push these characters beyond an acceptance of things as they are, so Senay finds work as a chambermaid in the mysterious 'Baltic Hotel' – where Okwe works as the night porter and receptionist. Following the romantic tradition, Okwe is the 'knight in shining armour' who must rescue the virgin in distress – Senay. After she is forced to leave her job at the Baltic Hotel because of harassment from the immigration police, she finds herself in a garment sweatshop where she is literally on her knees sucking the owner's penis. But she bites back and is once again jobless and on the run. Senay finds her way back to the Baltic Hotel where she is finally willing to sell her kidney for a passport and her chance to escape to New York, where 'there are lights in the trees'.

The irony is that Okwe is to perform the operation, and the price Senay must pay to 'Sneaky' includes her virginity. Unfortunately, Okwe is unable to fulfil his traditional role as romantic saviour, but with the help of his fellow travellers, Juliette and Guo Yi they turn the tables on 'Sneaky', Okwe removes one of his kidneys and sells it to the black-market dealer. Despite the fact that the duo have new passports in hand, a sentimental ending in which Senay and Okwe dissolve, hand in hand into a New York skyline is rejected. Instead, Frears gives us what might be more realistic – Senay goes to New York and Okwe back to Nigeria. Yet, this ending also seems problematic, because it suggests that there is really no legitimate way for aliens to become truly human. When the British organ dealer asks, 'How come I've never seen you before?' Okwe responds, 'Because we are the people *you never see*' (emphasis added). The finality of this utterance, followed by the departure of Senay and Okwe to their respective destinations at once suggests that law and order is restored, and business goes on as usual, once the troublemakers, this latter day Adam and Eve, are expelled from the post-colonial 'garden' of London. The poetic justice that we witnessed seems at once too neat and too troubling, since there is nothing to indicate that Senay has a better chance of finding fulfilment in New York than she did in London. Okwe has no assurances that he will not become a victim, for the second time, of those forces that drove him into exile in the first place.

For Mara of *Beyond the Horizon* most of the choices she is given are, in fact, ultimatums. She may cling to the past, the ways of the village and become a footnote in history, or accept the new dispensation and be remade in an alien image. There is, however, one choice that Mara makes of her own volition and with full knowledge of what its consequences will be. Mara's conscious decision, towards the end of the novel, to flee from Akobi, her husband, even though it locks her into the life of a professional prostitute in order to support her family back *home*, and perhaps earn enough money to break the chains of sexual bondage one day, reveals a changed Mara. This new Mara is definitely hardened by her experiences in Germany, and knows that her self-esteem will prevent her desire to return to her family and land of her birth:

> Kaye, I came here to you and Pee and all the others with thick bushy hair, which has now been exotically cut short, close to my scalp. My eyebrows have been plucked thin. I have mastered the use of make-up, so that my lips are never without their scarlet taint. And I have received into me the rigid tools of many men and accompanied them on sinful rides through the back doors of heaven and returned with them back to earth, spent men. *I am no longer green and you know it.* As for the morals of life my mother brought me up by, I have cemented them with coal tar in my conscience. If the gods of Naka intended me to live by them, they should have made sure I was married to a man who loved me and who appreciated the values I was brought up with. *I lived by these values until I could no longer do so.* The rot has gone too deep for me to return to the old me. (Darko 131, emphasis added)

There is no sense of defeat in Mara's words, rather there is a defiant acceptance of what fate has dealt her; she refuses to whine about her condition. Instead, she does not 'go gently into that good night' and she will not abandon those who depend on her for their livelihood. She still chooses an African communalism over Western individualism, no matter the cost to herself.

## THE ECONOMICS OF INVISIBILITY: SACRIFICE AND DEHUMANISATION

In their circumstances as undocumented aliens in foreign lands, Mara, Okwe and Senay are thrust literally and figuratively into estranging situations that initially evoke inadequate defensive responses. Mara must operate within the dictates of commercialised sex despite the moral system of family values and wifely obedience in which she was raised. Okwe is no longer able to openly represent himself without fear of exposure, and ironically, he is being seduced into covertly using his Western training as a doctor, firstly to treat the outbreak of sexually transmitted diseases infecting his fellow mini-cab drivers, and secondly as he is being drawn, however reluctantly, into the human body parts trade. Senay, strict Muslim that she is, finds herself at the outset making small compromises, then bigger ones in order to exist within the host – London. With the very core of their personal and cultural values confronted with the possibility of total displacement by the Western values that were paradoxically the basis of their licit desires, Mara, Okwe and Senay struggle to salvage some remnant of self-esteem and their sense of self, their identity. As the Doorman of the Baltic Hotel tells Okwe, 'If you stay here too long, you begin to dress like them.' When the Doorman half-jokingly says, 'dress like them', he is not just alluding to a superficial or outward transformation, but rather of an essential inner one. Guo Yi, Okwe's friend and confidante, refers to Ivan, the Doorman as 'Poladis' [*sic*] when he actually means Charon, the ancient Greek ferryman of the dead. When the logic of their predicament becomes devastatingly apparent to them that life *Beyond the Horizon* is only *Dirty*, definitely not *Pretty*, and that they will all be reduced to the status of *Things* – objects to be sold, bartered and used, it is almost too late for salvation. The way in which the characters come to terms with their fates and how author and director resolve the respective narratives reveals more about the art of Darko and Frears than about the quality of the characters themselves.

Frears' own location as a Western male filmmaker is perhaps most evident in the subtle emphasis on the way in which the 'undocumented' status of Okwe and Senay's problematic position as Turkish refugee, denizens of the London netherworld, colour our response to their struggles to become 'citizens', or in other words, legally part of the human world. Okwe is the 'good doctor', who is moral to the core and acts in the ambiguous role of the darker brooding elder brother and maybe lover to Senay, whose Turkish origins marginalise and render her exotic in relation to both Europe and Africa. For the audience, Senay's fair skin, dark eyes and jet black hair suggest an indeterminate ethnicity, so despite the seemingly long road travelled from racial segregation and its attendant absurdities, the intimation of a more than platonic relationship between the tall and dark Okwe and the petite chambermaid Senay has all the hallmarks of a transgressive act. These liminal undercurrents ultimately move Frears' narrative in a direction that is safe for its primary Western audience. Indeed it seems that it is precisely in the unfolding of this primary relationship that the problems of nation, citizenship and humanness in the contexts of gender, educational background and ethical frameworks under conditions of globalisation are erased.

Darko, on the other hand, seems unperturbed by the prospect of revealing the complex and ruinous manner in which women and men become victims and accomplices in their attempt to guarantee material security, to establish a legal relationship with the nation-state in the hope that they would be protected from the consequences of their own actions. Such a direct and unflinching gaze is perhaps too unsettling for some audiences (or readers) that see themselves as always-and-already humanitarian philanthropists; or perhaps, there is always-and-already a tacit agreement between the Hollywood-style storytellers and their audience not to insist too strongly that we acknowledge the presence of those aliens amongst us.

Prostitutes, porters, doormen and factory workers all comprise a segment of society that some would derogatorily refer to as 'the service industry' or 'help'. They are the people who function behind the scenes, cleaning, cooking and providing services to and servicing those in other classes of society. In both *Beyond the Horizon* and *Dirty Pretty Things*, 'the help' – men and women, skilled and unskilled workers – are most often a racialised underclass: this segment of society is not seen or counted as part of a normative white population or even working class; rather, they are the coloured invisible 'other'. It is precisely because of this conflation that those claiming normative status underestimate the potential for resistance and transformation by this racialised underclass. Okwe, employed as a porter and taxi driver, Senay as a chambermaid and seamstress, and Mara, a prostitute turned writer, are able to develop schemes that eventually help them to escape the bonds of dehumanisation inherently associated in their undocumented status. As members of the racialised underclass in each of their respective locations, Mara, Okwe and Senay exceed the expectations and limits that the Akobis and 'Sneakys' of their underworld have set for them. Both of these narratives clarify how citizenship is both trivial and substantial. By simply having documentation, a passport, stating that one is a Citizen, one is thereby able to *be* whom one claims, in short, *to pass*. Okwe and Senay are able to depart for their respective destinations *as citizens* only because their papers are of the highest calibre. Thus, citizenship is as paper-thin as a well-forged passport; or, put another way, it may not be worth the paper on which it is printed. For Mara, documentation enables her to exact vengeance on her husband, Akobi, and get him deported.

What preconceived notions do the citizens of England and Germany hold about illegal immigrants living amongst them? Furthermore, how do these stereotypes both aid and hinder the day-to-day life of the immigrant, illegal or in limbo, in her quest for the ever-elusive status of 'citizen'? While dominant stereotypes of the 'other' generally hinder advancement, there are times when the 'other' can and does exploit those widespread cultural assumptions to subvert the power structure. Akobi, Mara's pimp and husband, benefits immensely from a stereotype that his German wife, Gitte, holds toward Africans:

> 'And now let the spirits of our family rest a while,' he went on to Gitte. 'You have called up their names so much that they must be turning in their sleep if they are in bed, or clutching their stomachs in pain if they are having a meal.'

> Later I learned that this was a strategy of Akobi's. When the going got tough he would conjure up extravagant superstitions. Gitte, who, like most Europeans, believed that all Africans were full of primitive superstitions, always fell for it.
>
> As Osey would say, they have our own images of us: very rude, very rough, very low. We don't fight with them about these. *We use them to our advantage.* (Darko 102, emphasis added)

Moreover, one of the reasons why Mara has a thriving business as a prostitute is not only because she is described by Darko as a very beautiful woman, but also because European (and American) men tend to view darker skinned women as exotic, and thus a special prize to be had.[6] Since her customers are indeed operating on this stereotype, Mara, of course, benefits financially.

While both works use stereotypes, the manipulation of sexual ones raises a number of questions with regard to *Dirty Pretty Things*. Unlike Darko, Frears suggests that Okwe's personal values lead him to assume the role of protecting Senay's virginity and innocence. Admittedly, the film presents a certain ambivalence that we have alluded to earlier, and to be certain, the resolution of the tensions between Senay and Okwe are dealt with in a rather puritan self-sacrificing way. Senay, even though she has been raped by 'Sneaky', remains a 'virgin' so to speak, because she has *not willingly* given herself to Okwe, the subject of her affection. And Okwe, does not commit *adultery*, even though his wife is dead and there is no earthly reason for him to deny his feelings for Senay, except that such a union seems too much like Othello and Desdemona through the eyes of an Iago. This stands in stark contrast to the relationship between Akobi and Mara in *Beyond the Horizon* wherein Akobi is not only completely disinterested in preserving Mara's innocence, but is also quick to exploit her youthful sexuality and stereotypical assumptions of potential German male customers for his own profit and social advancement.

In exploiting Mara's sexuality, Akobi emblematically assumes the role of the European coloniser who is quick to capitalise on the undocumented immigrant's untenable position. Given the Hobson's choice of being a hapless casualty or making money and trading favours (or body parts) in order to survive and perhaps 'become' citizens, Mara is initially appalled by her work as a prostitute in Germany, and Senay is initially reluctant to perform obligatory acts of oral sex on her employer. Nevertheless, both Mara and Senay *accept an offer they cannot refuse*. For Darko and Frears the price of the ticket to citizenship is immorally high and corrupting, and it is the most vulnerable, 'the people you never see', who must pay that soul-destroying price of admission.

Senay and Mara, despite their different ethnic backgrounds and personal motivations, are equally objects of sexual desire for documented (white) men who seek them out. As feminist theorist and cultural critic bell hooks explains,

'When race and ethnicity become commodified as resources for pleasure, the culture of specific groups, as well as bodies of individuals, can be seen as constituting an alternative playground where members of dominating races, genders, [and] sexual practices affirm their power-over in intimate relations with the Other.'[7] hooks argues, 'getting a bit of the other' is a ritual of transcendence (23) for many men. Indeed, 'Sneaky' affirms his privileged position as a documented English citizen in framing his sexual demands as a 'deal breaker', effectively giving her an ultimatum: either submit to his sexual demands or she can forget about realising her dream of living in America. Thus, in 'getting a bit' of Senay, 'Sneaky' perversely uses his position as a wealthy, male citizen of the United Kingdom. He does so not only because Senay is a sexualised object of his desire, but also because he knows that he will ultimately be successful in his sexual pursuits, due primarily to the socially constructed power dynamic that protects him.

Mara and Senay illustrate the ways in which illegal alien women are so rapidly converted into sexual objects, and the employment opportunities available to these illegal immigrants are generally only those that dehumanise the individual. In the case of *Dirty Pretty Things*, Frears seems to communicate a cautionary and complex message: the cost of your dreams may be too high a price to pay, he warns the undocumented immigrant. And for the Western audience, this is the seductive, but awful penalty others pay for our pleasures. In contrast, Darko's seems to intimate in *Beyond the Horizon* that, for women, resistance is necessary, and the price is often humiliating and potentially soul destroying.

In the end, while there are substantial departures between the trajectories of both of these works and, indeed, the personal backgrounds of each artist, both offer scathing criticism on the ways in which Western countries construct and enforce the notion of citizenship. Moreover, both offer critical commentary on the political situations that have developed in the aftermath of the dismantling of the colonial system and the advent of globalisation. Both narratives leave their respective audiences to ponder serious questions about the nature and value of citizenship, nation and legal and illegal status in a global context of rapid flows of people, goods and services. *Dirty Pretty Things*, however, falls a little short of the kind of transformative resolution that *Beyond the Horizon* offers the reader. We are suggesting that *Dirty Pretty Things*, while encouraging our sympathy for Okwe and Senay as they struggle to be seen as human, and not as 'the people you never see', fails to free itself from the ideological moorings that bind us absolutely to notions of the state and its inviolability. *Beyond the Horizon*, on the other hand, suggests that engagement cannot take place in the periphery, in the former colonies, but must insist on remaining a thorn in the flesh at the centres of global flows. Or, to use Darko's narrative metaphor, our gaze must reflect back on itself; we must be willing to look as Mara does, on what she has become.

# Mary Ellen (Ellie) Higgins

## *Ngambika* and Grassroots Fiction: Amma Darko's *The Housemaid* and *Faceless*

Interdisciplinary discourses about Africa have in recent decades focused largely upon issues of traditional cultures under pressure from the forces of modernisation and globalisation and frequently have resorted to the simplified dichotomy of the rural (or traditional) and the urban (or modern).[1] Writers such as Amma Darko, however, have crafted 'grassroots fiction' to reposition and re-personalise the human context in which contemporary social struggles transpire.[2] I use the term 'grassroots fiction' to describe literary contributions and challenges to urban and rural development discourses that explore how social, economic and political forces influence individuals and communities. Darko engages with development debates by examining urbanisation, modernisation, economic instability, and migration at the microcosmic level. Through literature, she explores individual struggles with poverty, intricate webs of human exploitation, and possible strategies to alleviate the suffering of Ghana's underclass. As Obioma Nnaemeka writes, 'Development discourse and practice stand to gain from development in the particular. Until development assumes an individual, human face instead of the anonymity of the collective (the poor, the needy), it will remain an unrealisable goal in the 'third world' (*Nego-feminism* 375). The potential contribution of literature to this practice is rich, and from that perspective, Darko's novels can be read as grassroots fiction. Additionally, Darko's protagonists are often grassroots activists – her novels offer representations of ordinary women and men who demonstrate extraordinary strength to ameliorate contemporary problems as the author herself contributes artfully to the process of envisioning local solutions. Darko's work reinforces Celeste Schenk's assertion that literature can be 'read not only as an important contribution to interdisciplinary development studies but also as a kind of development practice itself' (236).

The Tshiluba concept of *Ngambika* illuminates the complex balance of power that affects women in relation to social, economic and political structures, and the possibilities for negotiations of local, national, and international responsibility. *Ngambika*, or 'help me to balance and carry this load', was selected for the title of Carole Boyce Davies and Anne Adams Graves' seminal work on African women writers, *Ngambika: Studies of Women in African Literature*. In her contribution to the discussion, Nnaemeka asserts, '*Ngambika* speaks against debilitating excess and unevenness and, on the other hand, it argues for balance and a fair share' (*Introduction*, 3). Emmanuel Awuah observes a similar Asante adage used in the Kumasi Market (and elsewhere) in Ghana; one that 'stresses the importance of cooperation and collective action': *dodo so a, emmia*, or 'when many people carry the load it becomes lighter' (407). Darko's second published novel, *The Housemaid*, and her third published novel, *Faceless*, feature characters who work as *kayayoos*, or porters, in the marketplace. These symbolic porters make a living by transporting others' loads. Akua (in *The Housemaid*) and the silenced *kayayoos* (in *Faceless*) also carry the burden of supporting their economically strapped parents. Darko's employment of market place porters and multiple protagonists in *The Housemaid* and *Faceless* provides a framework in which she explores the possibilities for cross-class cooperation and collective action, allowing for parallel construction and development of individual characters that invite comparison and contrast in analysis. Furthermore, through the characters Efia and Tika in *The Housemaid*, and Fofo and Kabria in *Faceless*, Darko explores the potential for solidarity between women – for the balancing of loads – across economic and spatial divides, in addition to the prospects for collective action across gender lines.

In all of her novels to date, Darko explicitly casts a critical lens on both the modern village and the modern city on national and international levels – 'modernisation' here is not associated with a particular rural or urban space, but an invasive and pervasive Eurocentric ideology obsessed with material wealth and consumption. Darko's first published novel, *Beyond the Horizon*, emphasises both internal migration within Ghana and external migration to Europe. Darko's protagonist, Mara, moves from her village, Naka, to urban Accra and then to Hamburg and Munich, Germany. At first, Mara embraces the 'been-to' myth; one that portrays Europe as the embodiment of both modernity and progress. Yet once she has travelled to 'Paradise' and her body is exploited as a sexual object of trade, the illusion is dispelled. Initially, the 'been-to' myth in *Beyond the Horizon* finds its local counterpart – one that is just as misguided – in the characters' naïve glorification of the city in *The Housemaid*. In *Faceless*, too, modern corruption and consumerism at multiple levels lead to devastating losses. As she rejects the representation of Europe as the site of progress, and as she interrogates materialistic consumerism in contemporary Ghana, Darko looks to Ghanaian traditions as alternatives. However, she simultaneously rejects the masculinist version of tradition that selectively and conveniently seeks to sustain privileges afforded to men. Alternatively, Darko reminds her readers of those traditions that emphasise community solidarity and balanced responsibility. In her narratives, traditions are not relegated to the past, but are viewed as dynamic, continuous, and transforming.[3]

Darko's novels do not conceive of villages and cities in dichotomous terms. Rather, Darko emphasises the spread of a modern consumer culture that destroys the community-centred values of both village and city inhabitants. In both locales, as Darko portrays them, the 'modern' invades minds more prominently than it does territories. Darko does acknowledge contrasts between rural and urban spaces – her attention is centred especially on economic disparities. Her work attests to Kwadwo Konadu-Agyemang's argument that mass migration to cities is largely a result of the uneven distribution of resources across rural and urban lines, an imbalance that dates back to the colonial era.[4] Darko's three novels demonstrate that the glorification of the 'modern' or the 'urban' is tied to economic survival, colonial legacies, and the espousal of Western materialism over more human-centred values. The relentless pursuit of wealth is most dramatically represented through stories of daughters who are viewed primarily as vehicles for profit. As fruitful as it may be to interpret Darko's work within the context of globalisation and the plight of those stranded beyond the horizon in Europe, I shall limit my exploration here to her two latter works that remained fixed 'at home' in Ghana.

*The Housemaid* commences with the discovery of the corpse of a newborn baby girl on the outskirts of the village of Braha. In the first few chapters of *Faceless*, the body of a murdered young woman named Baby Tsuru (or Baby T.) is found behind a hairdressing kiosk. Rather than craft her narratives in accordance with the usual whodunit formula of the mystery genre, Darko probes the social and economic circumstances of those who contributed to the abuse, and consequent deaths, of young girls. What follows is an exploration of myriad struggles for economic survival in villages and cities, as well as a commentary on sexual exploitation and contemporary corruption propelled by voracious, destructive consumerism. Darko's creative imagining of the stories of prostituted girls in Ghana is inspired by young women she encountered as she worked in an office in Accra close to the neighbourhood called Sodom and Gomorrah, which is featured so vividly and incisively in *Faceless*.[5] Darko imagines the lives of rural and urban women who are exploited sexually and whose suffering is hidden or silenced. The absence of their voices in the mainstream public sphere is underscored in the titles *The Housemaid* and *Faceless*: the first title speaks to those who are reduced to the service they perform and the second refers to those whose identities are effaced, whose stories remain untold.[6] And while human struggles to survive in Ghana are reported in professional documents and abstracted in statistical data, the more complex, individual narratives of those who battle for agency at the grassroots level are often omitted. Darko's grassroots fiction can be read as a means to address this intellectual imbalance.

In *The Housemaid*, the characters Efia and Akua migrate from their village of Kataso to urban centres. Efia travels to work as a housemaid for Tika, another central character whose deceased father is also from Kataso. In part because of sexual favours she offers her male business partners, Tika becomes a successful importer and entrepreneur in Accra. Akua, a minor character, leaves Kataso and later works in the urban Kumasi market as a porter. She locates shelter in unfinished buildings with the assistance of construction workers whom she repays with 'bribes of cash and sex' (32). Women's sexuality becomes a commodity; when Tika reflects on the use of her body for profit, she concludes, 'Business was business' (23). Business relationships predominate in 'modern' society; everything in it, including the human body and spirit, can be reduced to an article of commerce.

Because national development projects have prioritised urban spaces over rural areas, the villagers in *The Housemaid* have few options. Darko writes, 'Like most villages in Ghana, [Kataso] had lost its most successful sons to the cities, and these sons didn't return too often to help those they had left behind' (*The Housemaid* 27). The character Teacher chooses to work in the city because she cannot manage on the salary she would receive in the village. Kataso has 'no flowing water, no electricity, no entertainment centre, nothing' (29). The appendage of television to the list is significant; like actors in television commercials, characters in the narrative revel in the acquisition of commodities and later worship the purchasing power provided by 'fine sweet cash' that the city falsely promises (3). Several characters' migrations from villages to city centres within Ghana in *The Housemaid* echo Mara's transnational migration in *Beyond the Horizon*. Mara glorifies the urban sphere as she invents a new, more 'modern' (48) persona – 'Mara of the City' (50). Mara idealises 'been-to's' who have travelled to Europe; she would 'imagine Europe not to be just near Heaven but in Heaven itself' (34). Synchronously, Akua in *The Housemaid* believes that while she is still destitute in the city, in her village she will 'qualify as one of the soon-to-be-envied – a returnee'. (32). One porter asserts that women from her village compare their status by asking, 'How many of your children are in the city?' (31). Like Mara, Efia dreads the 'shame' of returning from the city 'empty-handed' (92). Through the counterpart to the 'been-to' myth – the 'returnee' myth – Darko exposes the politics of uneven development in Ghana. At the same time that she echoes Konadu-Agyemang's assertion that the stark lack of material resources in rural Ghana has prompted the flight to cities, Darko adds yet another component to the analyses of the flight to urban spaces: the glorification of the modern and its perceived apotheosis in the city.

In *The Housemaid*, the uneven distribution of economic resources is more prominent across spatial lines than gender lines. Women's location in the city, rather than their gender, is associated with wealth, though several urban women characters face quotidian threats to their survival. In Darko's narratives, women are not static guardians of tradition, but rather agents in a commercial setting that has become increasingly global. As Diawara has argued, the market place is emblematic of the dynamism of indigenous traditions; cosmopolitan African markets illustrate the continuity and transformative power of pre-colonial African trading practices (73–81). The contemporary informal sector is not romanticised in Darko's *oeuvre*, however. Women's economic success in the informal sector is recognised: Tika, like her mother Sekyiwa, is 'one of the wealthy market mummies' (18). Gender patterns are reversed as Sekyiwa purchases sex from 'good-looking male gold-diggers' (18). At the same time, several women characters – Tika, Akua, Efia, and in *Faceless* Baby T. – informally market their own bodies for profit in an economic system characterised by gender hierarchies and sexual exploitation. The expectation that women's bodies can be used as objects for profit recalls King Ampaw's portrayal of prostitution and migration to urban centres in his film, *Kukurantumi: The Road to Accra*. Darko participates in what Odile Cazenave recognises as a growing artistic discourse on African prostitution, one that critiques a system in which 'the woman is supposed to maintain the family by marketing her own body' (Cazenave 239). While Tika caves in to the expectation that she sleeps with business clients in order to prosper financially, Efia is prostituted by her own parents. When Tika brings Efia to the city to be her housemaid, her father, mother, and grandmother – who remain in their village – pressure her to engage sexually with Tika's clients in order to become pregnant. Their plan is to compel Tika, who is deemed a 'wasted woman' because of her hysterectomy, to adopt Efia's child. Afterwards, Efia's relatives expect that the child will secure an abundant inheritance for the family. The newborn child is celebrated as a promising financial investment rather than a cherished son or daughter. After the plot fails, the discarded body of the newborn symbolises the disintegration of the value of human life in the midst of a society that has become increasingly preoccupied with business.

The motif of the daughter who is sold for profit is one common thread in Darko's work: Mara is coerced into prostitution in Germany by her husband in *Beyond the Horizon*, and Maa Tsuru receives financial compensation for the prostitution of her daughter in *Faceless*. Like the prostitutes in Francophone African women's prose described by Cazenave, Darko's fictional prostitutes do not simply function 'to represent only the vices of colonisation'. Rather, the characters reflect the position of 'woman-as-object and body-as-merchandise' (Cazenave 42). Darko's work can be interpreted as a commentary on the degradation of African traditions in both contemporary villages and cities. Simultaneously, Darko's detailed imagining of women's economic struggles lifts the characters from the realm of the merely symbolic. Tika's exchange of sex for business favours may function to critique a neocolonial emphasis on materialism and the consequent loss of traditional humanistic values; yet Tika is also a complex character. She is a controversial figure who utilises her sexuality to get ahead. In order to succeed, Tika must play the game: she performs sexual favours within an economic system in which the rules are largely crafted by men. She wishes to share her resources with young people from her home village by contributing to their professional training. Amidst the pressure to acquire wealth and power, Tika searches for a means to balance the load.

Darko engages further with discourses of gender and modernity in *The Housemaid* through the figure of the witch. Diane Ciekawy and Peter Geschiere argue that witchcraft has been interpreted as a subversion of modernity, but also as a discourse that engages with modern methods to accumulate wealth (1–14). Concomitantly, they argue that 'witchcraft conjures up the idea of an opening, a leakage through which people or resources are withdrawn from the community and disappear into the outer world' (5). The village of Braha empties as a result of the steady outpouring of its inhabitants who migrate to the city; the widow proclaimed witch suffers an even deeper isolation. *The Housemaid* opens with a commentary on 'forsaken and forgotten' (3) widows who are condemned as witches: they are the scapegoats, or *bouk emissaries* who bear the blame for tragedies that occur within the community. Darko focuses on one unnamed grandmother/widow who is forced 'to live in an isolated hut on the outskirts of the village' (3–4). Here, witchcraft is placed in the context of gender politics: while several 'modern' men in the novel neglect their families in order to pursue wealth, women bear the blame for the calamities that visit those left behind. In his report on 'witch camps', or 'outcast homes' in Northern Ghana, Almuth Schauber writes: 'The accused women are more elderly than young, more deformed than healthy, more poor than rich, more barren than fertile, more outspoken than conforming with traditional roles, more peculiar in their behaviour they display because of their old age or sickness.'[7] Mensah Adinkrah links the persecution of alleged witches to practices of general violence against potentially subversive women (347).

In *The Housemaid*, the traditional reverence for elders is reversed as the agent of oral tradition, the grandmother is deemed a witch and ostracised. The grandmother does not passively accept her fate; she 'defie[s] her isolation' to draw attention to the body of Efia's abandoned newborn (4). The wrath of the community then descends upon another woman: a newspaper headline reads, 'Find the mother! Hang her!' (5). In her study of witchcraft allegations in Northern Ghana, Susan Drucker-Brown argues that '. . . the fear of witchcraft has grown as men's dependence on women has increased' (547-548). While waiting for Tika to conclude a meeting with one of her debtors, her cab driver remarks, 'Look at me, praying for my luck to shine, so that I can make some money off a woman. These market mummies are taking over the country . . . [They] aim for your power' (52). As she hints that accusations of witchcraft are entangled in men's anxiety about women's economic power, and as she demonstrates the absence of *Ngambika* through the constant placement of culpability on the shoulders of women, Darko's work concurrently recalls local controversies about the Ghanaian media's 'witch-hunting' – a term used by defensive government officials whom journalists publicly accuse of corruption.[8] In *The Housemaid*, Darko pursues her own line of 'witch-hunting' as she questions why villages have still not received government support in the form of electricity, running water, or schooling. As she calls attention to the imbalances in power between city and village, she also reveals the need for a more balanced assessment of community responsibilities.

Darko's narrative abounds with subplots about absent fathers and struggling mothers. Because she receives no assistance from her children's father, the character Mami Korkor hawks fish without respite to support them. Her daughter Bibio is forced to 'play mother' to her younger brothers while Mami Korkor labours. The narrative also features good fathers. Teacher's foster father adopts her and enrolls her in school; Nsorhwe cares for his wife's children even though they are not his biologically. In *The Housemaid*, fatherhood is not merely perceived as natural paternity; rather, men who take responsibility for the welfare of their children are seen as the only admirable fathers worthy of the title. Mothers are clearly agents in the struggle for economic survival, but, as Davies writes in *Ngambika*, women's agency is rendered more effective when there is assistance to balance the weight. Darko's work reminds readers of the Asante adage discussed earlier in this essay, *dodo so a, emmia*: 'when many people carry the load it becomes lighter'. Darko calls for collective responsibility as an alternative to the scapegoating of women. Male characters are not the only ones guilty of negligence; Darko depicts multiple women characters who abuse their positions as parents. Efia's mother and grandmother succumb to the lure of consumer comforts; instead of tending to Efia's needs, they encourage her to prostitute herself so that they may inherit Tika's material possessions. Efia's covetous mother sits in Tika's chair and thinks, 'how soft, how comfortable, how pleasurable! ... When, oh when?' (59). Darko also speaks to the responsibility of daughters to care for their mothers. In a relatively hopeful conclusion, Teacher tells Tika that she has alienated her aging mother and persuades her to make an attempt at reconciliation.

In my interview with Darko in 2003, she intimated that her stories are inspired from events featured in the local Ghanaian media, in addition to her research and her own imagination. She commented that her work is based 'on the story of so many people. I mix them, knead them and come out with my own story' (112).[9] Based on her own observations at the grassroots level, Darko's narrative balances abstract, generalising theories of development and social transformation with detailed accounts of individuals, families, and communities. *The Housemaid* is the imagined story of the everyday lives of several figures found in Ghana's newspapers: accused witches, abandoned infants, absent fathers, opportunistic mothers, exploited daughters, and market women, among others. It is also the story of those who manage to survive, and those who take responsibility for the care of their kin despite ceaseless hardships.

*The Housemaid* concurrently reflects on the dynamics of the 'modern'. It recognises lost traditions associated with village life: Teacher was 'born inside a traditional midwife's hut in village, and her umbilical cord had been placed in a calabash and buried by her grandmother in the brown earth of the village' (35). In contrast, Tika 'was delivered in a hospital in the city and had had her umbilical cord flushed down into the sewerage system with countless others' (35). In the village, too, traditions have been corrupted: when her scheme to siphon off Tika's wealth fails, Efia's grandmother irreverently asks 'where the hell are the gods and ancestors?' (90). Just as Darko represents migrating characters, she focuses on a widespread contemporary psychological migration away from familial and communal solidarity toward consumerism, business and profit.

While *Beyond the Horizon* emphasises international emigration and *The Housemaid* focuses on movements from villages to the city within Ghana, *Faceless* depicts the constant movement of urban, homeless youths who travel from one temporary dwelling place to another in search of shelter. The narrative is set in two very different landscapes within the urban sphere: one co-protagonist, Fofo, inhabits a squatters' enclave located in a suburb of Accra called Fadama (also known as Sodom and Gomorrah), and a second co-protagonist, Kabria, resides in a middle-class neighbourhood. The meetings between women across classes are set in Ghana's Agbogbloshie market. *Faceless* concentrates on internal divisions within the city: by identifying Sodom and Gomorrah as the site of sin, more privileged characters – with the exception of Kabria and other grassroots activists – attempt to divest themselves of any responsibility to alleviate the suffering of its poor inhabitants. The urban underclass is dismissed as an Other and their struggles receive little priority on the national agenda. The novel was published in the year after the Ghanaian NGO, The Centre for Public Interest Law (CEPIL), called attention to over 30,000 squatters who were delivered a two-week ultimatum to vacate their enclaves.[10]

Darko's narrative, like the Moroccan director Nabil Ayouch's film *Ali Zaoua* and the Senegalese film-maker Mansour Sora Wade's short *Picc Mi*, diverges thematically from previous narratives about African child protagonists who are caught between a traditional African education and a European colonial one. Darko critiques national indifference toward homeless children who must fend for themselves on the fringes of the city as they are apprenticed into 'the gospel according to street wisdom' (*Faceless* 28). Similar to Efia in *The Housemaid*, young women in *Faceless* are pushed into using their sexuality for the profit of greedy, negligent relatives. Fofo is also reminiscent of Hyacinth, the protagonist in Joan Riley's *The Unbelonging*; she cannot find refuge within her family or in her society.[11] For Darko's characters in *Faceless*, however, the site of unbelonging is not Europe but urban Accra.

In *Faceless*, the character Baby T. is prostituted and ultimately is murdered through a series of events in which multiple characters exploit her. As

Anyidoho writes, Darko's narrative offers 'a provocative tale of a society that has developed a tragic ability of guiding its young ones, especially the girl-child, into a life dedicated to prostituting every conceivable virtue for the sake of flimsy material possessions' (10). As Kabria investigates Baby T.'s death as part of a story she is pursuing for the NGO, MUTE, linked stories of abuse and exploitation unravel. First, Baby T.'s father, Kwei, tries to destroy her while she is in her mother's womb. When she is a young girl, she is sexually assaulted by her mother's lover, her 'new father,' Kpakpo (168). Afterwards, a trusted family friend, Onko, rapes Baby T.; Kpakpo and Onko then send her to a middle woman, Mama Abidjan, who claims to recruit girls to work as housekeepers but instead sells them into prostitution. Baby T. is placed in Maami Broni's informal brothel and under the surveillance of the streetlord, Poison. Kpakpo takes a portion of her earnings, and shares them with Maa Tsuru only after she suspects Baby T.'s real profession. Upon receipt of part of the profits, Maa Tsuru ceases her questioning and rationalises that the funds must be used to care for her younger children. Through Kabria's investigation into the murder of Baby T., Darko invites readers to contemplate modern, misplaced priorities through the theme of parental neglect. Through her narrative, she argues that children's economic and psychological welfare should be the responsibility of parents, relatives, and the wider community. Although Darko challenges 'the equating of the essence of womanhood to reproduction' (*Faceless*: 138), the primary target of her critique is not the idealisation of motherhood but parental remissness and abandonment. As in *The Housemaid*, reverence for parents in *Faceless* is not granted merely because of biological paternity or maternity, but rather it is earned through the traditional practice of responsible care and commitment.

Darko reiterates her argument in *The Housemaid* that parenthood should be defined by the practice of nurturing rather than biological reproduction. She critiques the individualistic practice of welcoming children for one's own aggrandisement; Kwei's mother celebrates Maa Tsuru's pregnancy because the child will 'make a nice impression in her obituary' (148). Instead of casting blame on mothers, Darko lends an insight into their complex predicaments through the voice of Ms. Kamame, a guest on Sylv Po's radio programme, 'Good Morning Ghana': 'A woman like Fofo's mother, whose "village" happens to be inner-city Accra, is more likely to lose her sense of onus rather speedily when pushed by joblessness and poverty and the non-existent male support' (140). In my interview with Darko, she links parental neglect to the loss of particular Ghanaian traditions in the wake of struggles for economic survival and urban migration. She asserts, 'Initially, in the community you were imbued with certain values... You were taught responsibility. But now, people are out of the villages, out on the streets, surviving, struggling.'[12]

While recognising social and generational changes, Darko draws upon the energy and intelligence of selected traditions to launch her critique of modern corruption. Like *The Housemaid*, *Faceless* tracks the corruption of tradition in the contexts of modern economic hardships and contemporary consumerism. Sylv Po describes inebriated mortuary attendants: 'an irony for a part of the world where the dead are revered, and the destinies of the living are tied to the apron strings of the ancestors' (178). After Kwei repudiates Maa Tsuru for getting pregnant with his child – a moment that echoes Akobi's rejection of Mara's child in *Beyond the Horizon* – she wonders, 'Since when did a fertile womb become a bad thing?' (151). Rather than engage in the practice of *Ngambika*, several characters in *Faceless*, like those in *The Housemaid*, cast the guilt for tragedies upon women. When confronted with accusations about his assault on Baby T., Kpakpo claims that 'it was she who started pushing herself on me... provoking me' (167). Maami Broni rationalises that she agreed to take Baby T. in as a prostitute because she was told that Baby T. was 'already giving herself to men freely' (219). Not only does Baby T. bear the burden of prostituting herself for her mother and stepfather's benefit, she is assigned the blame for the exploitation of her own body. Through the vehicle of fiction, Darko reassesses and reapportions responsibility to include the larger community, including the state.

In both villages and cities, Darko's women characters muster the strength to survive, yet seek assistance to balance their multiple loads. Darko's narratives speak to the absence of national intervention, and above all, the instrumental role of parents. *Faceless* functions in part as a commentary on the uneven division of domestic labour; Kabria carries a disproportionate load vis-à-vis her husband. Although both she and her husband work, Kabria is expected to perform the additional tasks of cooking, cleaning, and child-rearing. She recalls: 'A report once alleged that the African woman worked for an average of sixty-seven hours a week as opposed to fifty-five for the African man. So who really was the weaker sex?' (82). Ms. Kamame speaks of the effects of the sexual division of labour: 'the responsibility of the mother doubles. She becomes the only caretaker of the child's emotional or physical or financial needs... that means performing the tasks of two' (137). The exigency for the sharing of responsibilities – for *Ngambika* across genders – is a central motif in *Faceless*. Darko recognises that while the plight of the middle-class working mother is significant, street children have an even heavier burden to bear. Fofo cries with misery at 'the weight of it all' (189), and is drawn into drugs and theft. Several young *kayayoos* – a Hausa term meaning 'load' – migrate to Accra to work as porters in the urban markets. The *kayayoos* – young girls from Northern Ghana – are silenced by Poison because they carry part of the resolution to the mystery of Baby T.'s murder. While several young characters work as market porters, others like Baby T. are coerced into prostitution. Those who profit from the prostitutes euphemistically refer to a young woman's 'apprenticeship' (220). Poison personifies neocolonial exploitation and modern corruption; he views other humans only as a means to increase his wealth and power. He sees himself, above all other things, as 'a businessman', and his denial of responsibility a 'business ploy' (203).

Ousmane Sembène has stated that cinema can function as a night school. Concordantly through fiction, Darko blends elements of mystery and resistance literature to educate her readers. As Fofo brings Kabria into a critical awareness of 'some of the ingredients that go into the making of a street child' (103), readers, too, benefit from her perceptions. As they cooperate to solve the crime of Baby T's murder, the street-wisened Fofo, the committed members of the non-governmental organisation MUTE, and the journalist Sylv Po at 'Harvest FM' radio provide more optimistic models for future collective action and self-determination. *Faceless* critiques the absence of government-sponsored intervention on behalf of children – Fofo proclaims: 'I want government,' but receives nothing (73). The government does not assist her mother with funds to pay for her children's uniforms or schoolbooks, nor does it provide the police with the vehicles or phone lines they need to investigate Baby T.'s case. The novel contemplates the work of NGOs and popular radio programmes as grassroots alternatives to state or international intervention. MUTE's creation of the Alternative Library and Sylv Po's oral accounts of street children and AIDS mirror grassroots work 'on the ground'. The Alternative Library attends to the undocumented struggles of those who are discarded, rendered invisible, and an outcast.[13] Simultaneously, it provides research on the histories of areas on Accra's urban periphery that house generations of migrant adults and children.

MUTE's goal to 'salvage knowledge and facts about people and places that used to be handed down orally' (104) recall the 'textualisation of orality' in the work of authors such as Amadou Hampaté Bâ.[14] Dina, the head of MUTE, describes two elderly women as 'human libraries' (105), a description that recalls the proverb ascribed to Hampaté Bâ, *'En Afrique, chaque vieillard qui meurt est une bibliothèque qui brule'* [In Africa, every elderly man who dies is the equivalent of a library burning down]. Darko alters the adage slightly: the 'human libraries' are two women – plural, feminine *vielles femmes* rather than the singular, masculine *viellard*. Because Fofo's story is taking place in the present, Dina asserts that MUTE – and by extension, the Ghanaian community – 'cannot just make [Fofo] another documentation case' (105). In addition to emphasising parental responsibility, Darko calls for the wider collective to act. *Faceless* partakes in discourses of grassroots development as it remains mindful of the politics of international development: Kabria humorously pokes fun at her husband's unwillingness to repair her collapsing automobile, 'Creamy', by comparing his inefficacy to failed development programmes that attempt to 'modernise' or convert African countries. Adade 'lend[s] as much support and understanding as the World Bank and IMF lend to the world's developing countries' (191–192).

The travails of Kabria's beloved 1975 Volkswagen Beetle 'Creamy' mirror Kabria's efforts to bear her load. 'Creamy', in contrast to Adade's new Toyota, has 'been in and out of every kind of workshop' (39) and frequently rebels against its encumbrances. Like Kabria, 'Creamy' refuses defeat: when Kabria dreams of getting rid of 'Creamy', it takes charge of the dream and drives itself back to her. The vehicles of community action, like the determined 'Creamy', require consistent maintenance. The conclusion of *Faceless* points to the need for collective intervention and its potential for the rehabilitation of communities. Rather than provide a comfortable closure for her readers in which community solidarity and agency solve Fofo's dilemnas, Darko reminds readers that there is an urgent need for future action. At the novel's end, Fofo finds shelter, yet her AIDS test remains undisclosed and the fate of the characters in Sodom and Gomorrah still hangs in the balance.

In her three works, Darko's more privileged woman characters range from the ignorant, self-serving Gitte in *Beyond the Horizon* to the well-meaning, yet self-absorbed Tika in *The Housemaid*, to Kabria, who encourages Fofo to tell her own story. In *The Housemaid* and *Faceless*, Darko demonstrates possible grassroots solutions through cross-class cooperation of men and women. Darko's use of co-protagonists – Tika and Efia, Kabria and Fofo – provides a model for community action on the local level, one that engages the adage, *dodo so a, emmia*. Just as Germany is ultimately not a haven but a prison for Mara in *Beyond the Horizon*, the city in *The Housemaid* and *Faceless* has little to offer poor, migrant women. The city renders the underclass invisible; those who dwell on the streets are dismissed as 'not normal' (68), and those who meet their death in the city are 'buried in mass graves at Mile Eleven' (69). Yet Darko recognises an untapped potential in Sodom and Gomorrah: Kabria notes the creative space of Sodom and Gomorrah's marketplace. She remarks: 'The rest of Accra probably has a thing or two to learn from Sodom and Gomorrah about innovations and initiatives' (184). Through cross-class, grassroots action, Fofo – and by extension, other homeless children in urban spaces – could move toward a collective 'rehabilitation' (105) – one that remembers the lessons of tradition as it moves toward future change.

Darko attempts to render the lives of exploited women more visible through creative writing. She brings to the surface the forgotten, the repressed, and the taboo: poor Ghanaian girls who are coerced into local urban prostitution for the profit of family members, and the discarded bodies of infants and girls. Such an unearthing seeks a deeper collective understanding of the struggles of poor women. Darko provides her characters with an imagined literary history that stretches beyond their symbolic functions. Her narratives recall the work of earlier African writers who brought previously marginalised women's perspectives to the forefront of creative writing and literary criticism. Darko's novels can be read as a valuable contribution to an alternative, grassroots library

– an alternative library, like a conventional one, raises awareness and contributes to the production of knowledge. It also attempts to address the gaps in knowledge by documenting the struggles of those whose voices and faces receive scant attention in the public sphere. Theirs are stories of unbelonging, stories of oppression and exclusion, but also of agency and the quest for access to those mechanisms of grassroots 'development' through which they can change their own lives.

Darko's works offer a commentary on contemporary migration from rural areas, and a stark exposure of the sexual exploitation of women both in Ghana and in Europe. Using the popular genre of mystery and local stories cast in Ghana's newspapers and public radio programmes, Darko explores how community action and understanding across class and gender lines may work to spark a shift in the balance of unbearable loads. As Darko builds on indigenous knowledge through her collection of NGO reports, her characters lend human faces to development discourses. Her portraits of contemporary Ghana reveal the corruption of traditional parent-child ties in an uneven economy in urban, rural, and blurred settings. Hers is a call for change, but also a call for the continuity of a tradition, like *Ngambika*, that emphasises shared responsibility.

# Carmela Garritano

## Amma Darko's *The Housemaid* and the Gendering of Novel and Nation

For the first generation of African male writers, such as Chinua Achebe and Camara Laye, the novel offered a powerful narrative form through which to counter colonial representations of Africa and create a sense of national culture and identity. In its re-creation of what Simon Gikandi calls the 'signs of everyday life' (22), the African novel testified to the existence of dynamic and complex African cultural systems, defying the colonial construction of Africa as a dark absence without culture or history.[1] Benedict Anderson's provocative study of the nation links the emergence of the novel with the 'deep, horizontal comradeship' of the nation (7) and demonstrates that the novel's replication of national time and space enabled the invention of a cohesive national community. African writers, in appropriating a borrowed genre, effectively exploited its capacity to enact national identity in its presentation of 'simultaneity' (Anderson 24), which Anderson calls 'a precise analogue to the idea of the nation' (26).

As Susan Andrade explains, the novel provided the first wave of African male writers with 'an ideal means by which to consolidate racial, religious, ethnic and class differences into a single national identity' (250). Nevertheless, Michelle Burnham aptly notes in her critique of Anderson that consolidation through simultaneity and sameness, disregards the play of difference in the constitution of national identity. Quoting Homi Bhabha, Burnham explains that 'any identification with a likeable image or feature is always 'constituted through the *locus* of the Other' (54). Andrade makes a similar claim, arguing that the singular national identity presented in the first African novels represented a 'male-dominated nationalist ideology' (250) which, in its consolidation of an African identity, effectively erased 'women as subjects' (251). In the guise of a genderless African literature, these writers shored up a masculine national identity through gender difference. Although Andrade does not refer to either Anderson or Bhabha, her critique echoes Bhabha's reading of Anderson in that it insists on the recognition of what Bhabha has described as the ambivalence inherent in any consolidated national identity or discourse. For Bhabha, the people of a nation emerge within 'a double narrative moment' (Bhabha 145), a temporal 'in-between' space that 'interrupts the self-generating time of national production and disrupts the signification of the people as homogenous' (148).

This 'liminal signifying space ... is internally marked by the discourses of minorities, the heterogeneous histories of contending peoples, antagonistic authorities and tense locations of cultural difference' (148). Hence, the desire for identification with a homogenous national identity always entails the repression or displacement of difference, a supplement that destabilises the 'sociological solidity' of the nation (306).

Andrade's concern is to examine African women writers' efforts to antagonise and re-write this masculinist discourse by representing the sites of ambivalence and heterogeneity effaced within it. Taking a similar path, I argue that Amma Darko's novel *The Housemaid*, a text marked by discord and heterogeneity, interrogates the myth of a consolidated nation founded on comradeship and resemblance. The novel, in its re-enactment of the struggles of women living in contemporary Ghana, posits a discursive relationship between the nation and the bodies of women and presents a stinging critique of the failures of the Ghanaian nation. Yet, the novel does much more than offer a sociological account of the nation's failures at the level of narrative content. Darko's novel, through its structure and mode of address, at once produces and deconstructs what Anderson, borrowing from Walter Benjamin, has called the 'homogenous, empty time' through which the imagined community of the nation is played out. Darko's novel constructs a different temporality, one similar to that which Bhabha calls a post-colonial temporality; a temporality which 'forces us to rethink the sign of history *within* those languages, political or literary, which designate the people as "one"' (153). Darko writes a novel that proclaims itself as such and yet, simultaneously, destabilises the very conventions that define the novel. Her text, in its form and content, is a decidedly feminist one, a counter-narrative of the nation, at once 'evok[ing] and eras[ing] its totalising boundaries' (Bhabha 153) and, in this way, revealing the gendered displacement and ambivalence on which any national narrative depends.

*The Housemaid* explicitly defines itself as a national narrative, and one centred on how women experience the space of the contemporary Ghanaian nation. Darko's female characters are historical subjects, not signifiers that stand-in for Africa, or tradition, or the nation. The novel might be read as a de-mystification of the trope of the nation as woman, or what Florence Stratton has described as the 'mother Africa trope' (39), describing mothers who struggle against the material and historical realities of post-colonial Ghana and often make choices that turn their daughters against them. Tika is estranged from her mother, Sekyiwa, whom she blames for her father's death. Mami Korkor, a fish hawker, must work long hours and leave her children in the care of her young daughter, Bibio, who resents her mother for her poverty. Efia's mother and grandmother use their daughter to obtain Tika's money, forcing Efia to have sex with men so that she might become pregnant while she is in Tika's care. Within the 107 pages of *The Housemaid*, a novel told almost entirely through dialogues among the thoughts of its female characters, an old widow is declared a witch, a woman has an abortion which leaves her barren, a young unmarried girl gives birth to a Down's Syndrome baby girl, the child dies, and the young mother is pursued as a murderer. For women without economic power or the protection of their families, the Ghanaian nation is a threatening place, offering few prospects for happiness and presenting many dangers; dangers that manifest themselves on women's bodies. The first words of *The Housemaid* place the reader 'in Ghana', and in the paragraphs that follow, the narrator qualifies for the reader what 'Ghana' represents for its female citizens. Darko's novel begins:

> In Ghana, if you come into the world a she, acquire the habit of praying. And master it. Because you will need it, desperately, as old age pursues you, and mother nature's hand approaches you with a wry smile, paint and brush at the ready, to daub you with wrinkles.
>
> If, on top of this, your children, waging a desperate war of their own for economic survival, find themselves having too little time for you, count you among the forsaken and the forgotten; and if, crowning it all, cash, fine sweet cash, decides it doesn't really fancy your looks and eludes you in all nooks, crooks and crannies, then know for sure that you are on route to qualifying grandly as a witch. (Darko 3)

The narrator describes the vulnerability of women who do not occupy secure positions in a patriarchal system which locates them as either passive members of a patriarchal family or as objects of men's desire.[2] Here and throughout the novel, the narrator invokes the space of the nation as a gendered space offering vastly differently realities to men and women. It is the discovery of the dead body of a *female* baby which 'was on the lips of every Ghanaian' (6). Tika learns that 'in Ghana' women exchange sex for reduced tariffs (23), and at the end of the novel she proclaims: 'God help Ghana's poor, old, lonely women' (106).

Although invoked in these and other passages as if representing a unified 'people', the idea of the homogenous community of the nation is continually undercut in the novel. Ghana is represented as a site of contestation and competition, housing a multiplicity of voices inflected by the gender and class positions of its citizens, who speak different languages from dramatically different locations and economic situations. The discovery of 'the gruesome, decaying corpse of a newborn baby girl' (Darko 4) unleashes within the nation, and the novel, an unrestrained and irresolvable heteroglossia. At the market and the taxi station, two of the busiest locations in the city, men and women dispute the meaning of the body, and their interpretations vary dramatically depending on their gender. The men chastise the mother and suggest that when she is caught 'her womb should be removed, cut in two, and given to her to swallow by the count of three' (6). The women, on the other hand, sympathise with 'the poor baby's mother' and criticise 'the irresponsible man who impregnated the poor woman' (6). Disputes about how to interpret the body occur in the newspaper; one headline reads: 'Find the Mother! Hang Her!' and another: 'Why Did she Do It?' (5). The deformed and abandoned corpse of the female child, like the nation itself, is a site of conflicting interpretations.

Jonathon Culler, referring to the work of Doris Summer and Franco Moretti, remarks that one of the ways the novel advanced a national image was through its capacity to describe *and unify* the heterogeneous voices and interests that comprised the nation in order to 'symbolically represent the resolution of national difference' (4).[3] Darko's novel, on the other hand, refuses, or is unable, to give its readers closure, offering no solutions to the problems it describes, nor bridging the gender and class divisions the mystery has opened up. *The Housemaid*, instead, represents discord and division through its description of how the nation has failed women.

Consider the beginning and end of the novel. In its opening pages, the novel presents itself as a mystery novel, a narrative form driven by a desire for resolution. In Part One, the rapid unfolding of dramatic events rendered in a staccato syntax, lead the reader to expect a novel that will crescendo to a dramatic climax when the truth of the mystery of the baby in the bushes is revealed. Yet, within the first thirteen pages, *The Housemaid* spoils the reader's anticipated pleasure by disclosing who the baby's mother is and, in a sense, solving its mystery. The narrator explains that after the discovery of the corpse, the police compiled a description of what the suspected mother was wearing when last seen. Two boys scavenging in a rubbish dump find bloody and soiled clothes and take them to be salvaged by Bibio, the sister of one of the boys. When Mami Korkor, Bibio's mother, learns that the clothes might be essential to a murder investigation, she takes them to the police station. At the end of Part One, the police officer introduces Mami Korkor and the reader to Akua, 'the one who gave us the vital clue about the clothes. She was living with a friend called Efia, who took off unceremoniously one day wearing these same clothes. And at the time she left, she was very pregnant' (Darko 13).

In the opening lines of Part Two, when the reader is introduced to Tika and her maid Efia, she, perhaps, knows already that Efia, Tika's housemaid, is the woman who left the corpse of her baby in the bushes. It would seem, then, that the point of the novel is not to solve the mystery of the corpse. In fact, the plot of the novel, at various moments, seems incidental to this end. Mami Korkor's character, for example, threatens the believability of the plot, which bends almost to the point of implausibility to justify the existence of her character. She is briefly introduced to the reader in Part One and is never seen again. The reader is told that Mami Korkor is a fish hawker 'helplessly wishing she could have afforded a better life' for her daughter, who resents her mother for the poverty in which they live. The narrator wonders: 'But how could she change things? She has to hawk fish from dawn to dusk to earn enough to feed herself and her four children. They all depended on her. Not a pesewa came from their father' (11). Her character serves to illustrate how very hard it is for a poor and uneducated single mother to survive in Ghana and to stand in stark contrast to the life of Tika as it is developed in Part Two. While Bibio resents her mother for having children she cannot afford to care for properly, Tika worries that she is 'single and childless at the ripe age of thirty-five' (17). Tika concerns herself not with buying food to feed her family, but the lack of fun afforded by 'living only with Efia, her maid, in a two-room estate house, and travelling frequently all over Africa to scout for goods to sell in Ghana' (17).

The novel, too, ends in an extremely ambivalent manner. Efia, who has spoken very little throughout the novel, finally tells her story, explaining to Teacher and Tika that her baby was a 'bad child', a Down's Syndrome baby, which she believed signified that a curse had been placed on her and her family for all of the evil they had done to Tika (Darko 102). For this reason, she knew it was important to take the body back to her people 'so that the necessary rituals could be performed' (103). On the way to her village, the bus in which she was riding broke down and she was forced to leave the body of her dead baby in the bushes. Teacher remarks that if the baby had been born in Kataso, 'the village would have been thrown into a frenzied orgy of witch-hunting. And only God knows how many poor lonely old widows would have been spared' (106). Efia's tragedy, not the first of its kind and not the last, merely prevented other women from experiencing their own tragedies and, in the novel's concluding lines, Tika and Teacher speculate on the unhappy, and unchanged, fate of 'wrinkled old women' in Ghana (106). No harmony or solution is found at the novel's end, and this is further demonstrated in the series of questions Tika considers, but cannot answer: 'Should she reunite with her mother? What would her father want her to do? Has he been watching her? Would he approve of her business?' (107). In a tenuous and rather feeble attempt at resolution, the narrator tells the reader that Teacher and Tika 'laughed and cried; laughing and crying away their pain, their disappointment, their anger, their fear. And laughing with hope' (107). Yet, the novel has given the reader no reason to be hopeful, and the concluding sentences remain entirely unconvincing.

The resolution of conflict is one strategy through which the novel makes possible a sense of national community; another is its construction of narrative time and space. For Anderson, the novel provides 'a precise analogue of the idea of the nation' (26) in its construction of 'a solid community moving steadily down (or up) history' (26). The structure of the novel functions as a device for the presentation of simultaneity in 'homogenous, empty time' (26). Readers, in the act of reading a novel, read about and experience themselves as beings within the 'meanwhile' the novel creates. In the reader's engagement with the novel, she both comes to understand as a reader, 'the idea of a sociological organism moving calendrically', and to take away from that reading the experience of imagining herself as one among many members of a nation: she 'has complete confidence in their steady, anonymous, simultaneous activity' (26). Both inside and outside the world the novel creates, the reader imagines and enacts the idea of the nation. In a careful examination of Anderson's argument about the novel and the nation, Culler fleshes out the narrative elements of the novel that are crucial to the production of the imagined community of the nation. They are 'the formal structure of the narrative point of view, the national content of the fictions ... and finally the construction of the reader' (22). Following Culler's reading of Anderson, I want to sketch the structure of narration in *The Housemaid* and suggest that Darko's novel represents an attempt to reconfigure the time-space of the novel.

As explained earlier, Darko's novel displays the plot within a defined national space by reminding her readers, again and again, that events transpire 'in Ghana'. The content of the fiction is national in that it is 'geographically situated or bounded' (Culler 22). However, the text, simultaneously, disrupts the 'homogenous, sociological landscape' (Anderson 30) of the nation. The bounded space of Ghana is fractured into two parts, the city and the village, and the plot moves back and forth, repeatedly and sometimes jarringly, between these locations (the cities of Accra and Kumasi and the villages of Braha and Kataso). From the discovery of the body in the village, the narrative jumps to the city of Kumasi, where the story of the dead and abandoned baby and 'the name of an unknown eastern village was on the lips of every Ghanaian' (Darko 6). The narrative seems pulled between the village and the city, and although the movement between the two locations might have suggested a linkage of the landscapes, the novel, instead, uses movement to emphasise the separate and conflicting identities of the two sides of the nation. Arranging travel back and forth requires a considerable amount of discussion and planning, and a mediator, Teacher, is needed to facilitate communication between Tika and Efia's family. Furthermore, the narrator juxtaposes the lives of the women and the familial relationships of the 'villagers' and the 'city-dwellers' (Darko 41). The grandmother's pouring of libation and belief in the ancestors and ghosts, features of Kataso, are foiled by Nsorhwe's insistence on a scientific and 'modern' blood test. Efia's family's decision to use Efia's pregnancy as a way to acquire wealth is set against Tika's decision to abort an unwanted pregnancy to maintain her freedom and independence. In the village of Kataso, Efia's life is decided by her extended family, while Tika, the urban market women, moves and speaks freely.

The binary opposition between the urban and rural that Darko reiterates in the novel refuses to privilege either location as the true space of the nation and hence avoids the colonial and stereotypical teleology that posits the rural as traditional and the urban as modern. Escaping poverty and searching for a better life consume the energies of characters in both locations. If the village houses prejudice against women, the urban landscape presents women with obstacles equally challenging. Tika's fierce independence and successful business have come to her at great cost. Tika grew up in a 'loveless marriage' (Darko 26) and is estranged from her mother, Sekyiwa. Forced to trade sex for business contracts, Tika is dumped by her true love, Owuraku, who disproves of her business dealings. She becomes impregnated by one of her married business associates and has an abortion that leaves her barren. Profound feelings of dislocation and dissatisfaction trouble Tika because, the narrator explains, she was born 'in a hospital in the city' where her umbilical cord was 'flushed down into the sewerage system with countless others' (35) instead of being buried in her village. Tika seeks a connection with the village of Kataso as a symbol of the family and community for which she longs. She recollects her father telling her of the village, 'That is where my umbilical cord was buried' (29), and therefore wants her housemaid 'to be from my father's extended family' (37). Yet, the village and the kin relations found there provide neither solace nor support for Tika. The village does not represent the pristine and unblemished world of 'tradition'. Indeed, Tika's romanticised image of the village is soon spoiled by the events that transpire there. Her father's kin set out to manipulate her and scheme to gain access to her wealth, using the matrilinial 'traditional' network to inherit her riches.

If, for Anderson, the novel replicates the time of the nation in its reproduction of simultaneity, then Darko's novel might be said to inscribe another temporality, one that self-consciously 'disturbs the contemporaneity of the national present' (Bhabha 295). Bhabha challenges the time of the nation as Anderson describes it. For Anderson, the 'synchronicity of time' represented by the realist novel 'gives the imagined world of the nation a sociological solidity' (308). This synchronicity can only be achieved, Bhabha claims, by ignoring 'the distracting presence of another temporality' (295). This other time is what Bhabha calls 'another time of writing' (293); it is a time split between two moments: 'the continuist, accumulative temporality of the pedagogical, and the repetitious, recursive strategy of the performative' (145). The seemingly present and homogenous nation emerges only *in discourse* and therefore within a double-narrative movement; it is simultaneously the *object* of a national discourse and the *subject* of a process of signification. It is this other double time that Darko's novel enacts. Part One of *The Housemaid* locates the reader at the moment of enunciation, the present moment during which the story is being told. Bhabha might describe this as the time of the performance of the narrative. The narrator functions like a storyteller in this section of the novel, speaking from an extradiegetic location and engaging her audience in the telling of the tale. The opening paragraphs of the novel, quoted previously, exemplify this narrative stance. The narrator addresses the reader in the second person in the immediate present, placing herself outside the story, but in the time of its recitation.

In Part Two of the novel, the reader slips into the time of the pedagogical, the homogenous, empty time of the realist novel. Here, an absent, omniscient narrator constructs, unobtrusively, the real world of the story, providing details about setting, character motivation and plot and entering into the thoughts of her characters. Yet, the moment of enunciation, the moment of the performative, haunts this other, historical time. Narrative interjections peppered throughout the novel remind the reader that the story unfolding before her is, in fact, a narrative shaped by the presence of an opinionated and often ironic narrator who stands outside the narrative and assembles it. When Tika explains to Efia that 'the men who regularly called on her were business partners', the narrator adds: 'That, of course, was not entirely false, but Efia was no fool' (Darko 49). This information is completely extraneous to the plot of the story because the reader has already been told that Tika's business transactions often include sexual amenities. The comment is not filtered through Efia's consciousness, as it might have been as a means of providing insight into her character, but simply serves to call attention to the narrator's telling of the story and to remind the reader where her sympathies lie. This is not the omniscient narrator of Anderson's novel, who speaks in an imagined, empty time, but an interested participant revealing her position in relation to the telling of the tale. This narrator defines a third space of articulation or writing, a space always inscribed in any discourse of the nation, but one that, as in Anderson's analysis, is missed, ignored, or concealed behind a linear and progressive historical time that appears to unfold in a homogenous space. Darko's text refuses to conceal its constructed-ness. It, instead, maps what Bhabha calls 'the alienating and iterative time of the sign' (310) and experiments with a narrative form that calls into question the very possibility of a uniform and inclusive narrative of the nation.

The use of irony in the above and many other such interjections further complicates the text's reproduction of national/novelistic time and space. To whom does the ironic narrator speak and from what location? Anderson argues that the novel, in part, laid the foundation for the emergence of a national community by addressing its readers 'as nationals' (Culler 30), but Culler challenges this assertion, illustrating that in the very examples Anderson cites, a national community is not addressed, but sought after as 'an object of readerly desire' (30). Of Anderson's reading of Rizal's *Noli me tangere*, for instance, Culler demonstrates that the narrator, by 'offering a veritable anthropology of Manila and its ways, with references that would not have been necessary for Manila readers', speaks 'anthropologically, as if to an outsider to whom these things need to be explained' (28). Darko's novel, read against Anderson's contention, further elucidates the shortsightedness of the claim. The novel, in its mode of address, shifts between a readership seemingly inside of Ghana and an audience of outsiders. Darko's narrator speaks to the reader with a degree of familiarity and, as I argued above, places herself in close proximity to this reader in time and space. Irony is shared between reader and narrator, not between the narrator and her characters inside the world of the story. Its articulation plots a location somewhere between the exterior and interior of the story, where the reader and narrator see from the same perspective and share the same point of view. Darko also assumes that her reader has a certain degree of insider knowledge. The novel does not include a glossary to offer definitions of words such as 'akpeteshie' for readers who are not Ghanaian.

At other places in the novel, however, the text addresses an audience of outsiders. Several examples clarify this statement. Ga is defined as a 'dialect' (13) for readers, one would presume, not familiar with what languages are spoken in Ghana. The narrator explains to her reader that 'Like most villages in Ghana, it had lost its most successful sons to the cities, and these sons didn't return too often to help those they had left behind' (27). The reader is told: 'Kataso, a village in the eastern hills, had no flowing water, no electricity, no entertainment centre, nothing... A privileged few, who could occasionally afford batteries, owned pre-set radios, the kind imported from China in the 1960s' (29). A Ghanaian national would not need this information. Rural Ghana, in these passages, is foreign and strange and in need of the narrator's anthropological gloss. 'The young men, when they could no longer stand this bland, grey life, would leave for Accra, Kumasi and Takoradi, to work as shoe-shine boys, truck pushers or hawkers of items such as popcorn, dog chains and air fresheners along the cities' busiest streets' (29). 'The girls, in contrast, were sent for by relations or contacts in the cities to work as housemaids and babysitters, though many eventually ended up as iced-water sellers and prostitutes' (30). Urban life, too, merits explanation with the inclusion of 'objective' knowledge that might enable a reader situated outside of Ghana, outside of Africa perhaps, to make sense of the text. The narrator states: 'Life as a porter in Kumasi was not what a normal person would call living. It was survival' (32).

Of course, *The Housemaid*, because it is a post-colonial novel, complicates any examination of audience. Timothy Brennan calls the post-colonial novel a great 'paradox':

> For under conditions of illiteracy and shortages, and given simply the leisure-time necessary for reading one, the novel has been an elitist and minority form in developing countries when compared to song, television, and film. Almost inevitably it has been the form through which a thin, foreign-educated stratum (however sensitive or committed to domestic

political interests) has communicated to metropolitan reading publics, often in translation. It has been, in short, a naturally cosmopolitan form that empire has allowed to play a national role, as it were, in an international arena (56).

Brennan understands this tendency – expressed by writers like Darko, who on occasion live outside the nations about which they write and address the international reading public – as 'the lament for the necessary and regrettable insistence of nation-forming' and reflect the sense of alienation post-colonial writers feel when they are away from their home nations (56). It seems that for Brennan the outsider stance of the narrator is a sort of limitation.

The situation, for Darko, I think, is different. In reaching toward an audience at once inside and outside of Ghana, Darko tries to imagine a transnational and transitional readership and, perhaps, to construct a new feminist community. The novel opens the lives of Ghanaian women to 'outsiders' in terms of the nation, but speaks to her audience as members of a community of women. She, in effect, hails her readers as women, or, one might say, as feminists, and so in the act of reading her novel, one must participate in a transnational and transitional women's movement. By so doing, Darko effectively re-genders the novel's narrative form, interrogating both the homogeneity and the simultaneity of its time-space and calling for new kinds of reading and a new kind of reader.

# Gervase Angsotinge, Kari Dako, Aloysius Denkabe and Helen Yitah

## Exploitation, Negligence and Violence: Gendered Interrelationships in Amma Darko's Novels

On the evidence of her first three novels, what can be gleaned about the way Amma Darko sees the Ghanaian female? What thematic connections are there between the story of Mara in *Beyond the Horizon*, the stories of Tika and Efia in *The Housemaid* and the tapestry of females in *Faceless*? What links are there between the middle-class professional, Kabria, and her daughters Obea and Essie to the resourceless, cursed and downtrodden, Maa Tsuru, and her daughters Baby T. and Fofo – or, for that matter, between the ancient Naa Yomo to the procuress, Maami Broni? Although written by a woman and about women, these are not simplistic feminist novels in the sense that their main themes are of female solidarity and the suppression of women in a patriarchal society. Even though the exploitation and marginalisation of women is central to her work, the women in Darko's first two novels all have choices, but they are trapped in a warped society in which everything, including all human relationships, is commodified. In her third novel, *Faceless*, however, Darko turns even more militant. The main characters, Baby T. and her sister, Fofo, are underage and are thus denied any choice. Baby T. is removed from her home with the connivance of her own mother, who then benefits from her daughter's earnings as a child prostitute, and Fofo runs away from home to avoid a similar fate.

Juliet Mitchell (1986) and Onipede Hollist (2001) have suggested individually that the quality of the relationship between the sexes is what determines the humanity of a society. If one sex denigrates the other, then all are losers. From that perspective, the additional absence of any dignity in either the intra-female or the male-female relationships portrayed in Darko's works would deny the novels a conventional feminist reading. These novels 'force us to look at the reality of women's roles and lives' (Hollist 2001), but do not propose a theoretical or ideological resolution. They are descriptive, rather than prescriptive. Darko's feminism may therefore be described as unconscious, in that it lacks a political edge and tends to dwell on the wider issue of the quality of social relations between women and men in contemporary society.

Darko may have had something like this in mind when she observed in an interview with Ellie Higgins: 'I should think that if a country is going through a crisis, and people are writing around that time, they will be drawn to writing stories that would deal with those crises...' (p.115). Moreover, her feminism may thus be taken to be cultural rather than political, in the sense that it is linked to her view of the Ghanaian, male as well as female – a sinister and a cynical view relayed as much in the content as in the form of her narratives. The life-stories of her female protagonists in *Beyond the Horizon* and *The Housemaid* are told with little compassion and with a scant show of female solidarity. While the use of a non-intrusive narrator buttresses this by allowing her characters to speak for themselves, make their own choices or let themselves be manipulated into having decisions made for them, it is quite clear that by plot, narrative design and selection of characters, Darko is deeply implicated in this cultural criticism of Ghanaian society.

In *Faceless*, however, where the most exploitative traits of Ghanaian society are flung in our face, there are redeeming female characters and redeeming female relationships: Kabria and her colleagues in MUTE work together for the common good; Kabria endures an indifferent marriage in order to secure a materially adequate environment for her three children and her maid, Abena; the friendship between the two homeless girls, Fofo and Odarley exhibits trust, care and loyalty, and even Maame Broni, the madam, exhibits some compassion towards Baby T. According to Amma Darko, it is hazardous, even dangerous to be female in Ghana – you might end up as does Mara in *Beyond the Horizon*: a physical and psychological wreck of a whore, addicted to drugs, owned by your pimp, or you may be declared a 'witch', as is the old widow in *The Housemaid* and be lucky to survive the ordeal.

> A dejected widow, once upon a time a vibrant *akpeteshie* seller in the village of Braha, now penniless, aged and lonesome, started toward, 'witchdom' when one of her grandchildren developed *kwashiorkor*. She had turned herself into a snake and lodged inside the poor child's stomach, they said.
>
> Then another grandchild got goitre. And all eyes in Braha saw red (*Housemaid*: 3).

Or you might end up dead, as the child prostitute, Baby T., in *Faceless*, mutilated and defaced, dumped behind a kiosk close to an open sewer.

> I saw her. Unbelievable. Her face so mutilated...And her head...ah! That too was completely shaven...In fact, all the hair on every part of her body (*Faceless*: 67).

This paper deals with the Ghanaian female as seen by Amma Darko. Mara, Tika, Efia, Fofo and Baby T. are all tragic examples of the worst fates that can befall a Ghanaian woman: Mara becomes a prostitute hooked on drugs, Tika is a barren woman betrayed by her only companion, the housemaid of the title. Efia produces a deformed stillbirth and lives in extreme poverty. Fofo is but a child when she has to leave home to make room for her mother's male-partner, who threatens her sexually, and Baby T., never given a proper name and not living to adulthood, is pushed into prostitution, suffers a gruesome death and is not even given a human burial.

Despite the bleak portrayal of the present, however, there is no nostalgia for bygone times in Darko's novels. The answer to Ghana's problems is not to be found in some idealised distant past and its lost communal values of nurturing, sacrificing mothers and upright proverb-spouting fathers. Darko's novels instead deal with the present, and the metaphorical stench from rotten entrails seeps into everything. *Faceless* is even set amidst the excreta on a rubbish dump in Sodom and Gomorrah, Accra's most deprived slum. Darko states that:

> I take the trouble to investigate the realities. When I write about Sodom and Gomorrah... I want it to be authentic, because Sodom and Gomorrah does exist in Accra. So scenes have to be authentic (Higgins: 112).
>
> It's such a terrible place, Sodom and Gomorrah (Higgins: 116).

She is thus concerned with a reality that she has set out to portray with fidelity and without idealisation – the essence of everyday 'normal' Ghanaian life, presented not in the classical realist sense of a quest for objective truth and accuracy, but with some exaggeration, even sensationalism in order to establish a motif that then mediates the realistic concerns of the writings. In this respect her 'realism' is reminiscent of that of her male compatriot Ayi Kwei Armah in *The Beautyful Ones Are Not Yet Born* where the representation of Ghanaian reality is mediated through metaphors of decay, filth and defecation, what Gikandi (1987) describes as confronting 'the rotten underbelly of society' (p.74).

The background to this view can be found in Amma Darko's own experience of going to Germany as a young graduate. Once she returned to Ghana she was met with the question 'What did you bring?' (See the discussion in Higgins: 113). This was the same question that confronted Baako in Ayi Kwei Armah's *Fragments*, and in answering this question both writers contribute to a discourse that has been going on in the African novel since Achebe's *No Longer at Ease*. In this discourse, the story told is that of the African abroad in Europe for some time who now comes back home with the 'benefits' of Europe and high expectations of making an impact only to find both himself and his society increasingly 'no longer at ease'.

In Armah's version the protagonist returns home to find an Africa that is nothing more than a vulgar copy of the West, with no authentic values except those associated with money and consumerism. In Amma Darko's version, we are offered an updated rendering of this story. In this case, the protagonist is not an all-conquering male idealist, making a triumphant return with the trophies of Europe: education, status and economic power. Her protagonist, Mara, on the contrary, is stranded in Europe: defeated, victimised and bereft of any ideals. Writing at a much later time in the evolution of the post-colony, Darko is well-positioned to update this discourse especially with regard to the depth to which the cult of consumerism has eaten into the fabric of African society. As one woman boasts in a quarrel with her neighbour in *The Housemaid*: 'Who told you you can compare yourself to me? How many of your children are in the city?' (p.31) – implying that if you have children in the city, then they are a potential source of income. It is against this background that Amma Darko wrote her first novel, so to speak screaming at Ghanaian society: 'I'll show you how your "successful burgers"[1] earn their money'.

In the context of Ghanaian literature, Amma Darko's novels are not unproblematic. On the one hand they fit into the fiction of disillusionment such as Ayi Kwei Armah's *The Beautyful Ones Are Not Yet Born*, *Fragments* and *Why Are We So Blest*, Ama Ata Aidoo's *No Sweetness Here* and Kofi Awoonor's *This Earth, My Brother*, which have become canonical largely because of their perceived 'seriousness'. On the other hand, she also fits into the very vibrant tradition of Ghanaian popular writing in the way she deals in popular plots and character types as in her treatment of gendered struggles and coping strategies. Plots in Ghanaian popular fiction generally revolve around the ever-burning issues of bad marriages, female deviance, and romantic love. For example, the story of the tolerant wife who patiently awaits the repentance of her weak-willed husband after he has been 'tempted into sexual sin and drained financially by promiscuous city women' (Newell: 20) is a common template in this genre. In the world of such narratives the errant husband, the ideal (often betrayed) Christian wife, and her less desirable counterpart, 'the good-time girl' (the beautiful temptress who typically chooses money over love or marriage), are typical characters. Readers of these texts have recourse to such character types to 'make up their own minds' about situations in their daily lives, such as gender roles (Newell: 32). Darko generally dispenses with the romantic plot, but she does consistently respond to 'hot' issues such as marriage, the illusion of the successful 'burger' and the phenomenon of street children, and the sensational manner in which she handles her subjects, coupled with the in-text moral judgments (verbalised or implied) and commentaries that accompany it, which demonstrate her leanings towards the didacticism of writers of Ghanaian popular fiction such as J. Benibengor Blay, K. Bediako, Victor Amartefio, Ewura-Ekuwa Baddoe, and Akosua Gyamfua Fofie.[2] While her works may be said to problematise these issues in the manner of the canonical tradition, she also offers, in the tradition of the popular writer, positions and predicaments shown by such character types as the female who barters fertility for wealth (a version of 'the good-time girl'), the disloyal employee, the unfaithful husband, the betrayed wife, as well as the choices they make.

Both categories of Ghanaian writers (popular and 'serious') generally do not bemoan a glorious utopian past, so often lauded in early post-independence writing – rather they lament the loss of essential values in the world they live in now. But they do not perceive the solution to contemporary life and the future as lying in retrospection. Thus the times we live in dictate the strategies for survival. If we compare Amma Darko to Ama Ata Aidoo, another Ghanaian writer who uses similar material, the differences are startling. The rural-urban dichotomy as seen in *No Sweetness Here,* by Ama Ata Aidoo, has characters that reflect layers of complexity and have the saving grace of being portrayed with a sense of humour in that they can laugh at themselves in spite of the tragic dilemma of their lives. In Amma Darko's novels there is nothing to laugh about; the characterisation is humourless and the characters are, with very few exceptions, totally cynical in their endeavours.

The three books that currently make up Amma Darko's *oeuvre* already indicate the central concern of her writing: her preoccupation with the body as a site where a relentless and often brutal gendered struggle is taking place. These struggles between the sexes express themselves in many forms, but common to all is the issue of who gains power over whose body and for what purpose. How do women survive in this hostile environment? And what are their strategies in a thoroughly exploitative and materialistic society? We would argue here that women in Amma Darko's novels use essentially the interwoven biological survival strategies involved in fertility, sex, subservience and exploitation. The bitter irony is that the female self is quite often ultimately diminished and devalued by the nature of the gain in these struggles.

Amma Darko has written three expositions on her homeland, *Beyond the Horizon,* in which she calls our attention to the fate of many unresourced Ghanaian women abroad; *The Housemaid* in which she opens the lid of the proverbial can of worms, in this case, Ghana; and *Faceless* that deals with the tragedy of the street children in Accra. As Anyidoho says in his introductory essay to *Faceless*:

> '...taken together these three novels...tell one long and disturbing tale. Sadly it is a tale of a diseased society that seems to have lost its hold on the life of its children. It is a provocative tale of a society that has developed a tragic ability of guiding its young ones, especially the girl-child into a life dedicated to prostituting every conceivable virtue for the sake of flimsy material possessions' (pp.9–10).

Amma Darko's writing reflects the angst in contemporary Ghanaian society – they echo the stories that we read daily in the Ghanaian press. The headlines scream of abandoned babies, brutalised and murdered women: wives, mothers, daughters, sisters, girlfriends of ritual executions, of incest and rape, of sale of children, of child labour and of a general degeneration of society into one of oppression and violence. Despite differences of locale and narrative perspective, the three works she has produced so far relentlessly probe the nation's unhealed wounds.

## BEYOND THE HORIZON

*Beyond the Horizon* is the life story of Mara, her journey from village girl to traditionally married woman eking out a living in Accra, serving her abusive husband in every way, and then joining the same husband in Germany, where he has bigamously married a German woman. He forces Mara into prostitution and uses what she earns in the brothel to keep his Ghanaian girlfriend Comfort, in comfort and style.

We meet Mara, the protagonist and narrator of the work, 'this bit of garbage that once used to be me...' (p. 3), in skimpy red silk briefs sitting in front of an oval mirror in her room in the brothel where she works 'waiting to be used and abused by strange men' (p.1). She works for an 'overseer': 'He is my lord, my master and my pimp. – I am his pawn, his slave and his property.' (p.3) The story Mara narrates is ugly; it is a tale of physical and emotional abuse, as when Mara informs her husband, Akobi, that she is pregnant:

> 'I was by Mama Kiosk today and I told her that I haven't had my blood for two months and she says I am by all means carrying a baby...'
>
> 'Did Mama Kiosk sleep with you?' he asked, still in that disregarding tone... I felt cold sweat seep through my pores. I didn't answer. Then suddenly there was this angry roar of, 'Get up!' like an over-irritated boar and the next second I was up at attention on my two feet...
>
> 'And why did you get pregnant?'
>
> 'Pardon?' I replied spontaneously, and before I knew what was happening... Wham! First slap... Wham! Wham! Wham! Three more in succession' (pp. 16–17).

And it is a tale of exploitation, broken hopes and promises. It is the story of Mara's downward slide from what she confesses '[I] was before I was given away to this man who paid two white cows, four healthy goats, four lengths of cloth, beads, gold jewellery and two bottles of London Dry Gin to my family and took me off as his wife from my African village,... to him in the city' (p.3)... to our seeing her reflected in her oval mirror. For Mara has played a subservient role throughout her marriage. When Akobi vetoes Mara's leaving for the station with Mama Kiosk, Mara, anxious to prevent another quarrel, acquiesces subserviently only to do what she wants when he is not around (p.24) – and in Germany she uses the same strategy, ostensibly to keep peace in Akobi's bigamous household: 'I would be Akobi's hidden wife, so that harmony would prevail in the marriage . . . ' (p.26). And once she had accepted that role, she had to play it to the end.

In *Beyond the Horizon*, then, Mara fulfils the female roles: as a daughter that adheres to her father's wishes. She is a wife and lets her husband use her; she is a mother and uses her predicament as an addicted whore as an alibi to provide for her children left behind in Ghana – preferring an unreliable husband and the lure of the 'gold in Germany' to the role of mothering and caring for her children in Ghana. Mara thus oscillates between acquiescence, defiance and resignation – from victim to a woman who shows courage and fights back – but she lacks the tools to free herself from her predicament.

*Beyond the Horizon* ends with Mara looking back on her life and concluding unfinished narratives. Akobi is in jail. All he acquired in his German marriage has been confiscated by the bank. She knows there is no hope for her; she can never leave the brothel; money will compensate for her failing as mother and daughter: 'Now I can't go a day without sniffing "snow". I am hooked on it. I am fast sinking into a place hotter than hell. But I know this. And that is why I have decided that before I sink too deep I will make as much money as possible for my mother and sons back home' (p. 139). By providing her elder brother with a television and a video deck, and a younger brother with a car and building a house for her mother, she has purchased the loyalty of her family and the surety that they will look after her children. 'Material things are all I can offer them. As for myself, there's nothing dignified and decent left of me to give them' (p. 140). Mara thus obliterates herself for her children. That is the resolution Amma Darko seems to offer the reader. What awaits Mara 'beyond the horizon' is not education and a new life, but degradation and despair.

## *THE HOUSEMAID*

In *The Housemaid*, we are back in Ghana and the narrative focus shifts somewhat. This novel has a more complex structure. Whereas the stories of Tika and Efia, mistress and housemaid, constitute the narrative foregrounded in the novel, the background examines the reaction of the ordinary people upon the discovery of a decomposed newborn baby in the bush. The 'ins and outs' of this find and the accompanying violent and moralistic reactions, as seen against the otherwise callous interpersonal relationships in the novel, weave these parallel and intertwining narratives into a whole. The female characters and their stories are still central, but these are not women who are helpless victims of male exploitation. Used by men, yes, but also users of men. The central female character in *The Housemaid* is not 'the housemaid' but her employer Tika. She is not a Ghanaian version of Mara – Tika's tragedy is very different: 'It had never been Tika's dream still to be single and childless at the ripe age of thirty-five. Living only with Efia, her maid, in a two-room estate house, and travelling frequently all over Africa to scout for goods to sell in Ghana . . .' (p. 17).

How did Tika end up as an infertile, childless woman at thirty-five – the most dreaded fate for any Ghanaian woman? 'A very wasted woman . . . An unproductive womb is bad enough. But no womb at all? And that is what she is. A walking woman with no womb inside her . . .' (p. 46) Efia's grandmother rants. In Ghana, a barren woman is considered neither male nor female; she inhabits an undignified space peculiar to her state. What makes her situation even more tragic is the popular belief that successful businesswomen have bartered fertility for wealth. 'They say, you know that woman with a lot of money? Do you know she does not have a child?' (Higgins: 116). This is also a common theme in popular literature. Akua Julie, for example, the avaricious 'devil' in Asare Konadu's *Devils In Waiting* (1998) is also barren but very successful in business.

But, whereas a pregnancy was traditionally considered a blessing, in contemporary Ghana, it becomes a tool that is employed by almost every female in *The Housemaid*, with the exception of the barren Tika. Thus Tika's estranged mother, Sekyiwa, uses sex and fertility to entrap a wealthy man to set her up in business. She becomes pregnant to strengthen her hold on him in order to exploit him. When she has achieved what she wants, she discards him. Similarly, Efia is told by her mother and grandmother to get pregnant and have a baby who, they plot, would inherit Tika's wealth. Efia uses sex and fertility in her effort to gain wealth. The grandmother's advice prior to Efia's departure for Accra is utterly self-serving:

> '. . . So hear me! Be subservient, humble and very dependable . . .'
>
> 'Then get yourself pregnant.'
>
> '. . . Efia, you will live with her, win her affection, become indispensable to her. So that when you innocently become pregnant . . .'
>
> 'Innocently? How does she become pregnant innocently?' Efia's mother asked.
>
> 'By pretending she was forced into the sexual act,' the old lady replied (pp. 46–47).

So the only advice a young girl can get from her mother and grandmother is how she can craftily get herself pregnant and give birth to an illegitimate child so that these same women can benefit from her condition. When Efia's father hears about the plans connected with her going to work for Tika, his immediate response is: 'So, what is in it for us? . . . What are we getting out of our daughter's going away to the city to serve somebody?' (p.43).

In *The Housemaid* it is the women who control their men through sex. The matriarchs control Efia's father who is not reckoned as a man. Sekyiwa controls her emasculated husband and Tika sells herself for expedience and profit to Samuel, the customs officer in order to get her goods tax-free into the country; to the factory owner, Attui, 'to get good credit rates on the goods she bought' (p. 25); to Riad, the shop owner with several outlets to whom she can distribute her commodities for sale; then to Eric, the musician, whose elder brother holds a prominent position in Ghana Commercial Bank and can therefore give her credit. To the same degree as sex is a means of income in Mara's Germany, it serves as a means of exchange in contemporary Ghanaian fiction:

> '[This] left sex as the only really affordable entertainment in Kataso. Everyone – young, old, mature and immature – indulged in it freely, making the two midwives the busiest of the village professionals' (p. 29)...
>
> 'Thanks to bribes of cash and sex, workers at the building sites regularly tipped [the female porters] on the next place available for occupation' (p.32).
>
> 'Where to?' The driver asked curtly.
> 'Kumasi.'
> 'You have money to pay me?'
> 'No.'
> He grunted. 'So you won't pay me?'
> Akua unbuttoned her blouse. The driver's eyes blazed with consent. She removed her pants. He grinned, and stopped the truck in a secluded bend (pp. 30–31).

The theme of the female barracuda is then not new in Ghanaian writing and popular perception. Asare Konadu's *Devils in Waiting*, set in the 1970s, deals with a typical *kalabule*[3] 'business woman', Akua who rides roughshod all over Kumasi in her quest for wealth and the men through whom she can obtain this. The term *kalabule* which was coined to refer to unsavoury business practices during the Acheampong regime (1972–78), 'had been gendered as feminine' (Newell: 126) by the time Rawlings had taken over the country in the 1980s. Referring to Victor Amarteifio's *Bediako the Adventurer*, Stephanie Newell (126) also argues that there is a '... parallel... established between a man's loss of control over his wealth and his sexual abandon to a woman'. Just as Bediako loses the 'control of his conscience, savings and social status' (Newell: 122), so Tika's father, who is so insignificant that he is not given a name, suffers the same fate at the hands of his second wife, Sekyiwa. In like manner, Ama Ata Aidoo's male protagonist in *Anowa*, the infertile Kofi Ako, loses control of his life while blaming it on his wife, Anowa. Here the myth of the infertile wealthy woman is reversed – it is the infertile male who has bartered wealth for fertility.

In *The Housemaid*, Darko appears to have given up all hope of any redeeming factors in Ghanaian society – everybody exploits everyone else: mothers their daughters, daughters their mothers, girlfriends their lovers, maids their mistresses. Society is a web of exploitation that smothers and stifles any attempt at healthy human interaction. This web is somehow woven around Tika, who is as much the spider as the fly caught in the net, as is every other Ghanaian we meet in the book: a manifestation of our earlier argument that the self diminishes as it gains. Tika is the exploiter of males, the chess player *par excellence*. Amma Darko's feminism radicalises as she focuses on Ghanaian society. Men are here merely as a means to an end – they are commodities for sexual gratification: 'Sekyiwa had become one of the wealthy market mummies. Young good-looking male gold-diggers began to vie for her attention. Her husband's libido was waning anyway... She gave [the gold-diggers] good money; they gave her good sex' (p. 18); or, for financial expediency: Tika sleeps with four men to get what she wants; Akua offers herself to the truck driver for a free ride. In *The Housemaid* the men become the pawns in a female chess game.

For women to survive and be 'free' in a manner that is beyond male exploitation, they must play by the rules of the cynical world around them; they have to gain power and maintain it and therefore adopt the same exploitative practices as the men. Darko appears not to agree that the oppressed must not adopt the same strategies as the oppressor. Tika's maid, Efia, cast as the stereotypical disloyal employee, is as much a victim as a cunning strategist. She is pawned by her mother and grandmother and used to exploit her employer. With nothing more than the scheming manipulations of these older women to guide her, Efia survives by quickly changing status from pawn to player and back again. But the question then is, do women really have power in *The Housemaid*? And if they do, is it merely the power obtained by assuming male roles of exploitation? Tika for all her sexual promiscuity has assumed an asexual status by destroying her fertility and denying any female function that society might expect of her: she refuses to be a daughter, a mother or a wife. There is something wrong in a society where a daughter can blame her mother for her father's death, and as Tika did, dedicate her whole life to punishing her mother, Sekyiwa. There is also something askew when the market-women in Kumasi can only calculate an increase in their profit by short-changing their all-male truck-pushers. Similarly there is the same 'strategic thinking' in the female porters, the *kayayee*, who sell their bodies to survive and hoard enough money to travel to their rural homes to attend the traditional festivals in order to flaunt their wealth:

> As for Kataso, the ultimate is when the city-dwellers return for the yam festival. The household with the most returnees gets the most honours and

> attention. And as for the dance at the Quebec Inn . . . 'The dance that crowns the festival is called 'showtime', because that's when the returnees put on their best clothes and compete with each other' (*Housemaid*: 31).

Traditional festivals that used to be a thanksgiving for a good harvest have been reduced to 'showtime'. Thus even a religious festival has been defiled and commercialised. Everything is distorted and confounded in Amma Darko's Ghana.

An additional theme, that of the survival of superstition, of the belief in supernatural power, of the belief in witches causing havoc, permeates *The Housemaid*. It is used as a convenient strategy to shift responsibility for action onto someone or something else, in this case the weakest element in society: the old abandoned women. As Ghanaians show no compassion for each other, so there are no constraints on them in their self-serving quest for wealth and power. Even though some positive traditional beliefs linger – such as the burying of the umbilical cord to bind one's soul to one's birthplace – the predominant traditional beliefs are the ones that are sinister, like the belief in witches, like the belief in the power of curses to kill. Tika's father's first wife: 'cursed him with leprosy, should he defy her warnings, and had broken his feet to solicit the powers of the gods to see it through. It had proved too much for his heart' (p.20).

Predictably, *The Housemaid* ends on a similarly pessimistic note. The final chapter of the book links up with the opening, the belief in witchcraft, the tragedy of old, lonely women being declared witches and blamed for all the ills of society. It seems quite rare in Ghanaian life and literature to come across a young witch, the heroine in Aidoo's *Anowa* who is given this label being the only one that comes to mind. Darko's reiterates this point when she declares that,

> 'Ghana's "witches" are mostly women, old . . . so there is something with wrinkles here. . . . I have yet to find a young, healthy, good-looking woman who has been declared a witch in Ghana. I think apportioning blame, it's the easy way out' (Higgins: 117).

Teacher, the woman who initially facilitated Efia's being brought from Kataso to Tika's household, has been told the story of how Efia's baby came to be found in the bush in a state of decomposition. Teacher now returns to Tika to narrate what has happened and why it happened. Tika admits that Efia 'was as much a victim of her people's manipulation as I was' (p.105). This should have been the resolution for Tika's dilemma, namely her realisation that Efia's grandmother and mother caused this tragedy, but this eludes her because she appears not to transcend her own superstitions and fears of the power of the supernatural.

Another moment of insight is tossed away when the question, 'Can Tika make peace with her mother, now also old and poor?' crops up. Tika evades it, instead wondering what her dead father would have wanted and whether he has been watching over her all these years. She is not able to face her hostility towards her mother and her punishing Sekyiwa for the death of her father so many years ago, so she trivialises it by making the trite comment that she would not have wanted her father to witness '... the business discussions I used to hold in my bedroom!' (p.107).

The conversation between Tika and Teacher now veers into Efia's belief that Tika had used *juju*, and that she had cursed her, and that the dead infant was the result of gain. Both Teacher and Tika speculate that if Efia had delivered the baby at home, 'Kataso would have been thrown into a frenzied orgy of witch-hunting' (p.106). Human error is thus blamed on witches. The implication is that Ghana is unwilling to face her own inadequacies and to accept her own guilt. All failings and all disasters are transferred onto some old women casting them in the role of scapegoats. This is again seen in Tika and Teacher's typical reaction of pushing the blame for witchcraft onto someone else – in this case a man. The two women prefer to think that the manipulator of the witches is male: 'In which case, the crucial question is why he would want to appoint wrinkled old women as his ambassadors on earth. He certainly seems to, if the rate at which such women are declared witches in our society is anything to go by' (p.106).

The issue is of course not whether the chief witch is a man or a woman; the issue is that Ghanaian society is paralysed by its own superstitions and evasions. The two women end their conversation by '... laughing and crying away their pain, their disappointment, their anger, their fear. And laughing with hope' (p.10). We may wonder what they hope for. Ghana has not resolved any of its problems; it is as caught in its superstitions as ever; it is as crafty in its manipulations as ever. Whether Tika will allow Efia back into her household does not bring a resolution – it just brings the events full circle – we can either laugh or we can cry; it does in the final analysis amount to the same: no solution.

## *FACELESS*

Although Darko's third novel may be structurally the most complex, the central narrative in *Faceless* is that of the powerless and vulnerable Maa Tsuru and the tragedy of her life and that of her two daughters, Fofo and Baby T.. In *Faceless*, fertility has becomes a liability; there is nothing Maa Tsuru can achieve through her repeated pregnancies. Her children are no means of exchange; they are all 'condemned to the devouring jaws of the street' (Anyidoho 17). 'Look at them,... What have they done? Their only wrongdoing is that they came into the world through me' (*Faceless* 49). As a strong, but contrasting parallel to this dysfunctional household, we have the middle class nuclear version of family life as seen through Kabria, Adade and their three children.

Woven around these family portraits is a whole array of secondary characters – from the most depraved, like the paedophile, Onko, who is the cause of Baby T.'s tragedy, through the vicious parasites, Poison and Macho, who prey on the dispossessed children of Sodom and Gomorrah. There is Kpakpo, representing the brutal and abusive stepfathers who – 'only interested in the food and sexual services which they obtain by seduction or force from females of all ages' (Oppong 13) – elbow the children of their mates onto the street. We have the benign old Naa Yomo, somehow representing the old order of sanity and care in Agbobloshie – the care that is so obviously lost in the environment of Maa Tsuru and her children. We have the social workers, including Kabria at MUTE, who are representative of the new NGOs in Ghana and who have taken over the role of responsibility with which government and the churches can no longer cope. We have Sylv Po, the reporter representing one of Ghana's new investigative FM stations that have come to embody the conscience of the nation. *Faceless* exhibits a degree of balance between the forces of good and evil. Between these forces, Darko has placed the vulnerable street children.

> Perhaps the most frightening lesson in *Faceless* is the fact that having lost their moral authority over their children, parents like Maa Tsuru are totally paralysed by fear, the fear of terrors such as Poison. And it is left to the children to devise their own means of facing up to the Machos and Poisons of the world (Anyidoho 17).

In both of Darko's earlier books, sex is used as a means of control. In *Beyond the Horizon*, the men use sex to manipulate their women. Mara supports Akobi, his girlfriend, Comfort, and herself with her earnings from prostitution. Ghanaian men are shown as earning their living by exploiting their women. Though *The Housemaid* shows women as being more in control of sexual exchange, if to no higher end, in *Faceless*, corruption is more widespread. Poison and Maami Broni live off Baby T.'s earnings, but even her mother, Maa Tsuru, gets a commission.

Poison was the boss . . .
Maami Broni helped in the only way she knew how. She introduced her to the 'devil's weed'. It helped. Once Baby T. began to use it regularly, carrying out her 'duty' with several men night and day became bearable (p. 221).

Although her circumstances are by no means as stark as Maa Tsuru's, the 'independent' middle-class woman, Kabria, assumes a subservient role in her marriage. In this modern nuclear family, there is little equality. The 'head of the house', Adade, 'a paragon of paternal and conjugal virtue, in comparison with the other males in the story, who abandon their women and children . . .' (Oppong 13) is so 'exhausted' after a day's work that he barely has the energy to eat the food that his wife has both cooked and served after a full day at work and looking after her children. Like Ramatoulaye in *So Long a Letter*, Kabria in *Faceless* finds her marriage stifling but cannot find the courage to leave. This is the dilemma of the majority of contemporary African women – left out while the rest of the world moves on, she lacks education, the means, and the societal support to carve a role for herself as an individual and not as an appendage.

While she does have an education, Kabria is stuck in a low-paid job that gives her the necessary flexible time schedule to look after her children responsibly. And to cater for her children, she assumes the subservient role of a 'doormat' in her marriage. Adade's superior income gives him the power to arrange his home for the purpose of his convenience. His car is bigger and newer and more reliable, and ferries him to work and home via his beer bar, whereas Kabria has a daily battle with her unpredictable 'Creamy' as she ferries her three children to and from school and manoeuvres her way through the congested markets to do her household shopping for which she alone is responsible. Kabria effaces herself in order to secure a safer environment for her children.

In Darko's first two novels, school appears irrelevant; the women do not invest in education neither for themselves nor for their children. Tika drops out of school and is rewarded with financial assistance from her mother to start a business. Wealth is obviously more important than education. In *Faceless*, however, Kabria, who has had higher education, endures an indifferent relationship in order to ensure that her children receive a good education; she has additionally apprenticed her maid, Abena, to a dressmaker, and the professional women at MUTE offer Fofo, a school drop-out, the means to learn a trade so that she will be able to look after herself.

More obviously exploited, the lower-class Maa Tsuru, from childhood, has been conditioned to accept herself as worthless and allows herself to be used by the males with whom she interacts. She debases herself in her relationship with the man who happens to be her partner at any time in her life to the extent of sending her children away in order to create physical space for herself and her man and have enough food to feed him. The downward spiral of Maa Tsuru's life is blamed on a 'curse' issued by her mother at her birth. Instead of taking charge of her own life, she uses this curse as an alibi for all misfortunes that befall her. Even Naa Yomo explains everything through this curse:

> 'It is the curse'...
> 'Thirty-eight years ago, she was born in the very room inside which she has now locked herself in' (p. 117).
>
> 'It's the curse!' Maa Tsuru wailed from inside. 'It's the curse!' (p. 119).

Kwei, the father of Maa Tsuru's children is forced by his mother to abandon her because of this same curse.

> The young man grew desperate. 'Her dying mother did not curse her, mother!' he protested. 'That wasn't what I heard. She cursed Maa Tsuru's father; not Maa Tsuru . . .' (p. 147).
>
> The mother shook with fury. 'Shut your big mouth up. You call yourself a man? You think you understand the world better than I do? Yes, she cursed the baby's father. Your lover's father. But who told you she stopped there? Idiot! Let me tell you what she did. She went on and further cursed all of his descendents too. That was what she did. All of his descendents . . .' (p. 147).

So this curse can be used as a convenient excuse by a mother to force her son not to live up to his responsibilities as a father. It becomes the excuse for a man to abandon his wife and children, and it can be used by the abandoned mother to push her children out of the home and onto the street. Nobody needs to take responsibility for any action once supernatural forces are thought to be at play.

While the female is the victim of male abuse in *Beyond the Horizon* and *Faceless*, relationships exist between the females in both works that have some redeeming qualities: Mara trusts Mama Kiosk and sends money through her for her children; she can also turn to her fellow prostitute, Kaye, when she needs help. In *Faceless*, Fofo loves her sister Baby T. and wants the authorities to bring her murderer to justice:

'Government!' the girl cut in.

Kabria cocked her eyebrows. She wasn't sure she heard right, because it didn't make sense. 'What did you say?'

'I said government. I want government.'

Kabria roared with laughter. She laughed till she shed some tears and then laughed some more.

'You want the government?'

Fofo didn't reply. She wore a hurt look (p. 73).

> 'I said, the girl who was found dead last week at where I tried to rob you, was my sister' (p. 74).

Fofo also has the capacity to forgive her mother, and with Odarley she shares a deep and loyal friendship. Moreover the women at MUTE, Kabria, Vickie and Dina . . . work together actively for the good of society.

As was the case in the earlier novels, *Faceless* also offers the reader no solution. Nevertheless, there is some sort of just resolution in that Onko commits suicide. He had lost his business after his involvement with Baby T. had become known and not surprisingly seized on the strategy of blaming his misfortune on witchcraft. In order to have the curse lifted, he is told to obtain pubic hair from Baby T.. It is this encounter that causes Baby T.'s death. Maami Broni, who facilitated the meeting between Baby T. and her defiler, Onko, suffers from nightmares. She sees Baby T. everywhere and at all times. But we again see the conclusion degenerating into frivolity: Kabria's only nightmare is the imagined loss of her car, 'Creamy'. We may surmise that Darko has no remedy for Ghana's illness if the demise of a car can be discussed in the same breath as the aftermath of the murder of a child. But perhaps the impact of the novels should not be equated with their lack of an antidote to Ghana's percieved societal malaise. How then can we summarise the progression and significance of the works the author has published to date?

## CONCLUSION

Considering the role the novels ascribe to them in the gendered power struggles, the male characters are not explored beyond their asocial and absolutely amoral character: in essence, they have been written out of the narratives. The women in Darko's novels tend to be portrayed with no feminine aspect in the traditional sense. With the exception of Kabria, they are not caring and nurturing mothers, nor do they play the expected roles of daughters and wives. In the following excerpts from an interview with Higgins, Darko gives us her views on the reasons for and ramifications of this situation:

> 'There is this mentality that if you give birth, God will take care' (Higgins: 116).
>
> 'The babies have just become tools. I think we are losing a sense of something that is very African. On one side we want to feel this motherhood, our worth.... We want to fulfil that, and yet we are losing the essence of this whole motherhood thing to just have a child that you do not take care of' (Higgins 116).

Moreover in *Faceless*, the author has factored in the contrastive counterbalance to this depressing scenario. Kabria, the professional Ghanaian woman working with the NGO, MUTE, cares for her children and her maid, Abena, and she sets out to help Fofo, whose own mother has abandoned her. Is Kabria Amma Darko's *alter ego*? The author is obviously familiar with the behavioural pattern of middle-class school-going children in their teens and younger. She herself must, like many other Ghanaian urban working-women, have faced Accra's horrendous traffic with a rickety car. The picture of a woman coping with life in an unreliable car echoes that of Ama Ata Aidoo's Essie in *Changes*. Perhaps, taking these representations together, we might interpret the possession of a 'car of one's own' as a metaphor representing not simply essential transportation, but also a degree of social mobility, autonomy and power. After all, Darko knows that in the Ghanaian middle class household there is no equity in sharing household chores.

Does Darko blame traditional practices for this? Yes, because, as is perhaps most obvious in *The Housemaid*, the female has now adopted the tools of the male oppressor. The women who are traditionally entrusted with the role of raising children have themselves become lured by the trappings of this exploitative web which is why society is breaking down. Amma Darko's fictional world has become so materialistic that all human relationships are commodified in terms of personal gain. In *Big Men, Small Boys and Politics in Ghana*, Paul Nugent argues that 'superior learning, piety and wealth have all harboured the potential to deliver status and power. But Ghanaians have tended to treat wealth as the most reliable route to personal success' (1985: 3). This means that by deriving material gain from everything and looking at the world in terms of potential gain, you become capable of selling whatever you have: your body, your child, your honour, your conscience. As hooks (1984: 83) reminds us: 'Power is commonly equated with domination and control over people...' so that whereas the reader is persuaded to condemn the male exercise of power as domination in *Beyond the Horizon* and *Faceless*, the same reader is ambivalently not called upon to attack the same female exercise of power over males in *The Housemaid*.

Ultimately, the strategies in Amma Darko's novels, therefore, are as stark as the reality that spawned them. Thus ten-year-old Bibio can throw away her mother as another piece of useless rubbish because, according to her, the mother failed to supply what she wanted; 'she was to blame for their pathetic life' (Housemaid 11), which in this case was picking discarded food and clothing from the rubbish dump. There is an erosion of values when a child can discard her mother for not providing materially. In Darko's subsequent novel, *Faceless*, however, we do see a reversal of this tale in Fofo, who is pushed onto the rubbish dump in favour of her mother's male partner. Fofo does not entirely blame her mother for her situation: 'Her emotions about the woman who had carried her for nine months confused her sometimes. Deep down inside her, she felt some affection for Maa Tsuru. Yet an overpowering urge to hate her also consumed her at times' (p. 44).

But rather than resolve this conflict, she escapes into dreams of a better life:...

> 'You know something?' Fofo addressed Kabria, 'Sometimes I imagine myself to be outside of myself. I will float out of myself and watch with pity the miserable life led by this young girl called Fofo. Later when I reunite with

> myself, the weight of it all hits me once again. Then I'll shake with misery. And when I happen to be alone, I cry' (p. 189).

Fofo's despair echoes that of Mara, sitting in front of her oval mirror: neither offers a viable escape route.

Though we may not have been offered a solution which might absolve us of any responsibility save that of an observer, we cannot leave these novels without some kind of final response to the political and social issues that Darko's honest scrutiny of the contemporary Ghanaian situation raises. Like other African women writers such as Ama Ata Aidoo and Tsitsi Dangarembga, Darko's portrayal of the Ghanaian female seems to belie the idealised image of the African woman, especially in the Negritude tradition, as guardian of mythical and ancestral values and nurturing mother of Africa's male sons (see, for instance, Senghor's *Femme Noire* (*Poemes* 1984 16)). Negritude's 'Mother Africa' imagery has been the subject of much recent feminist criticism (Boehmer 1991, Ajayi 1997, Mitifu 1997) for its portrayal of the African woman as 'a motivational force constructed not in the active tense but in the passive' (Ajayi 39). These feminists have read into works such as Mariama Bâ's *So Long a Letter* and Flora Nwapa's *Efuru* and *Idu* the subversion of such imagery. In her discussion of Bâ's novel, for instance, Ajayi argues that in so far as Ramatoulaye 'endeavours to be the perfect nurturer who provides a stable home base' for her husband, 'an endless stream of in-laws', as well as for her twelve children, she fits the 'Mother Africa' image. However, Ramatoulaye also subverts this image when she uses the *mirasse*, the Islamic ritual that 'requires that a dead person be stripped of his most intimate secrets' (*So Long*... 9), as a cultural framework for revealing 'the day-to-day operation of the patriarchy and the marginalisation of women' (Ajayi 44).

In Darko's works, the 'Mother Africa' image is not so much subverted as it is discounted. Naa Yomo, the guardian of tradition; has very little time left to live, and yet all she can do is lament the failure of the younger females to take up her role. While both Mara in *Beyond the Horizon* and Maa Tsuru in *Faceless* are mothers, neither of them possesses the credentials of the archetypal Mother Africa as they both fail to provide a nurturing hearth for their children. Kabria more appropriately suits this role, but unlike Ramatoulaye, she is not 'married' to tradition, on the contrary, she is concerned mainly with the basic needs of her family. Common to all three mothers is the lack of (adequate) means to attain their independence from their men. The unmarried and childless Tika is by far the most economically independent, but even she must rely on her men in order to succeed. When we view the women's material realities against the background of the general lack of formal education among Darko's female characters, we are inclined to conclude that together with Aidoo, Dangarembga and others, she sees education as a means for women to escape dependency.

The symbolic 'Mother Africa' may be free from colonial domination, but the mothers of Africa still lack the basic tools to free themselves from material privation and male domination.

In conjunction with the liberation of the mothers from the image of the helpless and submissive 'Mother Africa' who sacrifices all for her sons, however, Darko also sees the survival of society as dependent, not on her taking over the tools of her male oppressor, but rather on her maintaining a balance between self-fulfilment and self-centredness, between independence and indifference. She suggests by her portrayal of her characters' material realities what Ajayi, in her discussion of *So Long a Letter*, terms 'a responsible individualism committed to a responsive collectivity' (Ajayi 48). The idea comes from the basic tenet in African cultural practice that the well-being of the individual is (or ought to be) the well-being of the whole society. One way Darko explores the question of individual responsibility is by forcing us to face the very issues that her characters evade by consigning to the supernatural realm of witches. Commitment to a 'responsive collectivity' (Ajayi 48) would for instance require the wealthy but barren Tikas to alleviate the misery of the biologically prolific but economically less fortunate Maa Tsurus and their children. In Nwapa's *Efuru*, a similar tradition is invoked that allows her society to benefit from the economic prosperity of the childless Efuru. To cite another example, in Burkinabe woman writer Monique Ilboudo's novel, *Le Mal de Peau* (1992) a suggestively named Ma Thérèse receives and cares for young girls who are cut off from their biological families for failing to conform to social norms. In *Faceless*, Kabria, not a wealthy woman by any standards, nevertheless reaches out to her housemaid, Abena, as well as to the alienated and bewildered Fofo, for whom she also secures help from MUTE. Thus, together with her colleague African women authors, Darko issues a call to compassion and fellow love that we must not resist.[4]

# Vincent O. Odamtten

## Amma Darko's *Beyond the Horizon*: Vending the Dream and Other Traumas for the Obedient Daughter

Some things are too dangerous to keep secret...
Every dream has its price. Steve Knight.[1]

Ghanaian writer Amma Darko's first novel, *Beyond the Horizon*, has proved to be at once too easy and too complex for many of its critics. Its shocking and timely exposure of the ripple effect of neocolonial economics and patterns of emigration and the stark conflicts between its characters, who are trapped in a local-global web that results in their arrested consciousness of determinate political, social and gendered forces, have claimed most of the attention, somehow deflecting recognition of the skill of Darko's presentation. The novel has been acclaimed, perhaps justly, as either an exposé of the fate of African immigrants to Germany – '*Beyond the Horizon* is a gripping and provocative story of the plight of African women in Europe, and the false hopes of those they leave behind'[2] – or, as 'a moving tale of the abuse of women in modern-day Africa', which is especially effective because of its lack of 'your typical male-bashing [...feminism]', the directness of its style and the simplicity of its message.[3] Nevertheless, such readings miss the book's nuanced narrative style, which addresses neocolonial reality with equal amounts of ironic distance and loving humour and introduces us to the confessions of a narrator whose act of narration at once restores voice to the silenced and draws in and controls the readers' perspective.

The problem that confronts Darko and the reader is how, in this neocolonial hegemonic new world order, do we write and read through the cracks, which the democratic materialist lure – the dazzling gleam of capital – hides from view? How do we look at or engage with the sordid underclass of globalisation that the world insists is not there? When will we be able to recognise the prohibitive cost of dreams that are not available to all, or maybe even most, of those who dream them?

### WHAT IS BEING SAID AND HOW SHE CAME TO SAY IT

In considering this debut novel such inquiries cannot hope to succeed without taking into account the vagaries of publishing and the question of language.

One of the fascinating aspects of this book's history is that it first saw publication not in English, the language of the original, but rather in a German translation by Schmetterling Verlag. This is at least partially due to the fact that Darko, a Ghanaian writer, whose protagonist/narrator is also a Ghanaian woman, chose to make Munich, the locus of the entire narration, (though not of all the events narrated). This is the 'confession' of Mara, presently a prostitute, who had been lured by her husband Akobi to what they envisioned as a paradise and trapped into permitting him to sell her into prostitution.

Even when she has thrown off Akobi's yoke, she remains in place living a lie and trying to fulfil the expectations of the family she has left behind. According to Louise Zak, Darko's manuscript came to the attention of a woman filmmaker in Berlin who wanted the film rights in order to bring it to the screen. Although that project never came to fruition, the manuscript caught the attention of Jorg Hunger of Schmetterling Verlag and in 1991 the German translation of Darko's first novel hit the literary stage, some four years before an English edition was published.[4] I do not wish to impugn the original decision by the English publishers to reject Darko's manuscript as unsuitable for inclusion in the canon of modern African literature they were in the process of constructing and marketing in the West, nor to suggest that the canon they had in mind allowed them an exercise, however muted, of cultural hegemony. However, one sees the critical response, particularly in the West, as, on occasion, tending to suggest that ex-colonial subjects are to blame for their gullibility: their men are deceivers, abusers and leaches and the women are naïve victims of multiple deceptions at best or doomed prostitutes. In any case, the claim might be made that as an accomplished storyteller, Amma Darko, while gripping us in the thrall of a powerful story, reveals the unvarnished truth about the social and moral corruption that plagues Africa's sons and daughters. If we in turn, or perhaps instead, are careless or gullible in our attention to the text, we might even be persuaded that there is some validity to colonialist claims that no good can come out of Africa for it is eternally the heart of darkness. Hopefully, this modest attempt to look beyond the mirage of the caretakers of our consciousness will reveal the true quality and significance of Darko's first novel.

The novel's titles in English and German, *Beyond the Horizon* and *Der Verkaufte Traum*, and Darko's linguistic and thematic concerns emerge and merge to reflect the predicament of those who have inherited the post-independence legacy of neocolonial suffering. The linguistic shuffle between English and German is emblematic of the dilemmas that confront the post-colonial writer attempting to publish such a work as Darko's. Yet, that original negative response by Heinemann has proved, in time, to be a positive benefit for Darko's overall development as a writer who speaks in a voice that only gets firmer. By forcing her to use an alternative avenue for publication, through Schmetterling Verlag, the gatekeepers revealed their feet of clay. One of the linguistic by-products of the new global hegemony is that there is an Anglophone bias in much that passes for literary discourse and exchange. German, in such a universe, hardly seems worth mentioning as a vehicle for launching the literary career of a Ghanaian woman; nevertheless, the linguistic odds were to favour Darko in ways perhaps unforeseen.

The German title, *Der Verkaufte Traum*, literally means 'The Vended Dream', but also carries with it a range of subtle shades of meaning, a complex semantic bouquet if you will, which the English title, *Beyond the Horizon*, only partly captures. In its place, the substituted English title suggests the pot of gold at the rainbow's end, a Sisyphean quest, the pursuit of a chimera, and a heroic venture despite the ever-receding horizon of infinite defeats. The lesson taught is that we never learn from experience, and like mice, we are trapped on a treadmill expending enormous amounts of energy in order to stay, at best, where we are. And yet, use of the term *Verkaufte* in the German title suggests a less than philosophical transaction; indeed, it almost insists on the peddling or exchange of material goods, even as it maintains in its variant, *weiderverkauft*, the implication of repetition or reselling. It is the marketing, trading and even overselling of goods and services; but for Darko's purposes *der Traum*, which is orthographically similar to the English words 'trauma' and 'tram', is at once the dream, the vision and an *oneiric* state akin to the effects of ingested soma of Zoroastrian rituals.

In the ranks of the global underclass encountered within these pages, the promise becomes a nightmare from which Darko's characters can hardly escape. The experience is like a waking dream, a Kafkaesque obsession. Still, the edginess of the hallucination must be mellowed by addiction, and Mara herself is an addict; the dependency must seem to be internally driven, and the characters must believe that this is their chosen path. This state is one where, with apologies to Oliver W. Sacks,[5] the personal and the political, the internal and the external, the instinctual and perceptual erupt in a sort of public phantasmagoria. Its result: a world in which the psychosocial processes of displacement, condensation, over-determination, etc. seek to render the hallucinatory quality of the *real* bearable and dreamlike: in short, the ideological work of control is illustrated and performed within the narration of the work.

The charting of Mara's movement from Naka, the rural town where she was born and raised, to Accra, and ultimately Munich, illustrates what I have called a reversal of the Conradian trip into *The Heart of Darkness*, a journey into the 'blank of whiteness'.[6] This is all the more appropriate when we consider that Conrad's work begins with the confidence of an unnamed narrator whose voice resonates with the ease that comes with conquest and empire in the name of Victorian civilisation's exquisite economic exploitation of Africa even as it brought light to that continent's benighted wretches.

Even though the comfort of the narration and its location frames Marlow's deceptively revealing tale of colonialism's naked brutality, the termination of

Conrad's narrative of moral inquiry ends with a hasty retreat, on the part of the internal audience, from *the real* ('the brutes'), from knowledge gained from Marlow's tale and by Marlow himself from his own experience. The uncertainty of what to say or do before the immensity of the horror of what has been narrated is not completely lost on the reader, for we recognise that Conrad, implicated in the very structures that he seeks to critique, cannot offer any political or social remedy; history goes floating on.

By contrast, Darko positions her narrator in the heart of the empire, in the blank of whiteness, not as a comfortable guest taking a recreational trip down the Isar River in Munich, but as a prostitute trapped in a brothel, seemingly doomed to sell her body for the pleasure of men ejaculating semen into her black body. She sits posed almost naked in front of an oval mirror examining her reflection and meditating on how she has become the woman she sees in the glass. Structurally, Darko's narrative design begins at its seeming chronological end and ends at a chronologically penultimate terminus. However, this is as deceptive as the opening paragraphs of Sembene Ousmane's *Last of the Empire*, in which we are invited into a reading or telling of a distinctly Senegalese novel only to discover, as we read the final words, the text that we have just read, does not yet exist.[7]

Thus, Sembene and Darko rehearse a move that echoes and re-inscribes the prophetic desire implicit in the title of Ayi Kwei Armah's seminal work, *The Beautyful Ones Are Not Yet Born*. In that 1968 debut novel, Armah painstakingly details the corruption, decadence and betrayal of the hopes that crested with the people's hard won Independence, and had figuratively and literally gone down the toilet of neocolonialism. Despite the novel's unrelenting assault on our senses and its negative representation of post-independent Ghana, there is the possibility of redemption, as Kofi Owusu notes: 'The hope is that "a new flowering" will emerge "out of the decay", and the novel's title suggests that this "new flowering" will correspond to the birth of the unusual "beautyful", rather than conventionally "beautiful", ones.'[8] As readers, then, we may end up with a position contrary to Mara's pessimistic, and often repeated declarations that the possibility for her own agency, of being *sujet-pour-soi* and altering her 'karma', was foreclosed at the moment when she, as woman, was commodified and '. . . given away to this man (Akobi) who paid two white cows, four healthy goats, four lengths of cloth, beads, gold jewellery and two bottles of London Dry Gin' (3). And if not then, the point of no return had been reached and passed when Akobi made the sex tape of her, and, most certainly the last bridge back to 'normalcy' was most definitely burnt down when she became dependent on 'snow' (139).

But I would suggest that the tone of 'bite your lip acceptance' really mourns the loss of her naiveté, a comfortable blindness that allowed her to accept her role as the obedient daughter. However, her experiences since her 'sale', that is marriage to Akobi, have systematically exposed the lie of obedience. Mara is forced to mature under the most brutal of circumstances and her ability to exact revenge upon her tormentors, to assert herself in the end by reporting them to the authorities evidences an internal strength hitherto not expressed: 'Comfort has been deported... Akobi is in jail... Gite, has divorced him' (138–9). The authoritative tone that ends the narrative speaks to a protagonist who, in reflecting and reviewing her image/life, doubles the process so we as readers/viewers looking over her shoulder see her back and the reflection of herself – her face.

Then we know her to be real, to be whole, because Mara in staring at herself reflects on her self, distances herself from the particularities of her nightmare and is therefore able, 'before [she] sinks too deep[ly]' into her addiction, to give us her narrative in all its poignancy and articulateness, even if, as the obedient daughter, she feels she can only give her family 'material things' and nothing 'dignified and decent' of herself. Ironically, by supplying her loved ones with what Ayi Kwei Armah has termed 'The Cargo' she contributes to the very same ideological siren songs that led Akobi and then her to Europe in the first place. The characterisation of this movement seems most appropriate because those who make that journey are, for the most part, either economic or political migrants, exiles and refugees. Yet, they are all attracted by the commonality of what the former colonial hubs and emergent neo-colonial dependencies of the new global order offer... namely, *Beyond the Horizon*, the well-marketed dream beckoning us from our villages to the towns and cities and finally abroad.

Amma Darko takes the familiar folk tale of the disobedient daughter, a character we have seen in such works as Ama Ata Aidoo's *Anowa* and Amos Tutuola's *The Palmwine Drinkard*, and turns it on its head. We have instead tales of the obedient daughter. This is the young woman who, because of a sense of duty, wilfulness, naiveté or just plain ignorance, feels compelled to obey the rules, to play the game as her elders and betters have taught her; and yet, by the day's end, the young woman finds herself still trapped in that neocolonial hall of mirrors, never sure if the image seen is the real reflected.

Even though at the very beginning of her tale, she claims to be the one most in need of sympathy, Darko's storyteller realistically cannot afford to wallow in self-pity or bitterness over the series of choices that led:

> from my little African village, Naka, to... This room in which I am sitting [in] a lone, isolated house on the outskirts of Munich... bought [by a] man I call Oves. Formally, to others, he is Overseer. He is my lord, my master and my pimp... I am his pawn, his slave and his property. What he orders, I do. It is my karma (2–3).

Such a confession, framing the narrative of the journey that is to unfold, suggests that for this obedient daughter, even if she were to rebel, to seek another path, to refuse the continued commodification of her body and soul – her reduction to *sujet-pour-l'autre*, she would ultimately realise that under these neocolonial arrangements – resistance is futile.

Although Mara makes this confession, by most external and materialist measures of success she has made it; she is able to supply her family back in Ghana with the means to a relatively good life. In addition, while she makes these self-deprecating comments that belie a tongue sharp enough to emasculate any man before he knows it, the fact that she is narrating her life-story creates an ironic dissonance in her audience's imagination. We experience this in her description of the 'good news' announcing her imminent marriage to Akobi. In response to her mother joyfully telling her the 'good news', she reveals that:

> All I did was *grin helplessly* because I clearly remembered the same *good news* as this that mother had given my older sister two years before. Found, too, by my father. And *my sister was now a wreck*. . . . Akobi's father, like most men in the village, was a farmer too. But unlike most men in the village, he was also *an undertaker* (4, emphasis added).

The collocation of 'grin helplessly', the 'good news', 'My sister was now a wreck', and 'an undertaker' suggest that Mara's fate in marriage is to be the clown who either suffers the indignity of being the second madwoman of Naka, or is immured by the overwrought materialist ambitions of a misogynistic under-achiever, Akobi. Our jaundiced narrator, like her literary foremother, Sister Killjoy,[9] creates this double-voiced quality in her narration, allowing us to experience events from the point of view of an annoying, almost childlike young woman. However, almost immediately, the experiential authority of the older disinterested self who contemplates her reflection, heightens our *dis-ease* as it accentuates this perspective.

We soon learn what motivates Akobi and his decision to marry the astonished Mara from among all the other young women of Naka:

> Life in the city, Akobi soon realized, was not the glamorous days and nights he had seen in his dreams. Reality hit him and it hit him real hard, and he realized that the furthest he could go with his level of education was a messenger clerk at the Ministries, at best. But the worst confrontation of all for him were the women, one of whom he had hoped to make a wife and bring to Naka to pompously introduce (5).

Thus his own shortcomings in the areas of education, upward social mobility and romance are the catalysts that propel him towards Europe and encourage his misogynistic behaviour. Our narrator reveals that it was a young woman 'a typist or a secretary' (5) who gave him 'a nasty cold shoulder' (6) after he had become smitten with her. Ironically, it is this same woman, Comfort, whom he has in his sights as he reaches for the promise of wealth and prestige beyond the horizons of Naka, Accra and finally Munich. His vanity and hubris is to be his undoing in Germany. But Akobi is not a tragic hero; he is the architect and victim of his own lust propelled by the 'come hither' charms of a capitalist system of which he is only partially conscious.

If we glimpse the inner demons that drive the venal Akobi to be such a repugnant figure, then we have to look more carefully for the determinations that push Mara to follow him, like a well-trained puppy, out of the familiar Ghanaian village, to a Ghanaian city, across two continents to Munich and a brothel run by a pimp called 'Oves' or 'Overseer'. This mysterious man we are told by Mara, '. . . materialised from nowhere . . . He is my lord, my master and my pimp. And like the other women on my left and right, I am his pawn, his slave and his property. What he orders, I do' (3). These remarks, in which dominance and subservience are paralleled, speak to the apparent concentration of power in this symbolic male figure, even as Mara comes to represent the anonymous mass of women who surround the protagonist-narrator. It is interesting that the word 'overseer', in one of its archaic meanings, is comparable to 'husband.' Thus an equivalency is established between Mara's father, Akobi, Osey and Oves as traders in human flesh as property, supervising its circulation and reproduction within a local and global web of exploitative relations. Yet, as vulnerable as Mara seems, she deliberately make her voice heard, elevating herself from being a mere victim to articulate actor. As she observes:

> It is my karma. *Once, long ago, I believed mother* when she said to me, 'Your life is your road, Mara. God puts you at the start of this road and propels you to walk on . . . and you must walk it with gratefulness because it's the best for you.' *Once, before I started to walk my road all on my own, I believed mother* (3, emphasis added).

Mara's distinctions indicate the depth and subtleness of her self-analysis and understanding of the social, economic and political world. Her experiences, as harrowing as they were, have led her to comment on gendered human relationships in a devastatingly powerful way. For instance, when our narrator, who has been experiencing morning sickness, asks Mama Kiosk for a prognosis, the older woman, in her worldly-wise manner, tells her that she is pregnant. But, as wise as Mama Kiosk may be, she misreads Akobi's character:

> 'Your Ministries man will be proud of you, Mara. Bet my neck. Men like him feel great when they see the results of their handiwork. I am sure . . . he won't forget so easily that you too have feelings. He will acknowledge your existence and start treating you well.'

> But somehow I couldn't bring myself to share Mama Kiosk's enthusiasm. It was fine that I was going to have a baby. At least it would prove to the world that I was fertile and bring honour to my family. But as to whether that would automatically mean Akobi would stop beating me, ... I wasn't so convinced. I did see all these things as normal, as I have said, but it didn't mean that I liked them... For me, not obeying and worshipping Akobi would make me less of a wife, just as having no menstrual periods would make me less of a woman. And I didn't want to be less of anything (15–16).

This rather lengthy quotation demonstrates that even though our narrator is an *obedient daughter*, she is not as naive as she might first appear. Indeed, Mara knows that her biology and socio-economic status are implicated in her sense of identity, and wishes above all else to be *normal*; yet, the world as she sees and experiences it, set against the rhetoric of her elders, convinces her that not only are these times out of joint, patently unjust, but she lacks the means by which to establish a benign order. Simply put, she is always-and-already hailed by the ideological forces that subject her and the other characters to this alienated existence as they are propelled on a road that promises whatever one desires at its terminus. She is caught between personal expectations and external demands, both of which are only partially defined. This confusion is further complicated by her emotional and intellectual trepidation, as evidenced by her conflictual response to Akobi's departure for Europe: 'I walked back into our room, took his old towel, hopped into the grass bed, clutched the towel intimately to myself and cried my whole God-given eyeballs out. I was an irony unto my self' (44). The questions: How does she negotiate these forces, survive and, perhaps, find happiness? Indeed, how do we understand this narrator who, despite her seeming defenselessness, has captured our attention so completely and affected how we see human beings, women, children and even men trapped in a world not of their making, yet of their making?

## HOW THE STORY IS TOLD

The answers to the questions that linger in our minds can come only from a clearer knowledge of the narrator's art. Perhaps we can only understand Mara if we recognise the essential irony of her narration, which both reports the victimisation of the innocent and obedient daughter she once was and recites that sad tale in the knowing tones of an apparently 'hardened' prostitute. Only then, too, can we understand the sophistication of Darko's choice of an initial narrative posture for the real frame and symbolic context for this narrative: a woman sitting almost naked in front of an oval mirror – a woman who has an obsession with things oval. In that regard, we begin with the frame that surrounds our reflections on the narrative before us: *Beyond the Horizon* and over a shoulder.

We might begin as onlookers, spectators if you will, furtively eyeing both the curve of the woman's back and the reflection of her face and naked torso in the reflection. We know immediately that our narrator is aware of her *self*, both reflected image and *real*, and it is this consciousness that proves to be the snare that will prove our undoing. And, since she insists upon it, we might guess why our narrator is 'obsessed with ovals'. What meaning do we attach to that obsession in the context of the tale? An oval, an ovoid or ovum are all etymologically related, and speak to both Mara's reproductive capacities, as a representative of this underclass of women and, symbolically, her existential state. The former should not need further elaboration. However, as we consider the latter, we should envision the oval or ovoid as the transformation of a circle or sphere. We can imagine the sphere's centre (the defining point of the shape – its *being*) as equidistant from the circumference. Thus, the object is able to keep all external and internal forces in dynamic balance. However, when more pressure is exerted at the equator from external demands, the elasticity of the sphere or circle adjusts into an ovoid or oval. The ability of the shape to maintain its new form, or some semblance thereof without collapse, that is to say, its identity, depends on its elasticity, its resilience or integrity and the strength of those external forces. The 'centre' is always-and-already threatened with assault from without and even desire from within, i.e. under especially extreme circumstances such as *Der Verkaufte Traum*, the centre cannot hold. It is the oval that contains the mirror and Mara's double, her reflection (reversed self?) that is the narrative from which she emerges a full-grown woman/ storyteller.

So even as we seek to embrace and give comfort, prompted by guilt or pity or fear, to this unfortunate 'friendless, isolated and cold' sister, we, like her, recognise that we are looking at an 'image' or 'what is left of what once used to be my [her] image' (1), or is it just a fiction, or fictional reflection? As Paul Lacan would observe:

> The specular image seems to be the threshold of the visible world, if we take into account the mirrored disposition of the *imago of one's own body* in hallucinations and dreams, whether it involves one's individual features . . . or we take note of the role of the mirror apparatus in the appearance of doubles, in which psychical realities manifest themselves that are, moreover, heterogeneous (Lacan, p. 4–5).

This obsession with the oval mirror and the reflected image that invites us into the narrative to witness the intimacy of a confession disrupts the traditional discourse of the patriarchal gaze by turning what was once furtive and glancing and has become the ogle of the voyeur, the overseer, and by reflecting it back to the viewer gazing over her shoulder. It is significant because it is the key to both the reading of the text and Mara's body, her identity. In a manner of speaking, this critique is a Lacanian meditation or critical writing on Darko's fictional representation through the *reflection(s)* of Mara, her protagonist-subject, on the *female* body of both *herself* and Ghana. Germane to my argument is Lacan's preamble to his lecture on 'The Mirror Stage as Formative of the "*I*" function as revealed in Psychoanalytic Experience', in which he states:

> It suffices to understand the mirror stage in this context *as an identification*, in the full sense of analysis gives to the term: namely, the transformation that takes place in the subject when *[she]* assumes (assume) an image – an image that is seemingly predestined to have an effect at this phase, as witnessed by the use in analytic theory of antiquity's term, 'imago'.[10]

Thus, on an etymological level, her reflection rooted in the Latin *'imago'*, meaning 'image', is also associated semantically with an insect in its sexually mature adult stage after metamorphosis. Yet the image we see in the mirror/text does not *seem* to include us, the readers/viewers; nevertheless we, the 'johns', are acutely mindful of our presence, our culpability in the reconstruction of the text/image. Such an association is emblematic of Mara's life as a prostitute even as the *'imago'* doubles as an insignificant creature in a species-centric world, and, in the psychological sense, with the idealised *image* of a person, usually a parent, formed in childhood and persisting unconsciously into adulthood. The latter appreciation of the word is in concert with our characterisation of Mara as *the obedient daughter* – the 'ideal-I'.

The oval mirror, like the text, Mara's telling/writing the narrative, becomes the reflective surface or medium that she/we engage in as the reading process, the praxis by which the construction, deconstruction and reconstruction of ourselves, our narratives are made possible, even in this transitory apprehension of the image or mirage as a centred fixed *gestalt*. Yet, the use of the oval as a device for focusing the viewers' gaze on the centre of the image/narrative, that is, the imagistic and narrative device draws the viewers'/readers' eye to Mara's predicament (as both child and adult) placing us as, perhaps, uncomfortable voyeurs caught in both her and our own reflected gaze, pondering now, with a great deal more knowledge and genuine empathy, the meaning of the tableau.

## CONCLUSION

Darko's work is successful due to the complexity and power of her major character/raconteur. The novel explores, in the reflective light of the confessional, the global trading in women's bodies, a fact that has often been denied, erased or discussed in terms of outside of the West – Thailand, the Philippines, the former Eastern European countries and Russia and less often Africa. Now, Darko unapologetically relocates the site of the crimes in the white blankness of Europe and the West where 'snow' is to be sniffed into black bodies so that the pain of the real trauma may be ameliorated. And yet the story has been told: some things are indeed too dangerous to keep secret.

If Mara tried to be obedient, we understand that a major part of her problem was that she was a slow learner, a late bloomer if you will. Yet what is desired, the 'cargo' that is sought, is commodified in the discourse of intercourse in this post-colonial context. Activities are similar to Robert Young's characterisation of 'colonial desire' and his conclusions that:

> sexuality is a direct and congruent legacy of the commercial discourse of early colonial encounters, the traffic of commerce and the traffic of sexuality being complementary and intertwined economic and sexual exchange more intimately bound up, coupled with each other, from the very first. The history of the meanings of the word 'commerce' includes the exchange both of merchandise and of bodies in sexual intercourse.[11]

In the case of Darko's novel, this fusion in commerce of the sexual and the economic is extended into the contemporary context, as has been described earlier in our analysis of *Beyond the Horizon/Der Verkaufte Traum*, and might appropriately be described as revealing the tensions created by the pursuit of sexual desire/material goods and the limitations imposed on commercially impoverished sectors of global and local population groups: the neocolonial hallmark established in an unequal but interconnected set of local and global relationships. Mara's attitude toward prostitution is utilitarian, but we arrive at knowledge through her complete telling of the metamorphosis of that naive, obedient daughter of Naka into the worldly-wise prostitute of Munich. Darko writes a novel that is the confessional equivalent of the naked self in the web of living – to be a *subject-lesson,* rather than an object lesson.

Ultimately, Darko's narratives reveal that, despite the overdeterminate hegemonic character of neocolonial ideologies, the outcome in character and behaviour of diverse subjects reflects a different set of laws. These are laws grounded, not in the totalising teleology of the New World Order, but in the indeterminacy and unintended consequences of fleetingly regarding those subjects we refuse to reflect upon in a more deliberate manner. In short, we must learn from the cautionary tale of Darko's obedient daughter that if we are to do more than survive, then we must lower the price of our dreams, even as we expose dangerous secrets about reading and reflecting on what really lies *Beyond the Horizon*.

# Naana Banyiwa Horne

## Sage, Muse, Crone: The Grandmother in Amma Darko's Novels

> Institutionalised rejection of difference is an absolute necessity in a profit economy which needs outsiders as surplus people. As members of such an economy, we have *all* been programmed to respond to the human differences between us with fear and loathing and to handle that difference in one of three ways: ignore it, and if that is not possible, copy it if we think it is dominant, or destroy it if we think it is subordinate. But we have no patterns for relating across our human differences as equals. As a result, those differences have been misnamed and misused in the service of separation and confusion.
>
> Audre Lorde, *Sister Outsider*

Taking our cue from Audre Lorde, we might very well question if it is by sheer accident that the prominence of the grandmother figure in African literature has received little attention or rather perhaps a part of the '[i]nstitutionalised rejection of difference [that] is an absolute necessity in a profit economy which needs outsiders as *surplus* people. Lorde's words are located at the beginning of this paper in order to contextualise the oppressive constructions of so-called racial minority identities in debilitating ways to foster their disenfranchisement, a disenfranchisement that has been centuries in the making.[1] The word 'surplus' as used here is synonymous with redundancy, with remnants, with dregs. All of these are words connoting devaluation of human worth, outliving one's usefulness, or one's relevance and conjure up images of the grandmother, the aging woman, and her diminishing significance in a material economy where worth is measured in speed and potency. In a hierarchical world that devolves on the exploitation of the underclass, the silence maintained regarding the aged is part of the systematised oppression of an underclass whose usefulness is compromised by physical and often mental frailty.

In a 1986 publication on women in African literature, Mildred A. Hill-Lubin laments the dearth of critical and scholarly attention to the black grandmother.[2] This lament is particularly poignant because, the grandmother, as Hill-Lubin points out, 'has been a significant force in the stability and the continuity of the Black family and the community' (Hill-Lubin 257). Further, literary representations of her have not been lacking; 'she re-appears as a central character in numerous novels, autobiographies, short stories, plays and poems' (Hill-Lubin 258). The centrality of the grandmother figure in black literature mirrors her central role in black society – African, Caribbean, and African-American – making the neglect by scholars and critics all the more disturbing. For, perhaps no figure represents so clearly the way in which traditional sources of cultural wisdom have been ruthlessly erased within dominant profit economies.

To bring some specificity to understanding this plight, we will be considering the case of Ghana where the grandmother has traditionally been a significant figure in the society and her image abounds in the national literature. Yet, critical and scholarly studies of this figure have been slow in catching up with the literary representation. Indeed, some of the memorable portraits in Ghanaian literature are those of the grandmother. Unfortunately, Hill-Lubin's 1986 criticism is still pertinent today, and critical and scholarly studies of the grandmother have not yet gained parity with literary representation, even though the grandmother's life continues to give impetus to the literature. Accordingly, this essay seeks to redress the grave neglect of this important literary figure by exploring the grandmother figure in Amma Darko's novels.

Of Darko's three novels, the last two, *The Housemaid* and *Faceless*, feature grandmothers in roles that are prominent enough to merit analysis. I would contend that in Ghanaian literature, fictional representation of the grandmother often reflects cultural models, and that even as Darko problematises that figure by interrogating the popular perceptions of the grandmother as derived from cultural imaging, she reveals that the grandmother, as an actor within colonial/ post-colonial society, is also subject to those forces of history that delimit freedom and autonomy within the ranks of the oppressed.

The cultural models upon which the grandmother's representation is based are the sage, the muse, and the crone.[3] Of course, in real life, individual grandmothers often manifest a combination of the three roles to varying degrees, but for the purposes of this analysis, the cultural models have been isolated for scrutiny. The first of these categories, the sage or wise one, is she whose wisdom stems from a life based on experience. Her experience and exemplary life make her a potential guardian/keeper/re-creator of the moral and ethical precepts of the community. This model has its basis in Ghanaian society's traditional veneration of elders, which is based in the recognition that the very process of living and overcoming life's challenges leads to the attainment of wisdom in addition to the honing of character that sharpens moral acumen. The possession of wisdom is a key component in the identity of the sage and the attribute that unleashes the veneration of the beneficiaries of her wisdom. This wisdom and ethical consciousness make the sage one who is listened to and deferred to in times of crisis. Hill-Lubin observes of the African-American grandmother that: 'her function, role, and importance can be traced to the revered status, position, and responsibilities which elders hold in West African society. The Black grandmother, then, represents the most tenacious survival of the African extended family' (257).

Tied closely into the image of the sage is that of the muse, the source of inspiration for others, especially the younger generation: all those who are motivated to lead exemplary lives as they seek creative solutions to life's challenges. The grandmother's identity as muse manifests in her role 'as the repository and distributor of family history, wisdom, and Black lore' (Hill-Lubin 258). She is the storyteller *par excellence*, who inspires with her narrative and performative skills as she entertains and educates. At one and the same time, she nurtures and instils courage, moral values, and creative choices in her wards, through her imaginative re-creations of cultural models for emulation.

The final cultural model of the grandmother, the crone, is the flip side of the first two images of sage and muse. The crone image emanates from the toll and the ravages of time that have exerted on the grandmother. Defined in *The Webster Collegiate Dictionary* simply as 'a withered old woman', a crone's being is situated in the diminution of the stature of the aged. Because life's vicissitudes leave their markings on her body and mind, the grandmother can become wizened and enfeebled physically and mentally. It is this dimension of aging that the 'profit economy' identified by Audre Lorde exploits in dismissing the aged as a 'surplus', that is of no material value (115). The status of crone is the cradle of the vulnerability of the aged. The grandmother's wizened, enfeebled condition renders her susceptible to victimisation, especially ridicule from abler bodies.

All three cultural models of the grandmother abound in Ghanaian literature with specific cultural models often predominating in the literary representations of a given writer. Writers such as Ama Ata Aidoo and Ayi Kwei Armah are well-known for their memorable portraits of the grandmother.[4] In Amma Darko's work, we turn our attention to *The Housemaid*,[5] and *Faceless*,[6] the two novels in which the grandmother figure appears. Both of these novels are set in post-colonial Ghana, in a nightmarish world in which total disregard for humanity is the prevailing order of the day. In the diseased world of both novels, the sexual exploitation and gross abuse of females, on all levels, remain the central preoccupation. Going back to Audre Lorde's words in the opening quotation the pattern of behaviour is crystal clear; we 'copy it if we think it is dominant, or destroy it if we think it is subordinate' (Lorde 115).

In the introduction to Darko's third novel, *Faceless*, Kofi Anyidoho rightly indicates that the author's first two novels, *Beyond the Horizon* and *The Housemaid*, 'have already attracted enthusiastic critical attention, most of it focusing on . . . [Darko's] considerable skill in portraying the plight of women and young girls in a merciless world dominated by greedy, irresponsible and often cruel men in their life' [sic] (9). Anyidoho proposes that Darko's three novels should be considered together, as a trilogy, with each harping on the same heartrending story.

> Sadly, it is a tale of a diseased society that seems to have lost its hold on the life of its children. It is a provocative tale of a society that has developed a

> tragic ability of guiding its young ones, especially the girl-child, into a life dedicated to prostituting every conceivable virtue for the sake of flimsy material possessions (Anyidoho 9–10).

The destruction of young females is, without a doubt, central to each of Darko's novels, and this dimension of her corpus is what garners the most critical attention. Nevertheless, Amma Darko's interest in the grandmother figure is made apparent by the fact that two of the three novels feature grandmothers and rather prominently in *The Housemaid* which portrays not one but three grandmothers, even if one only makes a cameo appearance.

In *The Housemaid*, the destruction of the life of a young country girl, Efia, by the greedy desires of her family, is the central story. Efia is presented with an opportunity to go to the city and better herself by serving as a maid in exchange for sponsorship to become an established dressmaker with the required training, and capital to pursue her vocation. Sadly, instead of succeeding in the city, she falls into disgrace and ends up at the centre of a gruesome scandal that ends in her abandoning the body of her dead baby in the woods.

Two of the three grandmothers in the novel are connected integrally to the gruesome events of Efia's life. Although Efia's tragedy is the central event in the novel, the opening passage chooses to focus on a compelling portrait of the grandmother figure, presenting a composite image of the grandmother in her various manifestations in order to establish her identity in all its magnitude. Its detail and positioning in the story suggest that we should not lose sight of the importance of the grandmothers in the working out of the narrative events:

> In Ghana, if you come into the world a she, acquire the habit of praying. And master it. Because you will need it, desperately, as old age pursues you, and mother nature's hand approaches you with a wry smile, paint and brush at the ready, to daub you with wrinkles.
>
> If, on top of this, your children, waging a desperate war of their own for economic survival, find themselves having too little time for you, count you among the forsaken and forgotten; and if, crowning it all, cash, fine sweet cash, decides it doesn't really fancy your looks and eludes you in all nooks, crooks and crannies, then know for sure that you are on route to qualifying grandly as a witch. (3)

Significantly, the world the novel opens into is a dehumanised world, one that has internalised the 'institutionalised rejection of difference' (Lorde 115) that results in the diminution of human worth through poverty and ageism. It is not surprising that the portrait of the grandmother in these opening paragraphs is neither that of the sage, nor muse, but rather the crone. In fact, these opening paragraphs offer a stark recipe for the making of the crone. It is a degrading process that is the outcome of a triple-edged victimisation that is jointly perpetuated by nature, oppressive political, social, and economic forces, and a debased humanity, the product of the oppressive institutions. Mother nature, portrayed here, not as a nurturer but as some perverted artist, approaches 'with a wry smile, paint and brush at the ready' to bestow the wrinkles (3) which bring about the physical diminution of the aged. Ironically, initiated by nature, this degrading process is buttressed by exploitative political and economic forces and callous indifference.

Lorde's explanation of the workings of oppressive institutions is informative in this context.

> In a society where the good is defined in terms of profit rather than in terms of human need, there must always be some group of people who, through systematised oppression, can be made to feel surplus, to occupy the place of the dehumanised inferior...[T]hat group is made up of Black and Third World people, working-class people, older people, and women (114).

The opening paragraphs of Darko's novel evoke the crone, a wizened figure who, on account of her enfeeblement in a world that determines human worth in terms of profit rather than need, pushes the aged 'to occupy the place of the dehumanised inferior' (Lorde 114). These same oppressive forces co-opt the very children born and raised by the woman when she was in her prime, so that instead of providing her solace and a haven in her old age, her children cast her out because she has outlived her usefulness in a profit economy that is insensitive to enfeeblement.

Ironically, the children who have become the instrument for degrading their aged mother are themselves victims of the same oppressive institutions. As intimated by Darko, there is a direct correlation between the children's relegation of the aged mother to the ranks of 'the forsaken and the forgotten' and the children 'waging a desperate war of their own for economic survival' (3). Oppressive institutions engender further oppression among its victims through the process of internalisation: They turn their frustration against those who are as oppressed or even more oppressed than themselves. The children of the aged, reeling under oppressive political and economic systems, turn on the enfeebled because the latter constitute an easy target. It is much easier for the children to take out their frustration on their enfeebled mother than to confront the more powerful political, economic and social forces that oppress them.

The world of Darko's novel is made ominous by the competing evils of exploitation and its concomitant impoverishment; it is a world completely bereft of nurturance. In the diseased societal context of Darko's novel, the grandmother's potential to function as sage and muse is sabotaged. Her construction as crone, an image that is fraught with vulnerability, looms large.

Nature forces the grandmother to age in a world of systematised oppression that is rifled with fear and distrust. In this dehumanised context, the wizened look of the crone, coupled with her enfeeblement, attracts upon her automatic suspicions of being a witch, the ultimate pariah upon whose head all the despair in a dysfunctional world can be heaped. The grandmother is reduced to a malevolent rather than a benevolent force towards whom are attributed all the ills of the society. Formally pronounced a witch, she is driven 'to live in an isolated hut on the outskirts of the village' (3–4).

What is it about the crone that easily attracts the label of witch? The answer to this question, which is undoubtedly embedded in the internalisation of oppression by its victims, is further bolstered by African philosophical thought. The belief system in question is the concept of life force, which is at the heart of indigenous African philosophy. Life force is the impetus behind animism. Simply put, all of life – human, animal, natural – operates through the life force. Everything has a life force – the energising principle that derives from the originator. It is the recognition of this principle that underlies the indigenous African world's reverence for all life, including natural objects such as trees, rivers, mountains, etc. To borrow an image from popular North American culture, the life force operates like the 'energiser bunny' of energiser battery commercial fame. In the television commercial, the 'energiser bunny' derives its activation from the energiser battery, that is, the life force provided through that battery. The power of the commercial resides in the notion that the 'energiser battery' is so packed with life force that the same set of batteries can keep the bunny energised forever. In the words of the commercial, 'It is the ["energiser bunny"] that keeps going, and going, and going.' However, in reality, we know that the power of the battery will run down and a new set of batteries will need to be put into the bunny to reactivate it.

The life force principle behind human life is just like the operating principle behind the battery; it will become diminished over time on account of use or abuse (the activities one engages in for good or bad) and require recharging. The spark for recharging life force comes from interaction with other 'living creatures' – human, animal, natural. Imbibing/consuming are principal means through which life force is replenished. The process of consuming food, for instance, is based in drawing life force from what is consumed. African spirituality devolves on this symbiotic relationship that recognises that imbibing/consuming entails borrowing from other sources of life force not only physical replenishment but spiritual replenishment as well.

How then does this belief system explicate the connection between crone and witch? The crone's enfeeblement predisposes her to being perceived as predatory, as one who consumes/imbibes the life force of others, particularly children. The witch, typically, is accused of preying on children. In Darko's novel, a connection is established between imbibing/consuming and journeying towards 'witchdom'.

> A dejected widow, once upon a time a vibrant *akpeteshie* seller in the village of Braha, now penniless, aged and lonesome, started towards 'witchdom' when one of her grandchildren developed *kwashiorkor*. She had turned herself into a snake and lodged inside the poor child's stomach, they said.
> Then another grandchild got a goitre. And all eyes in Braha saw red.
> 'What is she doing lodging in parts of her grandchildren's bodies like that?' they asked. And formally pronounced her a witch (3).

The crone, declared witch, is constructed into a parasitic creature that lodges inside the bodies of children for the purpose of sapping their life force. She is projected as a devouring creature, that is, a malevolent creature that is best ejected from the community for the good of its people. Nonetheless, the narrative provides clues that the proclamation of the grandmother/crone as a witch has its basis in the multiple oppressions of poverty and ageism. The 'dejected widow', proclaimed witch, was 'once upon a time a vibrant *akpeteshie* seller in the village of Braha, now penniless, aged and lonesome' (3). Significantly, one typically does not attract the designation of witch until one is old and enfeebled.

This grandmother, however, resists her oppression by reclaiming her agency as a sage. Her interventions lead to the uncovering of the decomposing body of Efia's abandoned baby. Even though she has been banished to the outskirts of the village, because she has been proclaimed a witch, when her suspicions are aroused by 'a thick trail of black ants travelling [*sic*] to and from the thicket behind her hut' (4), she alerts the community. Even when her expression of her suspicions elicit jeers and taunts, she is not deterred.

> . . . [T]he old widow persisted, insisting on a search of the thicket. And when she saw that no one responded, she defied her isolation and showed up on the steps of the village elder's home. His household was thrown into turmoil. *What else but ill luck could result from a witch showing up at dawn on your doorstep? Best to satisfy her and be rid of her. So a search was ordered* (4, Italics added).

This grandmother, reduced to the rank of pariah, is wise enough to know that she has agency despite her proneness to victimisation. As crone, she may be feeble and powerless; but as witch, the same people who have victimized her by branding her a witch are nonetheless afraid of the malevolence they have invested her with as witch.

Paradoxically, it is through her victimisation as crone and, by extension, as witch, that she reclaims her agency as sage, an identity that is embedded in the wisdom acquired through experience. In her capacity as sage, she knows that there is power even in the identity of witch forced on her, and she taps that power to effect action. The grandmother turns her victimisation around and reclaims her agency as muse also, that is, as one who inspires positive action. The search ordered to appease her as witch results in the discovery of the decomposing body of an abandoned baby. Thus, through the grandmother's own initiative, she is able to assert her multiple subject identities and to force her community to show community spirit.

The grandmother figure evoked by Darko in the opening chapter of *The Housemaid* embodies the multiple identities of sage, muse, and crone; but, at the same time, the author problematises the depiction to reveal that this figure is a product of post-colonial societies that have endured centuries of political, social, and especially economic exploitation and continue to reel under these oppressive forces. Consequently, the grandmother can become a victim of the multiple forces of fear, poverty, and ignorance. Notwithstanding this sad reality, Darko asserts, in the first chapter of the novel, that the grandmother has the moral obligation to serve as the beacon of morality, especially in a demoralised world that has lost its sense of integrity. As the repository of the value system of the society, she is duty bound to set an example of courage to help redirect society back unto an ethical path.

By contrast, Darko chooses to depict the other two grandmothers in the novel as exemplars of the ways in which the forces of oppression are deeply entrenched in post-colonial Ghana. The first of these makes only a cameo appearance and is shown standing in her 'simple doorway' beaming 'with pride . . . watching her [granddaughter]' (33). Akua, the object of the grandmother's pride and joy, is one of the returnees from the city, who are portrayed glowing 'in their outlandish kaba styles' ready for 'showtime' at the Quebec Inn (33). The material well-being exuded by the granddaughter is what moves the old woman so much to make her exclaim in admiration, 'My granddaughter!' (33). Meanwhile, it is evident that young women like Akua are pressured to leave Kataso for the city in search of greener pastures, not only by their own desires and the limited opportunities for advancement in the village, but by the material desires of family members as well.

> [Families rejoice when their girls are] . . . sent for by relations or contacts in the cities to work as housemaids and babysitters, though many eventually end[ed] up as iced-water sellers and prostitutes.
>
> One day, four years ago, Akua, frustrated and itching to leave Kataso, but seeing no prospect at all of being sent for, did what only one girl before her had done. She left home and headed out, saying nothing to anyone (30).

Penniless, she trades sex for a ride to Kumasi and joins a band of girls who have left homes like hers under similar impoverished circumstances to hang around markets working as porters.

Like most of the girls in the same plight, Akua's experience in the city is fraught with humiliation, and even danger. Darko provides us a peep into the condition of these girls.

> Like her mates, Akua had no regular home. They all lived in unfinished buildings; when final completion work started, they moved out. Thanks to bribes of cash and sex, workers at the building sites regularly tipped them on the next place available for occupation. Because they were living there illegally and the building owners occasionally stopped by, nothing that might betray their presence was allowed. Cooking was out; they ate strictly by the roadside. Water stored in reservoirs for construction work sufficed for their washing and bathing purposes. Drinking water was bought and stored in plastic bottles, and nearby bushes were their easing grounds (32).

Yet, back home for the yam festival, Akua does not reveal any of the horrors of her life in the city. Instead, she 'dazzled her people with tales of traffic lights, fly-overs, the latest cars on the streets, and exotic events such as visiting foreign musicians. And finally, when it got to 'showtime', she joined the crowd of returnees to Osiadan proudly' (33). No one, not even her grandmother who is depicted beaming with so much pride, asks how she survives in the city or how she earns her money. The only thing relatives left in the village seem to care about is the gifts and other material things the returnees bring home. Of course, we are made to recognise that the adulation received by the returnees is directly tied into the gifts and other material bounty the villagers get from them.

Notwithstanding the brevity of Akua's grandmother's appearance in the novel, her fleeting image and brief utterance effectively communicate the compromising of the grandmother's moral authority by her material needs and desires. Far from a sage, she appears as a doting crone whose waning moral consciousness has rendered her mentally feeble as well, because she seems to have lost sight of what truly matters. She has been forced by poverty to abrogate her agency to be the voice of wisdom and morality. However, Akua's grandmother provides only a glimpse into the effect the long history of colonial/post-colonial oppression can have on the grandmother. The one who truly epitomises the toll the ravages of centuries of oppression has taken on the grandmother figure is the last grandmother to appear in *The Housemaid*, Efia's grandmother, possibly the most perplexing portrait of this figure in Ghanaian literature.

In the nightmarish world of post-colonial Ghana, the growing impoverishment of the masses has pushed money-making into the only preoccupation that sparks any desire in its inhabitants. Sadly enough, not even the grandmother is inoculated against greed and the desperation engendered by the struggle to attain material wealth at whatever cost; and as revealed through the third grandmother, sometimes, she is actually the instigator, the advocate of immoral acts in the interest of financial gain. Efia's grandmother leaves a sickening feeling in the pit of the stomach, indeed, because she embodies the worst possible internalisation of post-colonial oppression. Her integrity is so eroded by greed and desperation that she blatantly manipulates the cultural models in a manner that both undermines the trust the society places in the grandmother and even endangers the very society the elder is obligated to protect through her guidance. Though she tries to take on the mantle of sage, and muse, this elder thoroughly abuses her authority and causes the unfortunate destruction of her granddaughter 'Efia [who] followed her grandmother's counsel to the letter (49)' and is doomed because her grandmother is a disturbingly perverted old woman.

On the eve of the day Efia leaves for the city to work as a housemaid for Tika, (a 'stinking rich'[7] Accra businesswoman whose father hails from Kataso), the grandmother wakes Efia up in the middle of the night 'for an important discussion' (44). This behaviour is a common cultural practice, and in that sense, the grandmother of Efia is acting in accordance with cultural norms and performing her role as sage and muse according to a traditional archetype. The young woman, leaving to work in the city, needs words of wisdom and inspiration to guide her, and the grandmother is the right person to provide this guidance. But in Efia's case, her grandmother exploits this time-honoured practice to manipulate her granddaughter into becoming the key player in a scheme hatched by the old woman to defraud Tika. What makes the old woman so deadly is the fact that she speaks from a position of authority that is based in cultural ideals. As an elder, she is regarded as wise and all-knowing and as having one foot in the ancestral world on account of her age, and, therefore, very close to the world of the ancestors. She capitalises on these cultural perspectives to present herself as the conduit of the ancestors, one whose visions are communicated to her by the ancestors as part of the grand plan to redress the evils in the society.

The grandmother formulates an airtight plot to defraud Tika with the aim of enriching herself and her society. She starts by seducing her daughter and granddaughter into buying into her diabolical plans. Since superstition ranks with poverty and ignorance as key factors in the oppression of the masses, she naturally resorts to these devices as vehicles for manipulation. Her initial energy goes into convincing her granddaughter that she is the main cog in the wheel designed by the ancestors, and she, the grandmother, is the chosen medium through whom the ancestors communicate their desires. The desire of the ancestors is to avenge the death of Tika's father, their illustrious son, and they have chosen to accomplish this objective by using Efia as the means for returning the wealth generated by Tika and her mother back to its rightful heirs, the people of Kataso. The grandmother asserts that she is merely the mortal who can hear and interpret the desires of the ancestors because of her proximity to the ancestral world on account of her age. Employing the Socratic method, she raises leading questions and answers them herself to mesmerise her captive audience:

> 'Of all the extended family members, why did Teacher settle on us? She could have gone to the family house, or? Look at all the girls cramped in there just waiting for an opportunity like this. Yet, Teacher took just one look at our Efia and decided she was the one. Why? Because the ghost chose someone who could hear and understand his distant voice – *me*... The way that evil wife [Tika's mother] hurried Tika's father so prematurely to his grave, I tell you, his ghost will never find rest till he settles his score' (45, Italics added).

In this excerpt from the grandmother's 'important discussion' with her granddaughter, the elder taps her agency as the muse, that is, as the historian, the disseminator of community-lore.

Tika's father, the so-called illustrious son of Kataso, originally marries a woman from Kataso; but once in the city, he abandons her on account of Sekyiwa, the woman who gives birth to Tika, and thereby becomes the beneficiary of his hard work and generosity.

> At the age of twenty-two she [Sekyiwa] began a clandestine affair with a married man twenty-four years her senior. His wife was barren and rumour had it that this was the result of an abortion she had had when they were courting. Then Sekyiwa got pregnant. And the man felt his obligation to his unborn child transcending his loyalty to his wife (18).

The man devotes himself totally to his clandestine lover, now turned mother of his child, and not only marries her but makes her 'stinking rich' (18). However, once Sekyiwa becomes 'one of the wealthy market mummies' (18), she cuckolds him and throws his impotence in his face to boot. He dies a broken man, leaving imprinted in young Tika's mind his overwhelming sadness and tears as well as his great love for her. The father is beloved by the daughter for being the one who 'cuddled her' and stayed home 'playing and laughing with her' (19). Sekyiwa, on the other hand, poisons Tika's memories as the mother who chooses money-making and the pursuit of sexual pleasure with more men that are virile over devotion to her daughter and husband. Naturally, when Tika's father dies, the whole world, including Tika, lays the blame at Sekyiwa's feet.

Efia's grandmother exploits the troublesome circumstances surrounding Tika's life, including a set of coincidences, and the cultural belief that the restless dead will not rest till restitution has been exacted, to feed her greedy desires. She invokes a false sense of urgency in order to sway Efia and her mother. 'Listen, the ghost wants to return to his family [the extended family] all that his evil wife stole from him. The money that Tika used to start her business, wasn't it part of her mother's blood money?' (46). The old woman incorporates enough facts in her presentation to make the fantastic believable by appropriating the role of the sage. Another fact is that, Tika's womb has been removed on account of a botched abortion. Efia's grandmother capitalises on driving home the significance of this fact. 'The woman you are going to live with is a rich but wasted woman . . . A walking woman with no womb inside her . . .' (46). Efia's grandmother harps on Tika's calamity as yet another manifestation of the workings of the gods and ancestors and suggests a fanciful way in which they may capitalise on her barrenness:

> 'So, my granddaughter, if you ask me, the present circumstances are no coincidences at all. It has been destined this way ever since that day that evil wife stole our illustrious son's [manhood and wealth]. . . . The gods and ancestors of this village of ours designed everything. And your going to live with her is an essential piece of that design. So, hear me! Be subservient, humble and very dependable . . . Then get yourself pregnant' (46).

Within the context established by the grandmother, the advice to Efia to get herself pregnant, though shocking, unsound, and outright immoral, takes on the face of altruism, an action taken for the common good. It acquires the weight of duty. In fact, through her grandmother's council, Efia paradoxically becomes, at one and the same time, a young woman misguided into perceiving herself as the handmaiden who is chosen by the gods and ancestors to be the vehicle for making restitution to Kataso, and a whore/loose girl – the usual designation for females who sleep around. The grandmother's plan is to convince Tika to adopt the child Efia bears: 'I will suggest that maybe all this happened with the blessings of our ancestors. And emphasise how her dear father too is now one of our beloved ancestors' (47–48).

The grandmother is a manipulative genius who claims the ancestors as the designers of this ploy only long enough to appeal to the inherent desire for wealth and power in her victims. Being an expert manipulator, she knows that even though the lure of money, especially for the poor, can have a stronger pull on people's emotions than any qualms about morality, superstition can have the strongest impact of all. Therefore, she starts with the ancestors but drops the ancestral charade as soon as she has Efia and her mother where she wants them – their lust for wealth and power aroused. Once she invokes in the two a hunger for wealth, she blatantly schools them in the art of manipulation. Proudly, she unleashes her full arsenal that incorporates blatant exploitation of the ancestors and even the crone identity of the aged:

> And this is the plan. Inevitably, that Tika will rush to inform us of what has happened [that Efia is sleeping around]. And that is where I shall also play my part. Old and wrinkled as I am, when I bombard her with the volumes of tears I shall shed, she will need an iron heart to turn down my fervent plea to forgive my granddaughter. I will sob like a child, go down on my weak old knees and beg her to have mercy on us (47).

Efia's grandmother lives by the precept that the means justifies the end. 'A good reputation is fine, but you can't buy with it in the market' (56) is a strongly entrenched belief among the people of Kataso, and the old woman recognises the impact of this truism, given the stark poverty of her family. Her plan is to arouse pity in Tika and then exploit that pity. 'I will urge her, in my low and shaky voice, to adopt the child, make it hers' (48). The highpoint of her deception is preying on Tika's childlessness in a society that is flagrant in its disregard for the childless woman by convincing Tika that Efia's mishap (getting herself pregnant) 'is the wish of the ancestors to bring the joy of a crying baby into her [Tika's] life' (48).

Efia's grandmother epitomises the evil genius; she leaves no loose ends. Firstly, the old woman cautions against 'the risk of some foolish man getting up one day to lay claim to the child after it has become the somebody it will surely become' (47), thus encouraging her granddaughter to sleep around indiscriminately. She is wise enough to know that no man will be too eager to claim responsibility for the pregnancy of a promiscuous woman. Secondly, she draws attention to a possible danger in letting Tika adopt Efia's child:

> '. . . Our task will be to make sure that the child never forgets who *her* real mother is. That way, the wealth will also belong to Efia, and therefore to us all. And we will let it trickle down and spread. We will transform Kataso' (48, Italics added).

Despite the hint of altruism in the grandmother, indicating the wealth will trickle down and spread to help transform Kataso, her true motivation is building a material base from which to wield power. The operative principle in her scheme is greed and self-interest rather than the well-being of the community. In a society where age is revered, the grandmother, as the head of the matrilineage, wields power through her authority over her descendants, that is, those descended from the females in her line. The real inheritors of the wealth that will fall to Tika's adopted child will be generations of women in the matrilineage beginning with the grandmother and descending through her daughter, Efia's mother, and then Efia, and finally the child who is planned to be offered to Tika for adoption, perceptively designated as female by the grandmother when she breaks down the inheritance plan.

One of the strongest ironies in *The Housemaid* is that Efia truly does stand a chance to become financially independent and a benefit to her society, but instead, her own grandmother corrupts and destroys her. Tika, for a number of reasons – some of them noble and some selfish – is desirous of helping her father's extended family in Kataso, which is why she decides on Efia for a housemaid. A combination of vindictiveness towards the mother who loved making money more than she loved her daughter, and a genuine desire to honour her dead father, the illustrious son of Kataso, Tika decided to offer an opportunity for a young woman from her father's extended family by employing Efia as a housemaid. She is propelled to act on these desires by her sudden hospitalisation brought on by the botched abortion.

Tika decides on Efia with help from Teacher, a Kataso woman in the city who has acquired a reputation for helping people secure reliable housemaids. Tika plans to reward Efia generously for her service. Upon Efia serving her for four years, Tika promises to pay for her training as a seamstress, buy her her own sewing machine, and provide her with ample capital to become an entrepreneur. This arrangement is based on mutual benefit for Tika, Efia, and the people of Kataso. Instead, the grandmother's greed gets the better of her and causes her to lead her granddaughter astray. The old woman gets so completely swept away by what she considers her own cleverness that she makes the plot too complicated and arouses Tika's suspicion. Tika decides to send her back to Kataso. The irony is that even though Tika decides to send her back, she still intends to do right by her. She confides in Teacher: 'I will continue to care for her while she is in Kataso. And one day, when her baby is old enough to be left behind, and circumstances allow it, I might still decide to put her through her dressmaking training. Because in spite of what she has done, the fact remains that she has served me well during her short stay with me' (77).

However, her grandmother's greed is too strong to leave well enough alone. In a desperate last move, she advises Efia to pin her pregnancy on one of Tika's lovers. Of all the men Tika consorts with, Nsorhwe, a man whose name connotes *temptation* in Twi, is barren – unbeknownst to anyone because he is married with children – and is the one named by Efia, under the grandmother's tutelage, as the culprit. Naturally, the scheme to defraud Tika and Nsorhwe blows up in the grandmother's face. The pity of it all is that she fails to accept responsibility for any of these actions:

> 'You fool, fool, fool, fool, fool!' the old lady attacked her granddaughter as soon as they were alone. 'Why of all your whore of a madam's lovers did you let us choose this little, ugly, square-headed man? You fool a thousand times over!' (91).

She also turns on her daughter, Efia's mother, and threatens her with exposure.

'And you . . . should it get out of hand, rest assured that I will be the first to visit the chief and tell him where the idea came from' (92).

Efia's grandmother has no redeeming qualities whatsoever. She is perhaps the most disconcerting portrait of the grandmother in Ghanaian literature. She violates everything that is sacred about this figure; the worst part is that she does this by consciously manipulating the cultural models of the grandmother as sage, muse, and crone to feed her greed. She comes off as a psychopath who has absolutely no sense of integrity. She drives home the extent of the depth of post-colonial Ghana's internalisation of centuries of oppression, of political, social, and economic exploitation. She becomes a true representation of the witch, the epitome of oppression turned-in on itself. In the end, the powerless are rendered even more powerless.

Significantly, Efia is the one character in the novel who ends up victimised the most and pays dearly for her family's deception. The grandmother is so busy blaming everyone that neither she nor Efia's mother realise the traumatic impact of the scheming on Efia. The real casualty of these unsavoury events, she becomes so distraught over the shame of being sent back to Kataso pregnant and with no means to take care of herself or her yet to be born baby, that out of desperation, she steals from Tika in order to have the means to run away to deal alone with her pregnancy. Ironically, it is other victims of their family's greedy desires like Akua who rally around Efia on the streets of Kumasi. Bereft of medical attention and good nutrition, she delivers her baby alone, in one of the houses still under construction. The newborn is a Down's Syndrome child who dies shortly after birth, making Efia believe she has been cursed for doing Tika wrong. Efia seeks to make restitution by taking her dead child home for the necessary propitiatory rituals to be performed to liberate the neonate from the curse her people's wrongdoing has brought on its head. However, putrefaction sets in while she is on her journey, and the stink from the decaying body becomes so strong that she is forced to get off the lorry and bury her child in the woods. Though doubly victimised by the callous society that is quick to condemn rather than seek solutions, she is ironically the only character who, in the end, shows true courage by going back to face the consequences of her actions.

It becomes truly frightening when the grandmother, who should be the conscience of the nation, ends up the one leading the young to destruction, and also when the young show more regard for human values than those who should be their guardians with the moral obligation to set good examples. Fortunately, Amma Darko, in her latest novel, *Faceless*, re-injects hope into post-colonial Ghana by retrieving the cultural relevance of the grandmother figure. '[A]s the preserver of the African extended family; second, as the repository and distributor of family history, wisdom, and Black lore; and third, as the retainer and communicator of values and ideals which support and enhance her personhood, her family, and her community' (Hill-Lubin 258), the figure of the grandmother finds a partial redemption in this otherwise bleak depiction of Ghanaian society. In a novel where little else is redeeming, the grandmother is evoked in all her complexity. Naa Yomo, who is appropriately named in accordance with her aged identity,[8] embodies the multiple subjectivities of the sage, the muse, and the crone.[9] She is a character who understands fully her duty as a source of wisdom and inspiration, her physical enfeeblement as crone notwithstanding.

The compelling focus of Amma Darko's *Faceless* is the problem of street children whose desperate longing for parental care and the comfort of home is subverted by the debilitating political, social, and economic conditions that prevail in post-colonial Ghana. Street children, who are left to their own devices, are the real casualties of a dysfunctional world in which parents have relinquished their agency as providers of the economic and emotive needs of their children. Some, like Fofo, are drawn into the streets by a combination of hunger and the lure of freedom from the control of oppressive and abusive parents. And others, like Fofo's friend, Odarley, are deliberately driven into the streets by desperate parents who have failed to exert effective agency in raising their children.

Into this depressing world, where most of the adults have lost parental agency, the grandmother is re-inscribed as the rock upon which a saner society can be rebuilt. In this novel, Darko locates her in that problematic space in which street children, seeking intervention from their parents, are threatened by demoralisation stemming from the paralysis that afflicts the adults. The grandmother figure is constructed as a bridge that becomes essential in negotiating that nebulous space between street and home. She emerges as the hope from the past that re-energises the present by asserting her agency as sage and muse in order to inspire creative choices for Ghana's troubled children.

In *Faceless*, the magnitude of the plight of street children is portrayed through Fofo, a fourteen-year-old girl who becomes estranged from a home that is anything but a safe haven. Naa Yomo is the grandmother figure through whose agency Fofo's ineffectual mother, Maa Tsuru, gains the resolve to attempt to salvage what is left of her broken family. In *Faceless*, Darko makes poignantly clear that homelessness has strongly gendered implications. Female children on the street are at the mercy of sexual predators. The novel opens with Fofo, the young female protagonist, narrowly escaping a rape attempt by Poison, a street lord reputed to be a vicious pimp. She escapes this ordeal momentarily by growing bold enough to physically beat Poison down. But being street-wise, she is aware her victory will be short-lived unless she finds some quick answers to arm her in her battle with Poison, for his motivation cannot stem from sheer desire. 'Poison doesn't go raping girls like us. He doesn't need to. When he wants it, he beckons, and the hi-life girls flood to him in their numbers' (33), Odarley vocalises what Fofo has already figured out – she will have to pay her mother a visit in search of answers. Interestingly, though Odarley's use of the word 'rape' here conflates sexual desire with rape, that word is problematical enough to indicate that the assault on Fofo does not make sense in the context of sexual desire. Hence, there is the need for Fofo to go to her mother for answers.

Fofo's situation epitomises that of children who are forced to flee from home because the men in their mother's lives turn home into an unsafe terrain. Though only fourteen-years-old at the time of the assault, Fofo is mature enough to recognise that her mother neither handles her own sexuality responsibly, nor is she capable of protecting her children, especially her girl-children, from sexual predators. Kpakpo, the new man in her mother's life, bodes ill for Maa Tsuru's children from a previous relationship. Their mother's desires as a woman usurp her ability to act in the best interest of her children. Sharing her bed with Kpakpo in the already crammed one room exposes the children to the sexual goings-on of the couple in addition to worsening the overcrowding. With Kpakpo's addition to the household and the mother's irresponsible behaviour, Fofo's two older brothers are pushed away from home, and Maa Tsuru's two daughters are also made vulnerable to being preyed upon. They are left alone one night with Kpakpo when Maa Tsuru is detained at the midwife's; he assaults Baby T., Fofo's older sister, taking the twelve-year-old girl into his bed to play her mother's role. When Fofo appeals to Onko, a supposedly kind uncle, to help Baby T., he ends up raping Baby T. and then silences Maa Tsuru with money and the threat to expose Kpakpo's earlier assault on Baby T..

Rather than fight to save her daughter, Maa Tsuru becomes further implicated in Baby T.'s victimisation by consenting, upon Kpakpo's recommendation, to send her sexually assaulted daughter to Maami Abidjan and Maami Broni, retired prostitutes who are supposedly 'recruiting young girls for work in chop bars and households' (167) in exchange for monthly envelopes filled with cash to support her new 'husband' and the two baby boys she bears for him. It is, in fact, Fofo's fear that she will be given away to Maami Broni for more money, just like her sister Baby T., that finally pushes her away from home into the streets. Fofo instinctively knows that Poison is in the middle of all these arrangements, having heard her mother and stepfather mention his name in their conversations and arguments before she takes to the streets. Now, Fofo decides that her mother must have some answers regarding Poison's attempt to rape her and therefore asks Odarley to act as scout to ensure that the coast is clear.

Amma Darko deftly weaves Naa Yomo's appearances into the resolution of the plight of street children. She is first presented as an 'old voice' croaking, demanding of Odarley, 'Girl, are your manners gone on holidays? Have you heard of something called "greeting" before?' (43). Her very first appearance, therefore, underscores her role as educator on and guardian of customary practices and moral precepts. Odarley, Fofo's homeless friend, is here cast in a John the Baptist-like role of going ahead to prepare Maa Tsuru for her street daughter's visit and to alert her to the 'big trouble' that Fofo is coming to see her about. Naa Yomo, the head of the extended family of Fofo's mother, is strategically positioned, almost directly opposite the latter's door in the twelve-room family compound, 'a house of many faces' (41). To reach the door of Maa Tsuru, Odarley must venture into 'the midst of angry mothers and screaming children and bleating goats and sheep' (42), and the first resident Odarley encounters and greets in the compound responds with so much hostility that she decides not to greet any more people.

Ironically, her decision to play it safe makes her fall foul of Naa Yomo, who makes it a point to reprimand the young girl for falling short on manners, even though the old woman acknowledges witnessing the encounter that makes Odarley decide not to greet any more members of the household, in the interest of safety. Naa Yomo is an elder who, unlike Efia's and Akua's grandmothers in *The Housemaid*, acts in a manner befitting her age and acquired stature:

> Naa Yomo at eighty-seven, was the oldest member of the household, and mother and grandmother and great grandmother to someone and everyone. If the washing-woman did not appreciate her [Odarley's] courtesy for whatever reason, Naa Yomo obviously expected it, for whatever reason. Odarley went over and greeted her politely. Naa Yomo responded and asked her how she was doing. (43)

As elder, Naa Yomo is not only knowledgeable of the protocol: she enforces it. Significantly, she teaches by example, enforcing tradition through her participation in the practice. Not seeing Fofo with Odarley, she queries if Fofo is not coming to visit her mother, and then prompts Odarley to remind her friend to greet her when she enters the compound, thus encouraging the young to consistently behave in accordance with the customary practices that hold our societies together.

The authority Naa Yomo wields stands in stark contrast to Maa Tsuru's pathetic demeanour. The mother's shameful wallowing in self-pity while her children languish in neglect and even danger also stands in marked contrast to her daughter Fofo's decisiveness in trying to extract from her mother what is really going on with her life and her children. Maa Tsuru's daughter, Baby T., has been killed; Poison, the street lord who was Baby T.'s pimp, has paid her a visit to warn her that he will replace Baby T. with Fofo if Maa Tsuru provokes him. Yet, all she can do is wail about having been turned into a leper by Poison in the same manner that she wails about 'the curse' and blames it for all her misdeeds. She cannot even tell Fofo the truth about Baby T.'s death; all she can do is plead with Fofo to go far away:

> 'I have nothing better to tell you, child. And no money to give you too,' Maa Tsuru cried. 'I looked on and allowed something to happen that shouldn't

have. My hands are tied. I have my finger between his teeth. If I hit him on the head, I'll make him chew off my own finger too inside his mouth' (49).

In this encounter between mother and daughter, the mother epitomises the paralysis that afflicts parents like her.

Maa Tsuru's failure to offer Fofo help to get away from Poison pushes her daughter deeper into the wasteland of the street. Desperate for money with which to leave Sodom and Gomorrah and the underworld into which she has descended, Fofo falls back on the pick-pocketing skills she perfected under Baby T.'s tutelage. While in the market, Fofo, disguised in boy's clothes, attempts to snatch a woman's purse. When the mob turn on the pickpocket, 'eager to make history of the boy' by 'whip[ping] him till he sees his guardian angel' (70), the victim feels compelled to save her assailant from possibly being beaten to death. Claiming the culprit as a wayward relative, she takes 'his' hand in hers to get 'him' away from the mob. Ironically, rather than running away to safeguard 'his' identity, the pickpocket – actually our homeless protagonist, Fofo, whose boy's clothes are all she received from her visit to her mother – reveals her identity to the woman and asks to be taken to the government. Fofo also claims the slain girl at Agbogbloshie Market is her sister, a detail that piques her intended victim's interest.

Fortunately for Fofo, her projected target is Kabria, one of four professional women working at MUTE, a non-governmental organisation that deals primarily with documentation and information build up (34). Dina, MUTE's founder, fondly refers to it as 'The Alternative Library' which is interested in '[e]very social, gender and child issue' (63). Ironically, it is at the very site where Baby T.'s body was dumped that Fofo attempts to rob Kabria and almost ends up being beaten to death by the mob. What could have been a tragedy, however, turns out to be an intervention by fate. Fofo becomes a beneficiary of the professional attention and nurturance of the four women at MUTE, and, through their dedication and effort, the plight of both Fofo and her slain sister are brought to the attention of the media and other helpful organisations whose collaboration helps unravel the mystery of Baby T.'s murder and the eventual rehabilitation of Fofo.

In this process, Darko casts Naa Yomo in the role of the preserver of the Ghanaian extended family as well as a storehouse and communicator of family history, wisdom and Ghanaian lore, including the ideals and values that sustain persons, families, and communities. She serves as the linchpin by which the old is hitched to the new. The epitome of indigenous knowledge and ways of knowing, she serves as the bridge linking her beleaguered community with the new structures of intervention, represented by MUTE and the media in the body of 'Harvest FM'. She is the medium through which MUTE collects pertinent historical and family information in order to gain an understanding of Baby T.'s and Fofo's situation, thus bringing about the exposure of the murderers of the former and the rehabilitation of the latter. It is also through her intervention that Maa Tsuru commences her own journey towards her own rehabilitation.

Naa Yomo's second appearance in the novel underscores her role as sage and historian. She gives Kabria and Vickie a crash history course that is vital in the understanding of the environment that they are positioned to benefit through their non-governmental organisation, MUTE. 'Do you know that this house stands on the original settlement of our forefathers when they came in from Niger country?... [T]his very spot here, where this stool of mine sits, is proper Accra' (116). To younger, upwardly mobile, educated women such as Kabria and Vickie, who wonder why anybody continues to live in the inner cities that are overrun by old dilapidated buildings, crime, and overcrowding, Naa Yomo brings the realisation that home is more than the physical structures. '[S]omewhere beneath this earth is my umbilical cord. The first two teeth in my mouth grew here. The last two would come out here' (117). She tells them about her resistance to being moved by her children who, because they fail to recognise that she lives in a house filled with history, want to move her from where she was born to live with them in their fine bungalows.

In the family house, she 'survived the great earthquake of 1939... Part of this house was levelled to the ground, but we stayed on. When they were re-settling others at Korle-Gonno and Kaneshie and Abossey Okai, we refused to move. We rebuilt this house with our sweat and toil. This house was built on a foundation of honour' (116). A true icon in her world, Naa Yomo's significance in her community is captured by the young girl who escorts Kabria and Vickie to Fofo's family home: 'No one can get lost going to that house. Everybody around here knows Naa Yomo' (114). Notably, upon meeting her, Vickie observes that that old woman 'knows so much', and Kabria acknowledges that 'if the contents in her head could be deciphered with a click of a mouse, she could fill up another George Padmore Library' (122).

One of the lessons Naa Yomo teaches is that knowledge of ancestry is crucial to our sense of identity and integrity. The granddaughter of 'one of a few Gold Coast men with whom the old governor, Sir Gordon Guggisberg, shook hands' (118), she is guided in her life choices by the recognition that she hails from a home that 'was built on a foundation of honour' (116). To the two visitors from MUTE who only see a dilapidated inner city house in the heart of the Accra ghetto, Naa Yomo explains with pride: 'This house was built by an honourable man, for his twelve sons. I am the daughter of one of those twelve sons. I am the only direct grandchild of the great man still alive in this house' (117). Armed with the sense of honour of her forebears, she makes it her business to keep the members of the household in line and maintain a sense of kinship with even people like Maa Tsuru and Onko, the child molester, who dishonour the family name by their actions.

Naa Yomo validates her authenticity as possessor of knowledge; she educates the modern scholars on indigenous systems of knowledge acquisition by sharing her practice with the two women: 'Every morning when I come to sit here, I listen and observe. Day in and day out, in all these past several years, I have been listening and observing. I have seen a lot and observed a lot' (117). She demonstrates that the oral system of disseminating knowledge is still an important mechanism for imparting historical lessons:

> 'As was told my great-great grandfather, who told my great grandfather, who told my grandfather, who told my father, who told me, my great-great-great grandfather was one of the early men of the Gold Coast who traded directly with the Europeans... Yes. He traded with them all: Swedes, the Danes, the Portuguese, the British. Hand to hand. Guns and gun flints for gold dust and palm oil and even slaves' (118).

While Kabria and Vickie wonder about Naa Yomo's motivations for referencing her familial links to the Atlantic Slave Trade and the trafficking in human beings, the old woman makes us realise that knowledge of the past – even unsavoury information such as the collaboration of our forebears with our oppressors through activities such as the slave trade – is integral to forging a meaningful path to the future. Acknowledging the good with the bad is imperative in preventing us from repeating the mistakes of the past while empowering us to emulate the strengths and achievements of our forebears.

Old, physically feeble, and somewhat of a crone, Naa Yomo is also the sage and muse *par excellence* who recognises the efficacy in accepting responsibility for our actions. She traces the root cause of children living on the streets to the loss of agency by parents who hide behind superstition to abrogate their responsibility to care for their children; to the absence of caring, responsible fathers; and to women whose desperate need for companionship supersedes their commitment to the well-being of their children. She speaks of the debilitating influence of superstition that exacerbates the problem of street children because it becomes a crutch that offers parents an escape from responsibility. Citing the case of Maa Tsuru whose embittered mother, a woman scorned, ushered her newborn into the world with curses heaped upon the head of the man who fathered her and his lineage, and caused Maa Tsuru to cling on to the belief that she came into the world doomed, Naa Yomo explains:

> [W]hen the seed of a curse finds a fertile ground in a human mind, it spreads with the destructive speed of a creeping plant. And while it does, it nurtures superstition, which in turn, eats into all reasoning abilities and the capability of facing responsibility (120).

A woman who gives birth to eleven children and loses five to death, Naa Yomo could have fallen a prey to superstition herself. Instead, she adopts a philosophical approach to reconciling herself to child loss. 'Do you know how many of my children I have buried? Five. Eleven, the good Lord gave me. And five He took away. The same good Lord. And not one of them did I send out onto the streets. So do I complain about the five I buried? No! I thank Him everyday' (115). She and her husband succeed in raising their surviving six children up to acquire education and attain good jobs because her husband stopped nurturing his superstitious mind and focused more on facing up to his responsibilities after the death of their fifth child.

Through Naa Yomo's parenting experience, Amma Darko disrupts the stereotyping of inner city parents as adults who fail to rise to the occasion of being exemplary parents. There are serious challenges that make child-rearing in the inner city an uphill battle. However, as Naa Yomo attests, dedication, commitment, and an unselfish embrace of responsibility are keys to successful parenting. Naa Yomo's experience with her husband affirms that good men are indispensable in raising good children:

> 'A good man would never say to his child: there is no food, go out onto the street and find some money for food. He would say: 'There is no food, so we'll all drink lots of water and go to bed. Tomorrow is another day. You will go to school and I will make sure there is food to eat when you return home' (115–116).

The positive picture of parenting presented here contrasts keenly with that of Maa Tsuru and her string of dysfunctional men who drive her children into the streets. The source of Maa Tsuru's woes, it becomes increasingly clear with the unfolding of the novel, is her using the curse as a crutch to justify the many bad choices she makes instead of taking responsibility for her actions.

It is no wonder then that, in the end, Fofo takes the mother to task and questions her inefficacy:

> Mother, why? What life have you been able to give those of us you already have? Look at the boys here? Look at me. We have no idea where the two older boys are. Are they dead? I often wonder. Are they alive? Are they in prison? Are they killing people to survive? You don't even know. And Baby T.? *You offered us all generously to the streets, mother. You made the streets claim and own us . . . You grew too used to living off the sweat of your children, especially Baby T.* . . . (188, Italics added).

Given this situation of parents abrogating their responsibility to the children they bring into the world, the grandmother becomes all the more the one upon whom the onus of restoring order falls.

In *Faceless,* Naa Yomo is the one person who is fully aware of the extent of Maa Tsuru's degeneration. After all she has known the younger woman from the time of her conception and was present at her birth where she witnessed the abomination caused by the mother who heaped curses upon the head and lineage of the 'no-good' man who impregnated her before her puberty rites and then publicly claimed he had no knowledge of her womanhood. She is horrified enough by Tsuru's actions to declare to Kabria and Vickie: 'She has lost her soul' because 'only a woman robbed of her soul would do what she was doing' (122). However, being the sage and muse that she is, she refuses to disclose the sordid details of Tsuru's misdeeds to the women from MUTE. Conscious of the healing impact of confessions, Naa Yomo declares Tsuru will have to redeem herself by asserting her agency to reclaim her life and her children. 'I cannot tell you yet. Fofo must know before others do. And Tsuru must tell Fofo herself. It's the only way she can salvage whatever is left of her soul' (122).

The mark of the revered elder is a commitment enhancing not just her own personhood, but her family and community. Naa Yomo is such an elder. She takes it upon herself to initiate the process of expediting Maa Tsuru 'salvaging whatever is left of her soul' (122). The younger woman stays locked up in her room, crying about the curse and not even answering her door. When repeated attempts by the women from MUTE to reach Maa Tsuru fail, the old woman walks across the compound to Tsuru's door and orders her to 'Open up!' (180). Tsuru snaps out of her paralysis and does not only open the door but obeys the older woman's summons to go to her room for a talk. Naa Yomo walking to Tsuru's door is depicted as a momentous occasion:

> As she ambled back, the children in the compound stared in awe at her back. Many of them could not remember when they had ever seen Naa Yomo tread across the compound from her own room to another's door. She always sat there and summoned. And when you did not respond fast enough, she dealt with you (180).

Cognizant of the depth of Tsuru's malaise, she steps outside her box, going the extra mile by handling Tsuru with kid gloves instead of the harshness she usually metes out to offenders.

When Tsuru does answer the elder's summons, she is treated kindly but firmly. Naa Yomo tells her about the organisation MUTE and 'Harvest FM' who are eager to help Fofo.

> Now I am telling you this: it cannot go on like that. It must stop. Listen. A woman came to see me... She is from the organisation that has been caring for Fofo. They want to know the whole true story. She will be back with a man from a radio station who has been working with them. They are people

> with good sense...The will come with Fofo. I assured them that this time you would open your door to them. Am I clear enough?' (181).

The 'it' Naa Yomo refers to in her talk with Tsuru is the younger woman's abandonment of her responsibility towards her children. Knowing Maa Tsuru cannot put her life in order without help, Naa Yomo takes on the responsibility of connecting the younger woman with the necessary resources that will aid her to reclaim her agency as a parent and make it possible to seek redress for her dead daughter and rehabilitate Fofo and herself. Naa assures Maa Tsuru: 'I shall be here, as always. And I shall observe and listen' (181).

A central problem with modernity is the rendering redundant of the aged by a profit economy that bases worth on prowess and youthfulness. Amma Darko, in *Faceless*, revamps the true usefulness of elders and their potential to assert agency as sages and muses. She propounds the significance of combining activism with knowledge acquisition in order to arrive at creative solutions to the problems of the community. By modelling Naa Yomo as a scholar/activist who does not sit on the information she has about Maa Tsuru but acts on it by taking it upon herself to personally call the young woman to action, Darko creates an alternative to her earlier representations of the crone. The feebleness of aging does not stop Naa Yomo from exerting her agency as sage and muse. The portrait of Naa Yomo serves as a refreshing foil to that of Efia and Akua's grandmothers in *The Housemaid*. In her depiction of the grandmother figure, Darko shows that, even though in colonial/post-colonial Ghana, the grandmother can be victimised by those forces of history that delimit freedom and autonomy within the ranks of the oppressed, she also has embedded in her enduring ideals and values that can sustain not just her personhood but her family and her community.

When attended to, the grandmother, therefore, can be a valuable ally to contemporary scholars and activists seeking to tap indigenous sources of knowledge and wisdom in combating the new problems facing post-colonial Africa that are so exacerbated by modernity and its fragmentation of indigenous African family structures. All that seems missing is a wider recognition of the value of the experience the elders bring to community. That recognition, as *Faceless* demonstrates once more, is not lacking in the work of Ghanaian authors, but perhaps we have failed to attune ourselves to what Lorde might see as a 'pattern for relating across our differences as equals'. Closer attention to our storytellers and our writers might help restore us to our past, and our past to us, not as a nostalgic longing but a critically constitutive part of our recovery and progress into the twenty-first century and beyond.

# *Rethinking Pan-Africanism*: Keynote Address Women Caucus Luncheon – Saturday 20th, May 2006 African Literature Association 32nd Annual Meeting and Conference Accra – Ghana

I took advantage of my workplace and the people of varied makes and dispositions, ranks and sizes, with whom I deal with daily at the office, to find out people's minds on Pan-Africanism. Some retorted their responses. Others shrugged off the question and smiled curiously, wondering what business I had, sitting in a tax office, coercing them to part with various sums of money in taxes, then daring to make them respondents on Pan-Africanism. A few however, did make known their thoughts.

Some of the responses were serious. Others were baffling. And yet others, rather sad. The question I put to them was simple: 'Do you have any thoughts on Pan-Africanism?' One man chuckled cynically, 'Ho! Don't mind Nkrumah. That was just one of his tricks to rule Africa'. I thought that to be sad. That someone could hold such a perception was very sad. Another snapped impatiently, 'What has that got to do with me? Ah! Isn't it the headache of the politicians? It is they who chop the big monies! Let them carry the big headaches too!'

I thought that quite baffling: Pan-Africanism a headache. Yet, maybe the guy had a point; considering it to be one of the very few serious responses I got. It came from a young man. 'The politicians have hijacked it!' he professed, 'They and the "book-long" people. They think it is all about politics, when it should be about people. That is why it hasn't made much impact.' By the way, for those of you not conversant with Ghanaian terms, 'book-long' is the snide term for highly educated people who think they know too much or who theorise a lot without putting their theories into practice.

I agree with the young man. Pan-Africanism should be more people-centred. It is a vision and a dream but it is also a movement. Numbers count. People need to be convinced about its ideals and become committed to its goals. As it stands now, it appears to be wrapped up in a shell. It appears to be nestling in the hands of a few politicians and learned men like a delicate and over- protected egg. Yes, political achievements made must be trumpeted. Like the peer review mechanism that African leaders have imposed on themselves, to help sanitise African politics and state corruption. Only time will tell what effect it will have on curbing the habit and hobby of smuggling stolen monies out of Africa to be stashed into various Swiss accounts. Hopefully it will also compel our men of power to care just a wee-bit more about us; such that they will formulate good and selfless policies in our interest to help put an end to the resultant images of our starving children on screens around the world.

So maybe we can dare to allow a little smile to our lips, albeit a cautious one. Lest we burst into loud laughter of hope too early and have it frozen in our faces. In the midst of all the violence and chaos in many parts of our continent however, a political stride like that, does offer a ray of hope. Yet if people are to endear themselves to the Pan-African dream, then due acknowledgement must be given to the reality that, even though politics does influence the thinking of a people, the people are first and foremost influenced by their culture. People are their customs and traditions and art and their beliefs. The ideals of Pan-Africanism must be stretched beyond the political arena into the cultural to complete the circle.

Let me cite an example. The debate over the issue of a common language for Africa appears to have fizzled away. Even a similar vision for Ghana alone, decades ago, generated fierce emotional reactions. That debate should not have been cooked in the political pot. It could have begun with the mass education of the people on the pros of it. Politicising it created suspicions. Because frankly, politicians do not rank among the most trusted of professionals.

We appear to dwell too much on the politics of issues instead of on what constitutes our make-up, namely our culture. So that on the issue of the common language, instead of people being encouraged to debate, argue, make suggestions and hopefully reach a consensus, one or two languages were thrown into the public arena through the grapevine which caused people to go on the defensive and question suspiciously why the language of ethnic group 'A' was being considered and not that of ethnic group 'B'.

Being what I am, a creative writer; put simply, a storyteller; may I tell you a short story:

> Once upon a time in a village called Koroye (in English: Unity) there stood a huge tree. Birds nestled comfortably in its branches. Lizards played 'hide and seek' along its stem. Maame Nsafufu dispensed calabashfuls of palm wine under its glorious shade to eager men, young and old and a few daring women too. Koroye was proud of its tree. Then one day, a great wind blew and to the dismay of the people of Koroye, their tree began to sway. So an order went out to all the village's strong able men to go into the bush and cut some long bamboo stems to prop up the tree. All obeyed. And very soon, one after the other, the men emerged from the bush with their bamboo stems, their bare upper bodies glistening with their sweat in the hot sun. They propped up the tree with the bamboo stems and soon, the swaying ceased. The men congratulated each other with glee and helped themselves

to more of Maame Nsafufu's palm wine. Soon they were all drunk. Just then an even greater wind began to blow. But by now the able men were all too drunk. Then a tune began to sound from the base of the tree:

'It's the roots.
There are holes in the roots.
The bamboo sticks
Only prop awhile
Till a greater wind returns.
And the swaying resumes
For it is weak in the roots
There are holes in the roots.'

It was the earthworm. The master of the earth that it was, it had burrowed and discovered the holes in the roots of tree. Now I ask you, in the midst of all the glistening bare upper bodies and long elegant bamboo stems, what attention would be paid to a small soft-bodied limbless invertebrate like the earthworm?

The physical enslavement of Black people is over. Its legacy on our psyche is the new weapon being used to wage the subtle war against us. The harangue grows ever louder about the inferiority of our culture. The same excuse that twisted minds used to justify slavery.

This continent is made up of over (50) countries. South of the Sahara alone is composed of over eight hundred (800) ethnic groups. Yet Africa is always treated like just one big country. Negative customary practices like Female Genital Mutilation is picked, highlighted, blown up and paraded as THE AFRICAN custom. One travels to other parts of the world and one has to deal with questions like: 'So has yours also been cut off?'

In certain societies of the world all that its people know about Africa is that, it is this one huge country of heat and dust, where fly infested children and their mothers with long dangling breasts, sprawl daily on a desert land somewhere, starving and waiting for free food from the U.N..

F.G.M. is cruel and wrong. And thank God for efforts to end it. Culture should be dynamic. Periodic modification and abolition of some customary practices is necessary and healthy. But it should be no basis to reduce our culture in its entirety to those few negative ones and use it to justifying branding it as inferior and primitive.

If the culture of a people is constantly so attacked and battered like ours is, will the psyche of the people of that culture not feel exhausted sometimes and beaten to a pulp? Such that sometimes all that they would find themselves doing is to stand and watch their culture hammered all the more? Will their confidence in that culture not give way sometimes? Consequently, would a vision rooted in that culture, not sometimes appear dented and devalued?

Ngugi could not have put it better when in one of his presentations he said, 'The loss of our languages appear to be the only one celebrated.' We take great pride in our ability to speak big English like the English themselves don't even speak. We rate intelligence and social standing with the ability to speak big English. Never mind if we sometimes get their meaning all wrong.

For whatever reasons that our forefathers instituted certain customary practices in their era, which, in our eyes today, are cruel and wrong, we must seek answers to our many *whys*, from our old folks who are the human libraries on our true history. Through that we would be giving our forefathers a fair hearing, because in their time they must have had reasons they deemed good and worthy to justify instituting such customary practices. The cruelty and wrongfulness of such practices like F.G.M., in our eyes today, probably allow our emotions to dictate too much to us. We have therefore, in our little ways, inadvertently sung gleefully along with the voices that seek to keep the holes in our culture, as in the roots of Koroye's tree, to feed the notion of its inferiority so that our faith in our culture continues to sway like Koroye's tree whenever a strong wind blows.

Won't it be more effective if instead of hammering on about its cruelty alone – which feeds the notion of our barbarism, and which puts those who still practise it on the defensive – to seek rather to establish the circumstances *for* the need *for* its practice in the eyes of our forefathers? And then go on to convince the practitioners of today of its irrelevance? Maybe then, when we have cause to be less ashamed of such aspects of our culture, we would begin to gain a firmer grip on it. Maybe then, where politics has proven less effective so far, we could employ culture to seal the holes. Maybe we should concentrate more on the common threads running through our ethnic groupings and less on the differences between our respective countries concerning our respective colonial masters. Our ethnic groupings stretch beyond the borders of our respective countries. Who knows? Maybe decades from now, our grand- and great-grandchildren would also be branding us as something dishonourable, for deeming it appropriate in our era, to assign defence lawyers to known paedophiles; or for allowing AIDS to destroy us so much when all we had to do was to change our lifestyles or use condoms.

The political strides made in the spirit of Pan-Africanism should in no way be underestimated. But they can be likened to the elegant bamboo stems that propped up Koroye's tree and the glistening bodies of the able men who brought it from the bush. For the tree to stand still even in the event of a strong wind, attention must be paid to the spineless earthworm. We must seal the holes to strengthen the roots. The roots are our culture, and the holes in the roots are the legacy of the past that is weighing down today on our psyche about our culture. Such that, as much as we strive to hold strongly onto it, a strong wind blows, then like Koroye's tree, we find ourselves swaying in our faith.

Many of the customary practices we deem cruel and wrong today in Africa were and continue to be directed against us women. So we women writers must have a greater stake in establishing from our old people, who are our human libraries, the answers to the *whys*. When we capture the responses to our *whys* in our stories to gain a better insight into the thinking and decisions of our forefathers instead of criminalising them, we would perhaps help calm some of their restless souls. And perhaps ours too. In the African Writers' Handbook, Walter Bgoya wrote under 'Publishing in Africa: Culture and Development':

> Some years ago in Dar es Salaam, Mrs. Shirley Du Bois, wife of W. E. B. Du Bois, the great African American philosopher and architect of the Pan-African movement, told an anecdote that I would like to share with you. After the coup that toppled Dr. Kwame Nkrumah of Ghana, a group of soldiers went to her house and demanded to make a thorough search of it. As they were about to enter her late husband's library, she stepped in front of them and challenged any one of the soldiers who was not afraid of the old man's spirit, which resided in his books and papers, to dare touch his things. The soldiers, who had come with much force and determination, looked at the impressive array of books and papers, thought about the matter, discussed it in their mother tongue, and decided it was too risky a business. They excused themselves, and left Mrs. Du Bois and her books alone.

To end, kindly allow me to read an excerpt from my upcoming novel: *Not Without Flowers* to serve as food for thought for us all, on the subtle games that the legacy of our past plays on our psyche today and dictates some of our thinking and attitudes.

> Akatasia was the pretty daughter of a wealthy Ghanaian entrepreneur who returned home from England where she had been residing, to get married. Akatasia was once quoted as having said that, when she first arrived at London's Victoria station, she thought that all of England was in mourning. And if England was in mourning, then it could only mean the death of a prominent member of the royal family. That was because everyone she saw at the station was in black: black trousers, black skirts, black jackets, black everything. By the time Akatasia returned to Ghana for her marriage years later, Akatasia had been effectively indoctrinated in the elegance of the colour black in the high echelons of fashion. On the day of her traditional marriage to her husband-to-be, Abrante, Akatasia wore an expensive and fashionable black designer-dress. Her grandmother, Aberewa, howled in shock at the sight of Akatasia. It was horrible enough that the dress was way up above Akatasia's knees with sleeves thin like cotton thread. Did she have to choose that day of all days to be so outrageously generous with her body

curves and feed the hungry and greedy eyes of the many males around with her near nakedness so free of charge? Thighs exposed to their possible uppermost upper and her bosom on such free display? On top of it all in the colour black too? 'Couldn't you have worn something in white which covered your thighs and bosom decently enough?' Aberewa wailed, but she was laughed at and asked to keep quiet. Akatasia was a modern woman, she was told, a virtual Londoner. And in Europe people wore black dresses even to weddings and outdoorings. It wasn't like Akatasia had donned a black wedding gown! Was this not just the engagement! The more important church wedding in two weeks' time was the special de luxe occasion. Aberewa reacted in horror to that assertion. This was just the engagement! The traditional marriage was just the engagement? Since when? Aberewa's horror was not without basis. Aberewa had heard that engagements in Europe often took place solely between the man and the woman intending to marry, sometimes even at a dinner in a restaurant. The man would bring out the ring from his pocket or wherever, often as a pleasant surprise to the woman and pose the question, 'Will you marry me?' Whereupon if she said yes, he slipped it on her finger and went on to announce to all that they were engaged. Finished. How on earth could that in even the minutest way, be equated with even a fraction, let alone the entire traditional marriage ceremony of Akatasia and Abrante? Their ceremony started at 11am and lasted till 6pm. The house of Akatasia's parents was filled with family members and friends and even gatecrashers. Akatasia's bride price of a big suitcase, pieces of cloth, headscarves, jewellery, assorted drinks and cash, were proudly presented. Her parents received their token compensation from Abrante for the 'loss' of their daughter to him. Akatasia's brother also got something for the 'loss'of his sister. The week prior to the marriage ceremony, three members of Abrante's family, came and performed the 'knocking ceremony' with the required bottles of Schnapps and a token fee. This was the symbolical knocking on the door of Akatasia's parents to formally seek their permission to be allowed to return the following week to marry Akatasia off to Abrante. How could all that be equated with a ring inside a pocket brought out at the dining table? No wonder Akatasia saw nothing indecent in her hideously exposing black dress. But the gods had seen all the wrongs. Aberewa feared this but kept it to herself because just as she had been shut up about the black dress, so too would she be shut up about this. After which she would be lucky not to be declared a witch. Then the gods reacted. The white wedding scheduled to come on in two weeks, never did. Three days after the traditional marriage that was belittled as just the engagement, a mammy truck loaded with bags of charcoal knocked down and killed Abrante instantly. 'A tragic accident!' wept some. 'Fate!' concluded others. But to minds like Aberewa's, Akatasia had tempted the gods. She had goaded them, so they had given her good reason to wear black. '... In conclusion the editor asked: should Akatasia have given Aberewa the benefit of the doubt and changed the black dress? Or would that have amounted to Akatasia giving in to primitive superstition just days shy of her deluxe white Christian wedding?'

Thank you for the honour done me by inviting me to deliver this keynote address. I hope I did not keep your lunch waiting for too long. Thank you.

**AMMA DARKO**
**Accra, Ghana**
**May 2006**

# NOTES & REFERENCES

**Vincent O. Odamtten**
Introduction: Beyond the Comfort Zone

1 See Louise Allen Zak's essay 'Amma Darko: Writing Her Way' which is an illuminating glimpse into the vagaries of the Western publishing world, especially as it impacts the career of a Ghanaian woman writer in Europe. It is thus fitting that this essay introduces the volume.
2 Apart from book reviews, of particular interest are these two notable critical responses, one to Darko's first novel, 'Women On Top: Prostitution and Pornography in Amma Darko's *Beyond the Horizon*' published in *Wasafiri* 37, Winter 2002, 8–13, by Maria Frias; and Edith Kohrs-Aissah's book, *Aspects of Feminism and Gender in the Novels of Three West African Women Writers (Aidoo, Emecheta, Darko)*, Heidelberg: Books on African Studies, 2002. See also, Miriam C. Gyimah's insightful review of Kohrs-Aissah's volume, in *West Africa Review* ISSN 1094–2254, v4, n1, 2003.
3 Amma Darko, *Faceless*, Introduction by Kofi Anyihoho, Sub-Saharan Publishers, Legon Accra, Ghana, 2003, p.9.
4 al-Tayyib Salih, *Season of Migration to the North*, Heinemann Publishing, 1966.

**Louise Allen Zak**
Amma Darko: Writing Her Way, Creating a Writing Life

1 Conversation with the author, 23 May 1999.
2 'Fostering' by an aunt is a common practice among West Africans, and Darko has never claimed to have suffered from it. Still, her relationship to her birthplace and family history seems to be a source of some conflict, which she has dealt with in her semi-autobiographical novel *Webs*.
3 Conversation with the author, 28 May 1998. It is a measure of the lack of attention to this new generation of writers that at the time of my dissertation on Darko (2001) there was not a single critical article in English about her or her works. All future statements attributed to Darko in this paper are from conversations with the author and public talks. They will be referenced parenthetically within the text by date.
4 As Alice Walker pointed out, Emecheta is a writer 'because of, not in spite of, her children'. *In Search of Our Mother's Garden* (San Diego: Harcourt, Brace, Javonovich, 1984, 66).
5 When *Beyond the Horizon* appeared in print, Darko took the book to her mother's grave as proof that she had accomplished something to be proud of, though it brought no material gain to her family.
6 Darko has an unorthodox take on critics' questions about how much of her work is autobiographical. Far from being annoyed, she says, 'I'm flattered! To write something so convincing that people think it's your own story – that's something!' (5 December 2000).
7 Chinua Achebe, 'What Do African Intellectuals Read?' (*Times Literary Supplement*, 12 May 1972, 547).

8 The popularity of the romance novel in Ghana may be judged by the fact that even a major figure like Ama Ata Aidoo began *Changes* as an attempt to write a romance of the 'Mills and Boon' type.

9 Adeola James, *In Their Own Voices: African Women Writers Talk* (London: Heinemann, 1990, 95).

10 James Gibbs and Jack Mapanje, *The African Writers' Handbook* (Oxford: African Books Collective, 1999, 188).

11 I am indebted to Amma Darko and Ama Ata Aidoo for explaining this proverb to me.

**Works Cited**


Achebe, Chinua. 'What Do African Intellectuals Read?' *Times Literary Supplement*, 12 May 1972, 547.

Darko, Amma. *Beyond the Horizon*. Portsmouth, NH: Heinemann, 1995. (First published in German translation by Anita Jorges-Djafari as *Der Verkaufte Traum*, Stuttgart: Schmetterling Verlag, 1991.)

—. *Colour Palaver*. Unpublished ms. (Published only in German in *Aller Menchen Wurde*, Frankfurt am Main: Saurlander Verlag, 2001.)

—. *Faceless*. Accra: SubSaharan, 2003. (Published in German translation by Anita Djafari as *Die Gesichtslosen*, Stuttgart: Schmetterling Verlag, 2003.)

—. *The Housemaid*. Portsmouth, NH: Heinemann, 1998. (Published in German translation by A. Jorges-Djafari with 'In Excess' as *Das Hausmädchen*, Stuttgart: Schmetterling Verlag, 1999).

—. *Verirrtes Herz*. (Published only in German translation by Anita Jorges-Djafari. Stuttgart: Schmetterling Verlag, 2000.)

—. *Webs*. Unpublished ms. (Published only in German translation by Anita Djafari as *Spinwebben*, Stuttgart: Schmetterling Verlag, 1996.)

—. Personal interview. Accra, Ghana. 28 May 1998.

—. Letter to the author. 18 November 1998.

—. Public reading and talk. Cologne, Germany. 2 June 1999.

—. Conversation. Cologne, Germany. 3 June 1999.

—. Telephone interview. 13 July 1999.

—. Telephone interview. 3 December 1999.

—. Telephone interview. 29 January 2000.

—. Telephone interview. 4 August 2000.

—. Telephone interview. 2 September 2000.

—. Telephone interview. 5 December 2000.

—. Telephone interview. 19 January 2001.

—. Telephone interview. 13 April 2001.

Gibbs, James, and Jack Mapanje. *The African Writers' Handbook*. Oxford: African Books Collective, 1999, 188.

James, Adeola. *In Their Own Voices: African Women Writers Talk*. London: Heinemann, 1990, 95.

Walker, Alice. *In Search of Our Mother's Gardens*. San Diego: Harcourt Brace, Javanovich, 1984.


## Monica Bungaro

Victims and/or Victimisers? Women's De(Con)structive Power in *The Housemaid*

**Works Cited**


Bungaro, Monica – Interview with Amma Darko, Accra, Ghana, 20th August 2000.

Caldwell, John (1968) *Rural-Urban Migration: The Movement to Ghana's Towns*, Canberra: Australian Nation University Press.
Darko, Amma (1998) *The Housemaid*, London: Heinemann.
Du Plessis, Rachel (1985) *Writing Beyond the Ending*, Bloomington: Indiana University Press.
Hadley, Janey (1996) *Abortion: Between Freedom and Necessity*, London: Virago.
Horne, Naana Banyiwa (1999) 'The Politics of Mothering: Multiple Subjectivity and Gendered Discourse in Aidoo's Plays', in *Emerging Perspectives on Ama Ata Aidoo*, eds. Ada Uzoamaka Azodo & Gay Wilentz, Trenton NJ: Africa World Press: 303–331.
Little, Kenneth (1975) *African Women in Towns*, Cambridge: Cambridge University Press.
Mohamed, Patricia (2001) *Gendered Realities: Essays in Caribbean Feminist Thoughts*, Kingston: University of the West Indies Press.
Ncgobo, Lauretta (1988) *Let It Be Told: Essays by Black Women in Britain*, London: Virago.
Nice, Vivienne (1992) *Mothers and Daughters: The Distortion of a Relationship*, Basingstoke: Macmillan.
Nnaemeka, Obioma (1997) 'Imagining Knowledge, Power and Subversion in the Margins', in *The Politics of (M)othering: Womanhood Identity and Resistance in African Literature*, London & New York, Routledge: 1–25.
Nwapa, Flora (1981) *One is Enough*, Enugu (Nigeria): Tana Press.
Oppong, Christine (1983) *Female and Male in West Africa*, Boston: Allen & Unwin.
Rich, Adrienne (1977) *Of Woman Born: Motherhood as Experience and Institution*, London: Virago.
Trump, Martin (1988), 'Black South African Short Fiction in English since 1976', *Research in African Literatures*, 19.1 34–64.
Wilenz, Gay (2000) 'Afrocentrism as Theory: The Discourse of Diaspora Literature', in *Passage: Journal of Translation and Transcultural Studies* 2–1: 37–60.

## Sean P. O'Connell and Vincent O. Odamtten

Licit Desires, Alien Bodies and the Economics of Invisibility in Amma Darko's *Beyond the Horizon* and Stephen Frears' *Dirty Pretty Things*

### References

1 The racialising of this underclass seems to serve at least two crucial purposes. Firstly, to divert attention from the class nature of the state's policies, since the 'other' is by definition 'alien'; and secondly, by so doing the 'citizens' feel their normative interests protected by the state, and thus they feel greater allegiance to the state than to the 'alien'. In addition, the term 'alien' conjures up images of the *extraterrestrial* and thus, the category of non-human is reinforced continually within the dominant discourse. See Katarzyna Marciniak's *Alienhood: Citizenship, Exile, and the Logic of Difference*, Minnesota, University of Minnesota Press, 2006.

2 The notion of these 'aliens' living and working in their various 'host' nations suggests their status as parasites or the smaller and weaker partner in a 'symbiotic' relationship; and yet, both Darko and Frears ironically suggest that the 'host' might properly be seen as the 'parasite' and that the relationship is definitely not symbiotic.

3 BBC Films/Miramax DVD back cover publicity information, 2003.

4 Darko, Amma, *Beyond the Horizon*, London, Heinemann Educational Publishers, 1995, p.10.

5 Collins, Patricia Hill, *Black Sexual Politics: African Americans, Gender, and the New Racism*, New York: Routledge, 2004, p. 28.

6 hooks, bell, *Black Looks: Race and Representation*, Boston: South End Press, 1992, p. 23.

## Mary Ellen (Ellie) Higgins

*Ngambika* and Grassroots Fiction: Amma Darko's *The Housemaid* and *Faceless*

### Notes

1 In interdisciplinary discourses about Africa, the village has frequently been represented as the privileged site of tradition, or as a link to more 'authentic' African identities. African cities, in contrast, have been associated – albeit uneasily – with notions of 'modernity' and globalisation. In recent decades, discourses that have assumed a strict dichotomy between village and city, between tradition and modernity, have been called into question. For example, in 'The Future of Tradition', (*Senegal, Essays in Statecraft*. Ed. M.C. Diop. Dakar: CODESRIA, 1992), Souleymane Bachir Diagne observes the emergence of 'a genuine *tradition of urban life* involving populations which for generations have known nothing other than urban civilisation' (273, my emphasis). One can also speak, *sans* oxymoron, of modern villages. The village and the city, rather than being static or homogenous entities, have their own eclectic mixtures of cultures and traditions.

2 I would like to thank Vincent Odamtten for his generous suggestions about developing the concept of grassroots fiction in this essay.

3 J.F. Ade Ajayi reminds us that history traces both change and continuity. The Western philosophy of progress, Ajayi writes, erroneously views modernisation in Africa 'not as a historical transformation of traditional society, but as something new to replace the old – development made possible only by the eradication of traditional societies and institutions' (32). The traditional, in his view, are both continuous and changing, both enduring and transforming. See *Tradition and Change in Africa: The Essays of J.F. Ade Ajayi*. (Ed. Toyin Falola. Trenton, NJ: Africa World Press, 2000).

4 See Konadu-Agyemang, *The Political Economy of Housing and Urban Development in Africa: Ghana's Experience from Colonial Times to 1998* (Westport, CT: Praeger, 2001), p. 186.

5 Darko elaborated upon the intersections between her experiences and her novels in my interview with her in Legon in 2003. The interview was published under the title 'Creating an Alternative Library: Amma Darko interviewed by Ellie Higgins', in the *Journal of Commonwealth Literature* 39.2 (2004): 111-120.

6 For a discussion of the invisibility of African children's labour in academic research, see Beverly Grier, 'Child Labor and Africanist Scholarship', in *African Studies Review* 42.2 (2004): 1-25.

7 Schauber's article, 'Ghana; Witches of the North – Tragic Story of Torture, Lynching' was published by *Africa News* online on November 12, 2002.

8 See, for example, 'Ghana; This Is Witch-Hunting – Baafi', in *The Independent* (Accra), February 23, 1999.

9 See the interview documented in footnote 5, p. 112.

10 At the time of writing, Centre for Public Interest Law has posted its case, 'Pending forced eviction of 30,000 dwellers at Agbogbloshie in Accra, Ghana', at http://www.cepil.org/casestory.asp?id=14.

11 See Joan Riley's *The Unbelonging* (London: The Women's Press, 1985).

12 Refer to my interview with Darko cited in footnote 5 above, p. 117.

13 I speak of Darko's work as an alternative library in my interview with her (see footnote 5 above), 111–120. The construction of an alternative library is explained in Darko's *Faceless*, p. 63.

14 Moradewun Adejunmobi discusses Hampaté Bâ's 'Textualisation of Orality' in 'Disruptions of Orality in the Writings of Hampaté Bâ', in *Research in African Literatures* 31.3 (2000): 27–36.

**Works Cited**

Ajayi, J.F. Ade. 'Tradition and Development', in *Tradition and Change in Africa: The Essays of J.F. Ade Ajayi*. Ed. Toyin Falola. Trenton, NJ: Africa World Press, 2000.

Ampaw, King. *Kukurantumi: The Road to Accra*. Ghana: African Diaspora Images, 1983.

Anyidoho, Kofi. 'Amma Darko's *Faceless*: A New Landmark in Ghanaian Fiction'. Introduction to *Faceless* (Legon, Accra: Sub-Saharan Publishers, 2003) 9–21.

Awuah, Emmanuel. 'Mobilizing for Change: A Case Study of Market Trader Activism in Ghana, in' *Canadian Journal of African Studies* 31.3 (1997): 401–423.

Cazenave, Odile. *Rebellious Women: The New Generation of Female African Novelists*. Boulder, CO: Lynne Rienner, 2000.

Ciekawy, Diane, and Peter Geschiere, 'Containing Witchcraft: Conflicting Scenarios in Post-colonial Africa', in *African Studies Review* 41.3 (1998): 1–14.

Darko, Amma. *Beyond the Horizon*. Portsmouth, NH: Heinemann, 1995.

—. *Faceless*. Legon, Accra: Sub-Saharan Publishers, 2003.

—. *The Housemaid*. Portsmouth, NH: Heinemann, 1998.

Davies, Carole Boyce, and Anne Adams Graves, eds. *Ngambika: Studies of Women in African Literature*. Trenton, NJ: Africa World Press, 1986.

Diagne, Souleymane Bachir. 'The Future of Tradition', in *Senegal, Essays in Statecraft*. Ed. M.C. Diop. Dakar: CODESRIA, 1992.

Diawara, Manthia. 'Toward a Regional Imaginary in Africa', in *World Bank Literature*. Ed. Amitava Kumar. Minneapolis: University of Minnesota Press, 2003.

Drucker-Brown, Susan. 'Mamprusi Witchcraft, Subversions, and Changing Gender Relations', in *Africa* 63 (1993): 532–549.

Eyango, Vijitha Mahadevan. 'The Classroom or the Marketplace: Survival Strategies of Ghanaian Women', in *Eye to Eye: Women Practising Development Across Cultures*. Ed. Susan Perry and Celeste Schenck. New York: Zed Books, 2001. pp. 106–118.

Konadu-Agyemang, Kwadwo. *The Political Economy of Housing and Urban Development in Africa: Ghana's Experience from Colonial Times to 1998*. Westport, CT: Praeger, 2001.

Mensah Adinkrah, 'Witchcraft Accusations and Female Homicide Victimisation in Contemporary Ghana', in *Violence Against Women* 10.4 (2004): 325–356.

Nnaemeka, Obioma. 'Introduction: Imag(in)ing knowledge, power, and subversion in the Margins', in Ed. Obioma Nnaemeka, *The Politics of (M)othering: Womanhood, Identity, and Resistance in African Literature*. New York: Routledge, 1997, 1–25.

—. 'Nego-Feminism: Theorizing, Practising, and Pruning Africa's Way', in *Signs: Journal of Women in Culture and Society* 29 (2): 2004, 357–385.

Riley, Joan. *The Unbelonging*. London: The Women's Press, 1985.

Schenck, Celeste. 'Developing Subjects', in *Eye to Eye: Women Practising Development Across Cultures*. Ed. Susan Perry and Celeste Schenck. New York: Zed Books, 2001, pp. 233–255.

**Carmela Garritano**

Amma Darko's *The Housemaid* and the Gendering of Novel and Nation

**Notes**

1 In his study of Chinua Achebe, Simon Gikandi has argued that it is the foreignness of the novel which, for the African writer, lends it force. He explains that 'the appropriation of the privileged discursive instruments of the West' gave the African novel its 'subversive force' (22). He writes: 'The power of the form – whether it is music or fiction – does not solely lie in its claim to be original, but in its irruption of the already-written discourse.

The borrowed instrument – which the dominant culture has discarded because it was supposed to have outlived its usefulness – is bent around and used against the culture that produced it' (22).

2 Nfah-Abbenyi describes the representation of African women in the male literary tradition as 'passive, as always prepared to do the bidding of their husbands and family, as having no status of their own and therefore completely dependent on their husbands' (40). Darko's female characters refute such a portrayal.

3 As Moretti has shown in his study of the European novel: '[The novel] is a form that (unlike an anthem, or a monument) not only does not conceal the nation's universal divisions, but manages to turn them into a story' (20) in providing the reader with 'a symbolic form capable of making sense of the nation-state' (20).

## Works Cited


Anderson, Benedict. *Imagined Communities: Reflections on the Origin and Spread of Nationalism. Revised Edition*. London and New York: Verso: 1991.

Andrade, Susan Z. 'The Joys of Daughterhood: Gender, Nationalism, and the Making of Literary Tradition (s)'. Lynch and Warner, 249–276.

Bhabha, Homi K, ed. *Nation and Narration*. London and New York: 1990.

—. 'DissemiNation: Time, Narrative, and the Margins of the Modern Nation'. Bhabha 291–322.

Brennan, Timothy. 'The National Longing for Form', Bhabha 44–70.

Burnham, Michelle. 'Between England and America: Captivity, Sympathy, and the Sentimental Novel'. Lynch and Warner 47–72.

Culler, Jonathon. 'Anderson and the Novel', in *Diacritics* 29.4 (1999): 20–39.

Darko, Amma. *The Housemaid*. Portsmouth, NJ: Heinemann, 1998.

Gikandi, Simon. *Reading Chinua Achebe: Language and Ideology in Fiction*. London and Portsmouth, NJ: James Currey and Heinemann, 1991.

Lynch, Deidre and William B. Warner, eds. *Cultural Institutions of the Novel*. Durham and London: Duke University Press, 1996.

Moretti, Franco. *Atlas of the European Novel: 1800–1900*. London and New York: Verso, 1998.

Stratton, Florence. *Contemporary African Literature and the Politics of Gender*. London and New York: Routledge, 1994.


## Angsotinge, Dako, Denkabe & Yitah

Exploitation, Negligence and Violence:
Gendered Interrelationships in Amma Darko's Novels

### Notes

1 The Ghanaian term 'burger' refers to someone who has been abroad and worked there to earn some money. The term is restricted to Ghanaian migrants on the Continent of Europe, especially Germany.

2 J. Benibengor Blay. *Emelia's Promise and Fulfilment*. Accra: Benibengor Book Agency, 1944; K. Bediako. *Don't Leave Me Mercy!!* Accra: Anowuo Educational Publishers, 1966; Victor Amartefio. *Bediako the Adventurer*. Accra: Amaa Books Ltd, 1967; Badoe, Ewura-Efuwa. *Beloved Twin*. Accra: Scorpio Books, 1973; Gyamfua Fofie, Akosua. *The Tested Love*. Kumasi: Beginners Publishers, 1989.

3 Unsavoury business practices, from Hausa *kare kabure* (don't open it).

**References**

Achebe, Chinua. *No Longer at Ease*. London: Heinemann, 1963.

Aidoo, Ama Ata. *Anowa*. London: Heinemann, 1971.

—. *No Sweetness Here*. London: Longman, 1970.

—. *Changes*. London: Women's Press, 1991.

Ajayi, Omofolabo. 'Negritude, Feminism, and the Quest for Identity: Re-Reading Mariama Bâ's *So Long a Letter*', in *Women's Studies Quarterly* XXV.3 & 4 1997, 35–52.

Amarteifio, Victor. *Bediako the Adventurer*. Accra: Amaa Books, 1985.

Anyidoho, Kofi. Introductory Essay to *Faceless*. Accra: Sub-Saharan Publishers, 9–21.

Armah, Ayi Kwei. *The Beautyful Ones Are Not Yet Born*. London: Heinemann, 1968.

—. *Fragments*. Boston: Houghton Mifflin, 1970.

—. *Why Are We So Blest?* London: Heinemann, 1974.

Awoonor, Kofi. *This Earth, My Brother*. London: Heinemann, 1972.

Ba, Mariama. *So Long a Letter*. London: Heinemann, 1972.

Boehmer, Elleke. 'Stories of Women and Mothers: Gender and Nationalism in the Early Fiction of Flora Nwapa', in Nasta, Susheila (ed). *Motherlands: Black Women's Writing from Africa, the Caribbean and South Asia*.New Brunswick, NJ: Rutgers UP, 1992, 3–23.

Dangarembga, Tsitsi. *Nervous Conditions*. Seattle: Seal Press, 1988.

Darko, Amma. *Beyond the Horizon*. London: Heinemann, 1995.

—. *The Housemaid*. London: Heinemann, 1998.

—. *Faceless*. Accra: Sub-Saharan Publishers, 2003.

Gakwandi, Shatto Arthur. *The Novel and Contemporary Experiences in Africa*. London: Heinemann, 1982.

Gikandi, Simon. *Reading the African Novel*. London: James Currey, 1988.

Higgins, Ellie. 'Creating an alternative library: Amma Darko interviewed by Ellie Higgins', in *The Journal of Commonwealth Literature*, Vol. 39. No. 2. 2004, 111–120.

Hollist, Onipede. E-mail to Kari Dako, 18th April 2001.

hooks, bell. *Feminist Theory: From Margin to Center*. Boston: South End Press, 1984.

Konadu, Asare. *Devils in Waiting*. Accra: Enowua Educational Publications, 1989.

Kwakye, Benjamin. *The Clothes of Nakedness*. London: Heinemann, 1998.

Mitchell, Juliet. 'Women and Equality', in ed. Juliet Mitchell & Ann Oakley, *The Rights and Wrongs of Women*, Harmondsworth: Penguin. 1986, 378–399.

Mitifu, Faida M. 'Zairian Novelists and Their Female Characters', in *Women's Studies Quarterly* XXV.3 & 4 1997, 97–108.

Newell, Stephanie. *Ghanaian Popular Fiction*. London: James Currey, 1999.

Nugent Paul. *Big Men, Small Boys and Politics in Ghana*. Accra: Asempa Publishers, 1995.

Nwapa, Flora. *Efuru*. London: Heinemann, 1966.

Nwapa, Flora. *Idu*. London: Heinemann, 1970.

Oppong, Christine. 'Social capital and systems of care: some contrasting evidence', forthcoming in Supplement 16, *IAS Research Review*, *Children at Risk in Ghana*, (25 pages).

Senghor, Leopold Sedar. *Poemes*. Paris: Seuil, 1984.

## Vincent O. Odamtten

Amma Darko's *Beyond the Horizon*: Vending the Dream and Other Traumas for the Obedient Daughter.

**Notes**

1 *Dirty Pretty Things* – Film directed by Stephen Frears.

2 Amma Darko, *Beyond the Horizon*, Heinemann Educational Publishers, 1995; first published as a German Translation under the title *Der Verkaufte Traum*, 1991.

3 Kofi S., barnesandnoble.com, <http://search. barnesandnoble.com/booksearch/isbnInquiry.asp?userid=nR3aHVGAIG>
4 Louise Allen Zak, 'Amma Darko: Writing Her Way' presented at ALA Conference at the University of Wisconsin-Madison, April 2004.
5 Oliver W. Sacks, *An Anthropologist on Mars: Seven Paradoxical Tales*, 4 n.8.
6 Vincent O. Odamtten, *The Art of Ama Ata Aidoo: Polylectics and Reading Against Neocolonialism*, University of Florida Press, 1994, 120.
7 Vincent O. Odamtten, '*The Last of the Empire*: Beyond The Manichean Aesthetic, in unpublished paper, presented at American Comparative Literature Association Conference, Ann Arbor, MI, 1986.
8 Kofi Owusu, 'Ayi Kwei Armah' entry in *Encyclopedia of African Literature*, edited by Simon Gikandi, Routledge, 2003, 29.
9 Ama Ata Aidoo, *Our Sister Killjoy: Or, Reflections from a Black-Eyed Squint*, Longman, 1988. We note that the protagonist-narrator of Aidoo's novel is named 'Mary' and the literary echo in Darko's work cannot be ignored.
10 Jacques Lacan, Bruce Fink (Translator), Heloise Fink (Translator) Russel Grigg (Translator), *Ecrits: A Selection*, W. W. Norton, New York, 2004, 4.

**Naana Banyiwa Horne**

Sage, Muse, Crone: The Grandmother in Amma Darko's Novels

**Notes**

1 See David Theo Goldberg's argument, referenced in *Nation, Empire, Colony* (1998) which affirms that underpinning the European liberal ideals of liberty, equality, and fraternity is a ruthless drive to attain hegemony and racial (and class) exclusivity (4). This statement lends support to Walter Rodney's assertion that Europe underdeveloped Africa to foster European development. Ruth Roach Pierson, co-editor of *Nation, Empire, Colony*, also speaks to the burden Africa and the so-called Third World has borne in order for the West to lay claim to greatness. 'The autonomy of European liberalism's free man rests on property and on the domination and exploitation of other classes and races – the colonised populations abroad and the working masses at home . . . The universal claims of the Enlightenment chafed uneasily against the competing militaries and capitalist imperialism of the so-called European Great Powers – culminating in the scramble for Africa of the 1880s and the outbreak of the First World War' (4).
2 'The Grandmother in African and African-American Literature: A Survivor of the African Extended Family', in *Ngambika: Studies of Women in African Literature*. Africa World Press, 1985, 258.
3 The terms sage, muse, and crone, which are employed here in developing a framework for analysing the various cultural identities upon which the literary images of the grandmother are modeled, were arrived at through the inspiration of Vincent Okpoti Odamtten. In a discussion with him on Amma Darko's *The Housemaid*, in which I vented my frustration with Efia's grandmother who turns my stomach by being so irresponsible and outright evil, because she blatantly manipulates where she should be guiding through her inspiration and wisdom, Odamtten suggested exploring the grandmother's actions through the various identities of sage, muse, and crone. His suggestion has proved invaluable in providing me with insightful explorations into the grandmother figure in a manner that is better suited for academic discourses.
4 Some of the memorable grandmothers in Ama Ata Aidoo's works are Nana in the play,

*The Dilemma of a Ghost*, The-Mouth-That-Eats-Salt and-Pepper in *Anowa*, and Nana, Esi Sekyi's grandmother in *Changes*. For his part, Ayi Kwei Armah offers us Naana, Baako Onipa's grandmother in *Fragments*.

5 Darko, Amma, *The Housemaid*. Portsmouth, NH: Heinemann, 1995. All references will be to this edition and will be by page numbers only.

6 Darko, Amma *Faceless*. Accra, Ghana: Sub-Saharan, 2004. All references will be to this edition and will be by page numbers only.

7 Even though it is Madam Sekyiwa, Tika's mother who is described as 'stinking rich' (18) in the novel, the evidence supports the same designation for the daughter. It is after all her enormous wealth that brings out the worst in Efia's grandmother.

8 The name of the grandmother in this novel is generic. Yomo is evidently derived from the Ga word for old woman, a designation that is informed by the aged nature of the grandmother or elder. 'Yoo' is woman; 'momo' is old. Yoomo, therefore, reflects mostly the crone identity of the grandmother which is based in old age and enfeeblement. However, it is also recognised that being aged, that is, becoming 'yoomo', comes with knowledge and authority to safeguard the family and community.

9 Refer to Naana Banyiwa Horne's 'The Politics of Mothering: Multiple Subjectivity and Gendered Discourse in Ama Ata Aidoo's Plays' for a more detailed analysis of the concept of multiple subjectivities. While this essay focuses on Aidoo's plays, the analysis of the political, social and cultural significations of mothering illuminates the multidimensional nature of the agency of the grandmother as it is embodied in Naa Yomo.

**Works Cited**


Aidoo, Ama Ata. *The Dilemma of a Ghost and Anowa*. London: Longman, 1995.

—. *Changes: A Love Story*. New York: The Feminist Press, 1991.

Armah, Ayi Kwei. *Fragments*. London: Heinemann, 1974.

Darko, Amma. *Beyond the Horizon*. London: Heinemann, 1995.

—. *The Housemaid*. London: Heinemann, 1998.

—. *Faceless*. Accra, Ghana: Subsaharan, 2004.

Hill-Lubin, Mildred Anderson. 'The Grandmother in African and African-American Literature: A Survivor of the African Extended Family', in *Ngambika: Studies of Women in African Literature*. Carole Boyce Davies and Anne Adams. Trenton: NJ: Africa World Press, 1986, 257–270.

Horne, Naana Banyiwa. 'The Politics of Mothering: Multiple Subjectivities and Gendered Discourse in Aidoo's Plays', in *Emerging Perspectives on Ama Ata Aidoo*. Trenton, NJ: Africa World Press, 1999, 303–331.

Lorde, Audre. *Sister Outsider: Essays and Speeches*. Freedom, California: The Crossing Press, 1984.

Pierson, Ruth Roach. 'Introduction', in *Nation, Empire, Colony: Historicizing Gender and Race*. Ruth Roach Pierson and Nupur Chaudhuri. Bloomington and Indianapolis: Indiana University Press, 1998, 1–20.

Rodney, Walter. *How Europe Underdeveloped Africa*. Washington, D.C.: Howard University Press, 1972.